Get Creative!

The Digital Video Idea Book

Todd Stauffer and Nina Parikh

McGraw-Hill/Osborne

New York / Chicago / San Francisco
Lisbon / London / Madrid / Mexico City / Milan
New Delhi / San Juan / Seoul / Singapore / Sydney / Toronto

The McGraw·Hill Companies

McGraw-Hill/Osborne
2100 Powell Street, 10th Floor
Emeryville, California 94608
U.S.A.

To arrange bulk purchase discounts for sales promotions, premiums, or fund-raisers, please contact **McGraw-Hill**/Osborne at the above address. For information on translations or book distributors outside the U.S.A., please see the International Contact Information page immediately following the index of this book.

Get Creative! The Digital Video Idea Book

Photos of Sony's DCR-TRV350 Digital8® camcorder courtesy of Sony Electronics, Inc.

1234567890 FGR FGR 019876543

Book p/n 0-07-223087-8 and CD p/n 0-07-223088-6
parts of ISBN 0-07-222929-2

Publisher	Brandon A. Nordin
Vice President & Associate Publisher	Scott Rogers
Executive Editor	Jane Brownlow
Project Editor	Elizabeth Seymour
Acquisitions Coordinator	Tana Allen
Technical Editor	Gene Hirsh
Copy Editors	Lisa Theobald, Cynthia Putnam, Lunaea Weatherstone
Proofreader	Stefany Otis
Indexer	Bob Richardson
Computer Designer	Carie Abrew
Illustrators	Kathleen Fay Edwards, Melinda Moore Lytle, Lyssa Wald
Original Design Concept	Kate Binder, Prospect Hill Publishing Services
Series Design	Carie Abrew
Cover Series Design	Pattie Lee
Cover Illustration	Jeff Weeks

This book was composed with Corel VENTURA™ Publisher.

About the Authors

Todd Stauffer is the author or co-author of more than 30 books on technology and computing including *Blog On: The Essential Guide to Building Dynamic Weblogs* and *How To Do Everything with Your iMac*. He is an award-winning magazine writer as well as the publisher of the *Jackson Free Press*, a news and culture magazine in Jackson, Mississippi. He has also worked as a cable television show host and writer.

Nina Parikh is deputy director of the Mississippi Film Office, where she works on commercials, TV series, and films such as *Oh, Brother, Where Art Thou?*, and the upcoming documentary series, *The Blues*. Off the clock, she is a filmmaker currently working on two documentary features and seeking distribution for several completed projects. She is a graduate of the University of Southern Mississippi with a degree in Radio, Television, and Film, and of New York University's 16mm film production continuing education program. She is a founding member of the Crossroads Film Festival and Mississippi Film and Video Alliance, who continues to work closely with both organizations.

About the Technical Editor

Gene Hirsh, a classically trained painter and illustrator, became involved with digital art in 1985 while working as a layout artist. That's when he discovered that desktop computers could actually make pictures interactively. Thus began his love affair with art and computers. Hirsh has worked in the corporate and advertising arenas art directing and producing digital video and animation for multimedia and training applications. He has worked as a graphic designer, layout artist, architect, illustrator, multimedia artist, computer gaming artist, art director, web designer, animator, fine artist and, most recently, has taken up writing in an effort to share his many years of experience. Hirsh is an award-winning artist, exhibiting his digital art in galleries and exhibitions around the world and on the Web. He is presently showing in a number of galleries in California. His art has been featured in Digital Fine Art Magazine and Digital Output Magazine. Hirsh is the co-author of *Photoshop Elements 2: The Complete Reference*. He received a BFA from California College of Arts and Crafts. He also studied at University of Arizona, George Washington University, and Catholic University of America.

Contents

Acknowledgments, xi
Introduction, xiii

Chapter 1	**Choosing Camera Equipment**	**1**
	Analog vs. Digital	2
	How DV Camcorders Work	2
	Choosing Your Camcorder Format	3
	Understanding CCDs	6
	Shopping for a DV Camcorder	8
	Videography Features	10
	Multimedia Features	12
	Renting vs. Buying	14
	Filters and Lenses	16
	And...Cut!	18
Chapter 2	**Computing Basics for Video Producers**	**19**
	What You Need	20
	PC Hardware and Software	20
	Mac Hardware and Software	25
	Working with Digital Video	30
	File Formats and Translation	31
	Saving, Backing Up, Archiving	33
	Adapting and Importing Analog Video	35
	And...Cut!	37
Chapter 3	**Home Movies**	**39**
	What You'll Need	40
	How to Stay Organized	40
	Some Dos and Don'ts for Shooting Home Movies	44
	Don't Narrate Constantly	44
	Don't Go Nuts With the Zoom Button	45
	Don't "Step On" Each Other	47
	Don't End Too Early	48
	Do Use Multiple Angles and Vary Your Shots	49

	Do Be Decisive About What You Shoot	52
	Do Keep the Camera Reasonably Steady	53
	Do Remember that Lighting Is Important	54
	Do Get Good Sound	56
	Do Practice	57
	Approaches to Editing Your Home Movies	57
	Finding the Beginning	57
	The Middle	59
	The End	60
	Post-Production	61
	And...Cut!	64
Chapter 4	**Wedding and Event Video**	**65**
	What You'll Need	66
	The "What" of Your Production	66
	The "Where" and "When"	69
	Pre-production	70
	Planning the Shoot	70
	Equipment Checklist	71
	Scouting the Location	72
	Stuff to Get from the Principals	73
	Equipment Planning	74
	Camcorder Placement and Techniques	74
	Choosing Camcorder Location	75
	Sync Your Camcorders	76
	More About Camcorder Settings	77
	Keep It Simple	78
	Getting the Shots	80
	Shooting Outdoors	82
	Shooting Parties and Banquets	84
	Editing the Event	85
	Standard Wedding Shots	87
	And...Cut!	88
Chapter 5	**Interviews**	**89**
	What You'll Need	89
	The Art of the Interview	90
	Choose the Appropriate Interviewee	90
	Setting Up the Shot	92
	Location and Seating	94
	Get a Name	96
	Ask Open-Ended Questions	97
	Changing Shots	99

Lighting, Sound, and Studios 100
    Lighting for Interviews 100
    Sound for Interviews 104
    Working in the Studio 106
Editing an Interview 107
    Technique 108
    Other Editing Tips 110
And...Cut! 111

Chapter 6   **Documentaries** **113**
What You Need 114
Documentary Styles 117
    Vérité Video 118
    Historical Documentary 119
    Personal Documentary 120
    Educational Reel 121
Writing and Planning Your Doc 121
Documentary Techniques 124
    Interview Before You Shoot 124
    Tricks for Nervous Interviewees 126
    B-Roll, B-Roll, B-Roll 127
    Hold Your Shot and Get Handles 128
    Protect Your Footage 129
Getting the Footage You Need 130
    The Rule of Thirds 130
    Be Aware of the Background 131
    Get Serious About Camcorder Stabilizers 131
    Get the Sound You Need 132
    Log and Work with Tapes 135
Historical and Stock Footage 136
Using Still Photographs 137
Editing Your Documentary 138
    The Sound Edit 138
    The Sound Mix 139
And...Cut! 140

Chapter 7   **Business and Organization Video** **141**
What You Need 142
Planning and Writing the Video 146
    Choose Your Approach 147
    Consider the Location(s) 148
    Communicate the Facts 150
    Make It Interesting 152

Directing and Editing the Shoot 155
    Using Multiple Techniques 156
    Shooting Meetings 157
    Shooting B-Roll 158
    Pulling it Together in Editing 160
And...Cut! 163

Chapter 8   **DV Feature (or Short)** **165**
What You Need 166
    Equipment Needs 167
    Other Needs 170
Writing Your Feature 171
    Adaptation 171
    The Treatment 172
    The Script 173
    Build a Story 175
Producing and Directing 177
    Breaking Down the Script, and Delegating 177
    Creating a Storyboard 180
    Choosing Locations 181
    Planning Your Scenes 183
    Directing 186
    Working with Actors 191
Techniques for Digital Features 194
    Lighting 195
    Depth of Field 197
    Shutter and Frame Rate 197
    Sharpness 198
    Style 199
Post-Production and Editing 200
    Watch and Log 201
    Create the First Cut 201
    Create a Rough Cut 201
    Work with Sound 202
    Create the Final Cut 202
And...Cut! 203

Chapter 9   **Basic Editing Techniques** **205**
Capturing Footage 206
    Manual Capture 207
    Automatic Capture 209
    Timelines 213

Editing It Together 217
        Making Straight Cuts 218
        Splitting Clips and Inserting Edits 220
        Inserting B-Roll Intercuts 222
        Adding Transitions: Fades, Dissolves, and Wipes 225
        Adding Titles 226
    And...Cut! 229

Chapter 10   **Audio and Music for Your Video** **231**
    Getting Good Sound 232
        Using External Microphones 233
        Recording Sound 237
        Recording Alternatives 240
    Adding Music and Soundtracks 241
        Choose Your Music 241
        Gaining Music Rights 243
        Using Music Libraries 244
        Making Your Own Music 244
    Foley Work and Sound Effects 245
    Adding Narration 248
    Editing Tips for Sound 250
    And...Cut! 253

Chapter 11   **Special Effects** **255**
    Special Effects Basics 256
        Filtering Colors and Appearance 256
        Applying Effects Over Time 261
        Fades in Adobe Premiere and Final Cut Express 264
    Adding Motion Effects 267
        Basic Motion 267
        Graphic Overlays 271
        Titles 275
        Compositing Video 281
    And...Cut! 286

Chapter 12   **Output Your Work** **287**
    Options for Output 287
    Output for Analog Delivery 289
        Getting Your Video on DV Tape 290
        Getting Your Video on Analog Tape 293
    Output for Digital Delivery 294
        Digital Movie Choices 294
        Exporting to a File 295

Getting Your Video on Disc 297

    Creating a DVD 298

    Creating a Video CD 304

Video for Internet Distribution 305

    Internet Deliverable 305

    Internet Streaming 308

And...Cut! 312

Appendix A   **Glossary** **313**

Index **325**

Acknowledgments

The authors would like to thank Jane Brownlow, Tana Allen, Elizabeth Seymour, and Gene Hirsch for their hard work and patience while editing and managing this project. We'd also like to thank the following people who helped us with advice, material for the book or CD-ROM, or who lent us access to their equipment, facility, or brain: Sam Watson and Sound By Sam (www.samwatson.com), Samuel Crow and F.O.C. Films (www.focfilms.com), Anita Modak-Truran and Questing Beast Productions (www.bellesandwhistles.net), Kent Moorhead and Forever Young Productions (www.foreveryoungproduction.com), Diego Velasco, Valerie Blakey, Tom Beck, Jerel Levanway, Joy Parikh, Upa and Nora Parikh, The Levanway Family, The Shilstone Family (Jack, Miriam, Anne, Mark), Turner Crumbley, Mitchell Moore, Hal and Mal's, Amy and Dakota Kraus, Ken Stiggers and PEG Network, Whitney Orr and Lisa Siegel, Darienne Wilson, Ward Emling, Lida Gibson, Remy Zero, (www.remyzero.com), Lhay Thriffily, Tom Beck, Chad Robertson, Shannon and Wayne Butler, Scott Lumpkin, and Tom McGraw.

Special thanks to Brian Hilburn of Avalon Digital (www.avalondigital.net) as well as to filmmaker Philip Scarborough for their help beyond the call of duty with clips, advice, camerawork, and even on-camera appearances. Thanks also to Monte Kraus of Krauscape Films (www.krauscapefilms.com) for access to his facilities, equipment, and permission to use some of his work in our examples.

Thanks to Gateway, Inc. for providing an excellent video-capable PC (complete with a Pinnacle Systems video editing package) for the Microsoft Windows-based screen shots. Thanks also to Apple, Inc. for providing Final Cut Express and to Adobe Systems, Inc. for providing the lastest version of Adobe Premiere.

Nina would like to thank Gerald, and Todd would like to thank Donna for putting up with the hectic schedules and crazy demands of getting this book together.

Introduction

The video world has gone digital; there's no question about that. Most home electronics sale flyers aimed at the consumer feature tons of digital video (DV) camcorders, with only a few older-style analog camcorders advertised. The reason is clear: with a slight increase in price, a DV camcorder affords a number of advantages, the most significant of which is how easy your digital video will be to edit with a computer.

With all of the features a digital video camcorder can give you, though, the camera itself can't help much with videography and technique. That's the idea behind this book; a book that the authors wish we'd been able to read a few years ago. Our collective experience and the advice of our peers are in here. This will not only help you to learn how to use your camcorder (which can be accomplished by reading your camcorder's manual) but how to capture *good video* of the events, moments, and scenes that you're recording. In particular, we show you how to get video that can be used to edit your project into an entertaining, informative, or useful final production that you'll be proud to display or distribute.

Editing is the key to most projects. With a digital video camcorder, you'll be able to record all sorts of events and load them into your computer. Then, using non-linear editing (NLE) software—ranging from free options such as Apple's iMovie to expensive "prosumer" editions like Final Cut and Adobe Premiere—you'll be able to edit that raw footage into a video presentation that communicates the information, ideas, or entertainment that you want to convey.

You'll find that "Get Creative! The Digital Video Idea Book" is essentially a guide to professional tips and techniques for capturing quality images and sound into your camcorder and then editing those images in an effective way. Some of the techniques and projects we'll cover include:

- How to choose the correct digital camcorder for your needs.

- What computer software and hardware to select for your editing.

- The Do's and Don'ts of home video.

- How to turn your home video clips into an entertaining presentation that your neighbors and friends will honestly enjoy.

- How to shoot events and weddings so that the edited project will woo and please the participants.

- How to set up and perform interviews that look and sound made for video.

- Recording and editing projects that communicate ideas and make money for small business or non-profit use.

- Filming your own documentary-style projects, including personal documentaries, "day-in-the-life" type documentaries, and even the sort of documentary you'd see on PBS or cable television.

- Using your digital camcorder to make a digital feature film—either a short feature or a long, independent movie. It is possible with a decent consumer or "prosumer" camcorder, a good script, some actors, and dedication.

In addition to these tips and techniques, you'll learn essential computer-based editing skills, and you'll garner advice on recording sound for your video, adding soundtracks, adding special effects and titles, and how to dig deeper into your editing software. You'll also find a bonus chapter on the companion web site which includes a discussion on marketing and promoting your projects and—if you've worked up a feature or a documentary— how to get it into a film festival or otherwise seen by the public.

Who Should Read This Book?

If you have a digital camcorder or you're thinking of purchasing one and want to improve the quality of your edited video projects, you should read this book. You'll find tips, techniques, and advice that will go a long way toward making the work you do behind the camcorder and in your editing software more professional-looking and productive.

This book is neither a replacement for your camcorder's owner manual nor is it an in-depth text on a particular video editing software package. While you'll quickly get a sense of the basics for both camcorder operation and software editing, both of these topics are too product-specific for the overview presented here. This book is about developing techniques and executing particular projects. You'll still want to learn about your camcorder and your editing software from their respective manuals (or other resources).

We also recommend that you be reasonably computer literate—you know Microsoft Windows or the Mac OS well enough to access the Internet, write documents in a word processor and, perhaps, have played with technologies such as digital movies or digital music files. If you've got a solid sense of how to use the mouse and keyboard, though, you'll have enough computing knowledge to take on the ideas presented in this book.

The CD-ROM included with the book features over 600 megabytes of sample clips that you can view to get a sense of what we're talking about, as well as entertaining sample projects to inspire you. Look over the "ReadMe.txt" file on the CD-ROM to learn more about it; the CD-ROM has an HTML (Web-style) interface that you can view in a web browser application such as Internet Explorer by loading the file **index.html** or **StartHere.html**.

We've also set up a site on the Web designed to support this book. Visit **www.digitalvideoideas.com** for updates, a bonus chapter and appendix, errata, and discussion with the authors of the book. We'll post additional projects, samples, and explanations that you'll be able to view online. If you have questions about the book, please consult the web site first to see if they've been answered. We'll offer a forum online where you can ask questions, as well.

Choosing Camera Equipment

You may already have the camcorder that you want to use for your video excursions. If that's the case, skim this chapter to see what other items you might want to consider adding to your videographer's arsenal, and then move on to Chapter 2's computing discussion, where you'll learn about the computer hardware and software that is necessary to accomplish digital video (DV) editing on your PC or Mac, and Chapter 9, where video and editing techniques are covered.

If you don't already have a digital camcorder, we'll walk you through some of the considerations that will help you get a good one. These days, digital camcorders (which record video directly into a computer-readable format) are available in a variety of price ranges and styles, so you're likely to find a pretty decent fit. Digital camcorders are still more expensive than common *analog format* camcorders, such as VHS and Hi8, but prices are coming down. Of course, you can always opt to use an analog format if you really want to—it requires an extra step for *digitizing* (turning the tape into a computer-compatible file format), but if you already have a camcorder or you have good reason to consider an analog format, you can still manage to edit the video. Let's take a look at analog technology first, and then we'll touch on some of the other considerations that can help in your camera decision.

focus

Throughout this book you'll find that we sometimes generically refer to the device you'll use to record images as a "camera" even though we're using camcorders. The word "camera" is used throughout the film and video world to refer to all types of motion, film and video cameras and camcorders, so it's tough to get out of our vocabulary. Just know that, in this book, they're synonymous unless otherwise noted.

Analog vs. Digital

For starters, you may be wondering what's the difference between analog and digital camcorders. An analog camcorder records a video signal to tape—usually a VHS-C (for *compact*) or Hi8 tape, although a number of similar standards (such as SVHS and Beta) are also available. That signal can then be played back by the camera or by a compatible playback device such as a VCR. The signal can also be played to special computer equipment, which can *digitize* the signal by analyzing the signal information and turning it into the 1s and 0s that a computer can understand and manipulate. In essence, the process is similar to the scanning of a photograph or the recording of a song to an audio CD—the recorded material is turned into a computer file so that it can be manipulated using your PC or Macintosh.

How DV Camcorders Work

What's unique about a digital camcorder is that the camera itself has enough electronics inside to make the jump from live image to computer file without the in-between step of digitizing. While most digital camcorders still record to a type of tape (although not *all* digital camcorders do so), they're recording digital information—basically, a computer file. This has a particular advantage in that it doesn't *degrade* when copied. The quality of the original image, as captured by the camcorder's lens and then translated into a computer file, remains within the file until that file is altered, and simply copying the file won't alter its quality.

Why is this? Any camcorder uses technology similar to a computer scanner, employing something called a *charged coupled device (CCD)*. This device registers various light levels and records them. With an analog camcorder, a continuous, modulated video signal is recorded on magnetic tape; by contrast, a digital camcorder records a computer file filled with 1s and 0s that represent the video signal—in the same way that a computer would store and read a word processing document, for example. That digital data—which is really a computer file that's in the standardized *DV Stream* format—is then stored to one of a few different tape formats from which it can be transferred easily to a computer or copied between camcorders without any loss in quality.

With a consumer digital camcorder, that tape format is most likely the popular MiniDV (Mini Digital Video) format, but you'll also find that Digital8 is common (it's a Sony-specific technology), MicroMV is gaining steam (another Sony-only technology), and the recordable digital video disc (DVD) camcorder is emerging on the consumer scene as a viable alternative to tape. Currently, however, MiniDV rules the consumer and "prosumer" (high-end hobbyist) market.

In professional circles, DVPRO and DVCAM formats are commonly used. They're similar to MiniDV in that they use the DV format for storing the data, but the tape runs at slightly different speeds and with different specs that sometimes make the professional versions a bit more reliable. Table 2.1 takes a look at both the analog and digital camcorder formats that you might encounter.

 zoom-in ————————————————————

It's important to realize that while the analog types represent various technologies for the **recording** process, the digital differences are mostly about the type of tape or media used. (MicroMV and DVD use different file formats as well, but the others all create DV Stream files.) In digital production, the underlying DV format technology is similar; what differentiates competing brands of digital camcorders is the media they use, the optics (lenses) that are offered, and the internal digitizing technology, which may be superior in some cameras compared to others.

It's worth noting that the Betacam and Betacam SP are common analog formats for professional video production—most local TV stations' news departments that haven't switched to digital are using Betacam SP equipment, which gives a much better color reproduction and overall warmth compared to other analog video technology. Digital Betacam (called "DigiBeta") is Sony's follow-up that uses digital technology but gives some great results that many videographers believe are very *filmic*, or film-like, in its tones and colors, making it popular for documentary and feature productions.

Choosing Your Camcorder Format

Which format should you choose? The easy answer is MiniDV—it's the standard for most consumer digital camcorders as well as for many professionals. The majority of camcorders that you can rent or borrow to film a digital video production use MiniDV tapes and technology. For the

TABLE 1.1

Various Camcorder Formats

FORMAT	DIGITAL OR ANALOG	RESOLUTION	NOTES
VHS	Analog	About 250 lines	Big tapes equal big camcorders
VHS-C	Analog	250 lines	Compact tapes, limited to 30 minutes
SVHS-C	Analog	About 400 lines	Small tapes and better quality
8mm	Analog	270 lines	An early favorite thanks to compact tapes
Hi8	Analog	400 lines	An improvement on the original 8mm format in quality
MiniDV	Digital	500–540 lines	Most common for consumer DV
Digital8	Digital	500 lines	Sony standard, uses Hi8 tapes for digital recording
DVCAM	Digital	500 lines	Sony's pro-DV format
DVPRO	Digital	500 lines	Panasonic's pro-DV format
DVD-CAM	Digital	520+ lines	Records MPEG-2 video directly to DVD media
MicroMV	Digital	530 lines	Sony-only technology, small tape with extra electronics

best compatibility and what many argue is the best quality in consumer and prosumer equipment, choose MiniDV.

But that's not the last word. If you're partial to Sony products or you're willing to veer a little off the beaten path, Digital8 is great, because the tapes are less expensive and sometimes a bit easier to come by in convenience stores and supermarkets. Then again, DVD-based camcorders are growing in popularity, partly because of the ease with which the media translates to the consumer setting—with the latest round of cameras you can record directly to DVD-R (DVD-Recordable) discs and then pop them in a consumer DVD player for playback. Check for software for editing compatibility, however, as these camcorders are pretty new on the scene.

Both DVD recording and MicroMV are newer technologies that aren't nearly as mainstream as the other two, so they're a tougher call. If you appreciate the advantages of those technologies, the only real step necessary before making the decision is to research the compatibility of a particular camcorder with the PC hardware and software that you intend to use for editing. If you can get the images from the camcorder into your software with a minimum of fuss, any of these recording mediums should be acceptable.

The MicroMV format and technology are interesting, as they allow Sony to create small camcorders that also take good *still* images. The MicroMV tapes offer additional memory for storing electronic information, such as on-screen catalogs, tape titles, and chapter markers, essentially making it easier to search the tape for specific scenes. The MicroMV camcorders tend to use higher resolution charged coupled devices (CCDs—more on them in the next section), making them an interesting alternative for still photography as well as for video—in a word, you could use a MicroMV camcorder for both video and for reasonably high-resolution photographs, negating the need for a second 35mm-style digital still camera.

DVD technologies are handy, too, for the simple reason that DVD-R media is reasonably inexpensive, durable, shippable, and easily played back in consumer equipment. DVD camcorders are just starting to appear on the scene, but they may have a bright future.

Finally, if you already have an analog format camcorder or you're swayed by the incredibly cheap pricing of SVHS-C or Hi8, you can use analog camcorders with your computer—you'll just need to consider the section "Adapting and Importing Analog Video" in Chapter 2 to get a sense of how you'll make that analog video work.

focus

This chapter focuses on digital video technologies, but plenty of good reasons exist for buying an analog camcorder if you're leaning that way. First, analog is much less expensive—good cameras can be acquired for a few hundred dollars, while comparable digital cameras are $400–500 more than their analog brethren. Second, VHS-compatible formats may be easier to view at home, since you likely have a VHS player connected to your TV. If that's the case, a VHS-compatible format is a consideration—with the right digitizing equipment (described in Chapter 2), you can still edit your videos on your PC or Mac.

Understanding CCDs

At the heart of any camcorder is the CCD, a small, solid-state chip that's designed to turn light information into an electronic signal that is then recorded by the camera in either an analog or a digital format. The analog formatted electronic signal can be read by special play heads (similar to a cassette player reading audio from a cassette tape) that turn the signal back into a presentation of light and color. That's how any standard-issue VHS-based VCR works in a home entertainment system. A digital signal is stored as 1s and 0s in a file format that can be played back or edited on a computer using applications that recognize the file format. In fact, because it's a digital file, the format of the *media* for that file becomes less relevant. For instance, a digital movie file can be stored just as easily on a MiniDV tape, on a computer's hard drive, or on removable media such as a DVD-R disc, as long as there's space for the file.

Likewise, that digital file is limited to playback on a computer: it can be played back by dedicated devices that have the processing capability to turn that digital file back into an electronic signal that, in turn, can be presented in light and color—that's what a consumer DVD player does. Aside from the media (tape versus disc) and some other feature tweaks, this analog versus digital distinction is the most significant difference between the older VCRs and newer DVD players.

But back to the CCDs: A CCD can be of varying quality, and many high-end camcorder manufacturers will argue that their CCDs—or the processes they use to manufacture them—are superior to others. That's something you'll have to test subjectively, or you can take the advice of professionals—depending on who you talk to, some will prefer high-end Sony equipment over Canon equipment, for example. Others will prefer certain qualities or characteristics of JVC over Sony, or Canon over JVC, and so on.

In addition to personal preference and qualitative judgments such as color reproduction and "warmth," some differences between camera types are measurable. Camcorders can show two basics stats that will help you as you shop for them: the *number* of CCDs used in the camcorder and the *resolution* of the CCDs.

These days, you'll probably shop for either a one-CCD camcorder (often called a "one-chip" camera) or a three-CCD camcorder (a "three-chip" camera). The difference is essentially that the single CCD in a lower end camera is responsible for capturing all of the colors, while a three-chip camera separates color responsibilities into red, green, and blue for each of the individual CCDs. The result is that, on the whole, three-CCD digital camcorders approach broadcast quality, while one-chip camcorders are pretty much stuck in the consumer category. (Plenty of people use one-chip cameras for a variety of professional and business tasks, but serious filmmakers and videographers grab a three-chip camera when they are going to shoot a DV project.)

The other issue that comes up when you're shopping is the *resolution* of the CCD, which is measured in *pixels*. A pixel is a "picture element," which is a sophisticated way of saying "a dot." The more pixels, or dots, in a given area, the better the resolution of an image, which generally results in better sharpness and detail. For analog consumer cameras, the CCD resolution can be relatively low—between 270,000 (270K) and 460K pixels. The typical consumer digital camcorder often has a CCD rated at 680K. What's becoming more common, however, is a higher resolution CCD, such as a *1 megapixel* (more than 1 million pixels) CCD or those at 2.1 million pixels (2.1 megapixels) or higher.

What's interesting about the pixel rating is that it generally has little to do with the overall quality of the *video* image—once you get much more than 400,000 pixels, the number of additional pixels won't alter the quality of video playback dramatically because of the limitations inherent in most of television and video playback equipment. Where the pixel rating is more significant is in *still* photography—in many cases, camcorder manufacturers are using these higher end CCDs so that still images taken with the camcorder can rival those taken with digital still cameras. It's also worth noting that a 2-megapixel CCD in a $1500-2000 digital video camera takes the equivalent of a dedicated digital still camera that might cost less than $200 at a local electronics store.

A camcorder or still camera equipped with a 2-megapixel CCD can take images that reach 1600 × 1200 pixels in resolution; for photos that need to be printed, that much resolution can look good when printed up to about 8 × 5 inches using a good inkjet printer and photo paper. However, that much resolution simply isn't necessary for video—even high-end DVD video is only 720 × 480 pixels in resolution (about 345,000 pixels), so for pure video purposes, these higher resolution CCDs aren't necessary. Unless you're really set on the convenience of taking both video and still images with the same camera, you might save money by sticking with a camcorder that has a lower resolution CCD.

focus

It's interesting to note that some camcorders at the highest end of the video spectrum—the $3500 Canon XL-1s, for instance—offer three CCDs that are rated at only 270,000 pixels each. Taken together, that's a lot of pixels, but it also shows that, when focused exclusively on video production, camcorders simply don't need the CCD resolution that high-end digital photography requires.

Shopping for a DV Camcorder

Nearly all of the innovation in the camcorder market is taking place in digital video camcorders, and digital is much more convenient for computer-based editing, which is what this book is about. We'll focus on how to make the decision to purchase a DV camcorder in this chapter instead of focusing on analog camcorders. If you've decided to stick with analog formats such as SVHS-C or Hi8 for your video work, that's great—you'll be able to use analog-to-video conversion hardware to edit that video using your computer. But since most of the analog camcorders still on the market are at the low end of the spectrum, buying a new one is a decision that should be fairly easy for you to make—choose a format and buy the most camera you can afford.

The wide-open DV market makes your choices a little more interesting. (Table 2.2 shows digital camcorder manufacturers.) The first decision you'll need to make about buying a DV camcorder is how much money you want to spend, at least in broad terms. Currently, there's a fairly significant break at the $1500 mark, which tends to dictate whether the camera uses a single CCD (below $1500) or three CCDs (above $1500) to record the picture. Some camcorders buck this trend, as usually is the case with lower end camcorders that are loaded with extra features that put them over the $1500 mark, even though they may have only one CCD.

TABLE 1.2

Digital Camcorder Manufacturers and Their Technologies

COMPANY	WEB SITE	DIGITAL TECHNOLOGIES
Canon	www.canondv.com	MiniDV
Hitachi	www.hitachi.com	DVD-RAM, DVD-R
JVC	www.jvc.com	MiniDV, DVCAM
Panasonic	www.panasonic.com	MiniDV, MPEG-4
Samsung	www.samsung.com	MiniDV
Sharp	www.sharp.com	MiniDV
Sony	www.sony.com	Digital8, MiniDV, DVPRO

One-CCD camcorders are useful for consumer applications—and their prices are getting lower all the time. Most of these single-CCD camcorder models weigh relatively little and are designed for home video or small business applications such as real estate. These cameras are fine for everything from shooting birthdays and vacations to shooting company video that you intend to present on the Internet—in fact, such a camcorder would do a great job for a piece you plan to use for a company or charitable banquet, or even, if the lighting and sound were well managed, as a sales video for your organization.

Pricier prosumer and professional models tend to be three-CCD camcorders that capture the red, green, and blue hues of the image that comes through the lens. This tends to give better reproduction, richer color, and better use of light and shadows; overall, there's simply more tone to the image. That said, the actual image quality and appearance relies greatly on the lenses that the camcorders use—which is the primary reason that DV camcorders can cost in the $2000–5000 range—the more you spend, the better the lenses and the more flexibility you have to change or augment the lenses and the camcorder's ability to get different shots.

Another reason that one-CCD camcorders can get to be a bit pricey is the feature set—anything from a higher resolution CCD for still photography to additional digital features for editing, image stabilization, night-time shooting, additional storage or connection technologies, or audio recording. In fact, the features on a consumer camcorder can take you in two directions—closer to professional-quality video or closer to a Swiss Army knife of computer multimedia. Which end you opt for depends on your focus on high-quality video versus how many options you want for still images, Internet video, and other such add-ons.

focus

When you're looking at extremely compact or some low-end camcorders, make note of whether the camcorder offers an **accessory shoe** (an on-camera connector that you'd find on high-end 35mm film cameras) for lighting, microphones, and other devices. While most camcorders include shoes, you might be sorry down the road if your camcorder doesn't feature one and you didn't check before you bought it. Likewise, not all camcorders have analog inputs (ports for accepting an analog connection from, say, a VCR), which enable you essentially to use the camcorder as a digitizing device for older analog sources by recording directly from that source via RCA or S-video cabling. Again, it's a feature you might want to have, particularly if you get serious about editing your videos into larger projects.

Videography Features

When you're shopping for a camcorder that promises to create the highest quality video, you can narrow down the feature set that you're looking for to some basic, but important, considerations, including the following:

- **Number of CCDs**   Three CCDs are almost always better than one, particularly for the serious videographer.

- **Lens quality**   One way serious, high-end camcorders are differentiated is by touting the name-brand lens manufacturer—it doesn't matter how good the sensors are if the lenses aren't equally impressive. Many new Sony camcorders use name-brand Carl Zeiss lenses, Canon uses its own highly regarded lens technologies, and Panasonic focuses some of its marketing on the fact that its cameras use the respected Leica brand lenses. At the upper reaches of the MiniDV camcorders, lenses are interchangeable, making it possible to change to a specialized zoom or wide-angle lens. Interchangeable lenses are also par for the course in professional DVCAM and DVPRO-format cameras. The Canon XL-1 series, shown in Figure 2.1, is regarded by many as the gold standard in MiniDV production cameras. The XL-1 is designed to support interchangeable lenses and was specifically shaped to have a look and size that give it professional cache for news-gathering or documentary filmmaking.

- **Optical zoom**   For camcorders with fixed lenses, the optical zoom capability of the camcorder is an important number. Low-end camcorders support 10x–16x optical zooms, while higher end camcorders are capable of 20x or better. (The *x* rating means the multiple of zoom—a 10x lens can appear to be 10 times closer to the subject than the lens's *widest* angle.) It's worth noting that a lower optical zoom number doesn't always translate into a lower quality camera—some high-quality lenses have a more limited zoom capability and some camcorders have limited zoom because they're ultra-portable. What you *should* know is that the *optical zoom number* is much more important than the *digital zoom* rating for a camcorder; digital zoom is an internal function that uses processing routines instead of physical focus changes to attempt to zoom in on portions of an image. Digital zoom always results in a loss in quality and isn't often recommended under normal shooting conditions.

- **Manual overrides**   While many digital camcorders are fully automatic in nearly every sense, the best camcorders for the videographer are

FIGURE 1.1

The Canon XL-1

those that let you make some of your own decisions concerning white balance, exposure settings, manual focus, and so on. (See the glossary in Appendix A for more on these terms—they'll also be discussed throughout the book.) Not only should you be able to make these settings, but you likely want these settings to be *easy* to override—not buried deep in a menu, but accessible on the camera's body itself.

- **16:9 support**   *Aspect ratio* (the ratio of width to height in the final video image) can be an important consideration when you're deciding how to film a project. Not all camcorders have a setting that enables them to shoot in 16:9, which is the aspect ratio that's used for film and for high-definition television (HDTV). While 16:9 certainly isn't mandatory even for professionals, it's something to consider if you plan to transfer your digital documentary or feature to film, or if you'd like to see your video in letterboxed format or appropriately formatted on 16:9 television sets.

- **Lighting and advanced audio**   Camcorders with stereo audio inputs, direct support for professional-audio three-pronged XLR connections (for instance, the Sony PD-150 and DSR-250 models, as well as some JVC and Panasonic professional models), and those with hot-shoe or built-in support for on-camera lighting can be helpful to the professional or prosumer photographer who uses the camcorder in the field for news or documentary work or sophisticated home movies.

focus ───

XLR doesn't really stand for anything. According to the site www.nullmodem.com, a company named Cannon created the connector and then called it the "XLR series." The letters stuck when the connector style became a standard in 1982.

Multimedia Features

Camcorders that skew toward multimedia features are meant to be jacks-of-all-trades for the consumer market. (By *multimedia*, we mean camcorders that are designed to record in media other than typical video and sound—those that offer special features for still photography, Internet video transfer, voice recording, and so on.) The calling card of such a camcorder is a higher resolution CCD that's meant for still photography, but you'll find camcorders that offer additional features such as the following:

Flash

Some photo-capable camcorders include a built-in flash (like the Panasonic shown in Figure 1.2) that can be used to add fill light to a subject for a still photographer or to eliminate red-eye and similar effects. Some camcorders use an onboard *key light* for flashes, and some offer flash capability only when you're taking still shots.

focus

An onboard key light is usually used for filming in low-light situations, when it turns on and stays on while you're recording. With some multi-purpose camcorders, that light can also be used as a flash for still photos.

MPEG and Compressed Video Support

Some camcorders can be set to record directly to more highly compressed file formats that are more appropriate for sharing over the Internet. Instead

FIGURE 1.2

Panasonic includes a flash on many of its photo-capable models—shown is the PV-DC352 model. (Photo courtesy of Panasonic.)

of recording directly to DV Stream—the dominant file format for DV camcorders—a camcorder that records a more highly compressed scheme can cut out the middle steps of translating and compressing the video for transfer via e-mail or posting on the web. The downside is that compressed video is of markedly less quality than pure DV footage, so it's not ideal for actual broadcast or television-based playback.

focus

In this context, **MPEG**, which stands for the Motion Picture Experts Group, refers to a method by which a video file can be **compressed** so that it takes up less computer storage space and is therefore easier to transmit. We'll discuss that in much more detail in later chapters, particularly in Chapter 12.

USB, Wireless, and Removable Media

While most DV camcorders have an *IEEE 1394* port (also called *FireWire* or *i.Link*) for connecting directly to computers, those that have still photo capability will often offer *USB* (universal serial bus, a lower speed technology) connections as well, for transferring images easily from the camcorder to your PC. Likewise, camcorders with a still-photo capability will often offer a secondary method for storing those photos, separate from the camcorder, usually in the form of a memory card of some kind such as a MemoryStick, CompactFlash, SmartMedia, or a similar standard. These cards are used to save still images (or, sometimes, audio and compressed video) instead of storing those images on the same tape as the video images.

 *zoom-in*

More and more camcorders offer **Bluetooth** technology for transferring still images and compressed video feeds wirelessly. It may sound a little too high-tech, but it's become a reality—transferring data such as these images without wires is part of what Bluetooth is all about.

Digital Editing Effects

Digital effects can be as simple as being able to shoot in a simulated black-and-white or sepia mode or being able to add the types of transitions you're used to seeing in movies and TV shows—fades, washes, and graphical transitions—using nothing but the camcorder's menus. Having special in-camera editing and effects capabilities doesn't necessarily mean your camcorder isn't good for videography, unless it appears that those effects are made available at the expense of optics. That said, choosing a camera with digital editing effects in the camera is important if you don't plan to use a PC for your editing but you do want to be able to do some transitions, titling, and so forth. If you're planning to use a PC for editing, you can ignore most digital editing features—you'll likely want to shoot your video as cleanly as possible and add effects in software.

Audio Recording

Clearly, good audio-in is an important feature for a quality camcorder. Beyond this basic sound-gathering feature, however, some cameras offer the ability to use the camcorder as a voice recorder, for example, saving your speech digitally either to tape or to a memory card. This is something a reporter might be interested in using rather than something that would ensure professional sound gathering for video. Still, the feature might be handy for taking notes in the field or for recording someone talking in situations where you don't want to point a camera at them.

Renting vs. Buying

Another issue to consider when it's time to procure a camcorder for your videography is whether you actually need to buy the camcorder. Too often, the first stop for an amateur videographer is the consumer electronics store, which is probably the effect of reading one too many Sunday newspaper circulars and getting worked up about shooting videos. If you haven't yet made that particular plunge, we suggest that you pull back from the precipice and consider some other possibilities.

Renting a camcorder rather than buying is a good idea if you're not sure what camcorder you want or you're not sure that you want a camcorder at all. The cameras *are* pretty expensive, even for a basic consumer model. While you can spend a lot of time shopping for a camera and playing with it in the store, it can be worth your while to get your hands on the camera and spend some time with it in the field. Of course, that's not practical with many inexpensive one-chip cameras, but you should consider whether you can borrow such a camera from a friend to get a sense of how it feels. For pricier three-chip models, you can often find a place that will rent you the camera for a few days—that's a great way to get to know whether you like the camera's setup and operation.

focus

One counterpoint to this argument is that if you try a number of different cameras, you could end up with a few different tape or storage formats. If the footage you're shooting is important, you might experiment only with MiniDV camcorders, for instance, so that the camcorder you eventually buy is fully compatible with the tapes you make in the interim.

Another reason to rent a high-end camcorder is so that you can use a better camcorder than you can afford to buy. If you're not going into business as a videographer (or if it won't at least be a serious avocation), you may not be ready to drop thousands of dollars on a camcorder. (In fact, we wouldn't recommend it.) If, instead, you can get away with a less expensive camcorder for much of your shooting, you could opt to rent a pricier camera for important outings.

For instance, a small one-chip camcorder might cost $750 and be useful for a lot of your home video or video that's destined, for instance, to be published on your real estate web site. Then, after some months of experience with the camera, if you stumble into a project or assignment where you'll be asked to video a friend's corporate project or a wedding rehearsal, you could head to your local camera shop and see if you can rent a three-chip camcorder and perhaps an appropriate lighting rig or sound recording setup.

Obviously, whether or not you need to get a high-end MiniDV camera is a numbers game—if you buy a lower-end camera first and then realize you need a more serious camera, you might believe that you could have saved money by skipping over the little guy. But consider three possibilities:

- Once you've opted for the more expensive camera, you've still got the cheaper camera for secondary footage that can be useful for editing. (For instance, you might put a friend on the task of getting some wide shots or exterior shots with the small camera while you run the large one closer to the action.)

- The less expensive camera can sit in your camera bag (with a fully charged battery, of course), ready to be pressed into action as a backup if you have trouble with your main camera. Yeah, you'll feel a little silly walking around with that consumer model on your tripod at a wedding, but it'll beat getting no video at all.

- You've always got eBay. If cash is tight, a well-kept camera won't lose too much value on the used market, particularly if you've got a name-brand camcorder that's still relatively current. The big-time auction sites have a large enough and knowledgeable enough audience that prices generally get bid up to good prices on well-maintained equipment.

 zoom-in

Certainly the reasons to buy a camera are a little more obvious—you need access to it at all times, you're already committed to a brand or model, or you've crunched the numbers and found that it makes more sense to buy the camera for a single project than to rent it for that duration. (If you know you'll need a $2500 camera for 25 days at $100 per day to rent it, you've just broken even and you still own the camera at the end of the shoot, which is a good deal.) If you fit into that category, you should definitely consider buying a high-end camera and leaving the rentals for equipment you're going to need for short projects.

Filters and Lenses

One element of the camcorder purchase that a lot of amateurs don't think about is the issue of filters, adapters, and lenses that they might want to use. In fact, professionals always have a filter attached to their camcorders, if only to protect the lens from scratches and the sun—but we'd wager that a large percentage of consumers don't do the same. Another component to add to your camcorder shopping experience is to find out what filters and lens adapters are available for your camcorder, how much they cost, how universal they are, and which you might like to purchase immediately.

The most basic filter is an Ultraviolet (UV) light filter, which is used primarily to keep UV rays from damaging your camcorder's lens over time—although it has the additional benefit of being in the line of defense against possible damage to the lens, offering a thin, inexpensive barrier that can be the first to crack when a stray rock bounces into the lens and the lens cap is off. You'll also find that some camcorders offer a lens hood that can be screwed on over the lens to protect it from the sides while shielding the lens from glare (and giving an overall more professional appearance).

Aside from a UV filter, you'll find that many camcorder manufacturers and third parties offer polarizing filters, which are used to change the angle of light that enters the lens to help avoid reflections when you're looking through glass or water, for example. A skillfully used polarizing filter can actually help you shoot through the surface of water at the fish below, for instance; the filter is commonly used for shooting objects through windows.

Finally, a neutral density (ND) filter is a popular add-on for outdoor shooting, as it decreases brightness and increases contrast in bright sunlight situations. Some camcorders, in fact, offer a built-in ND mode that turns on a digital ND filter that can be handy for a similar effect, but the actual filter, like a UV filter, can be used to protect the lens as well. In fact, with many camcorder models, you can stack the filters on top of one another— the camcorder's lens housing is generally threaded to enable you to screw the filters onto the camera (see Figure 1.3).

In addition to filters, many camcorder manufacturers offer other screw-on or mounted add-ons that attempt to make up for the fact that lenses on consumer camcorder's aren't generally interchangeable. You'll find that the manufacturers offer zoom and wide-angle adapters that often augment the camcorder's ability to see different angles of a picture—the zoom might work with the 10x optical zoom of the camcorder to give it an effective 20x zoom, for instance, which beats going into a digital mode. Such adapters are sometimes offered in different *grades* (Sony, for instance, offers some $50 wide-angle adapters and some at nearly $200 for its mid-range camcorders) that can affect the overall quality of the shot.

FIGURE 1.3

Todd's Canon GL-1 has a screw-on UV filter that he leaves

And...Cut!

In this chapter, you learned a bit about the various camcorder technologies you'll encounter and how to choose the one that's right for you. We also discussed some camera lens accessories you might consider purchasing—other accessories will be discussed throughout the text. In the next chapter, we'll move on to a discussion of the computer hardware and software you'll need to edit your videos on a PC or Mac.

Computing Basics
for Video Producers

ONCE you've acquired your camcorder and associated equipment, you'll need to consider the computer and software that will serve as the platform for your video editing workstation. In this chapter, we'll take a look at some of the options at your disposal, including a consideration of the hardware you'll need for editing; the software you'll need for editing and storage; and, along the way, some extra tidbits you might simply *want* for your setup.

We'll then move on to look at some of the basics of computing and digital video, including a discussion of the file formats and some of the methods you can consider for dealing with your digital video files. Finally, we'll take a look at a few of the solutions you can use for getting analog video into your computer if you already have a library of VHS or Super8 tapes that you'd like to work with.

What You Need

In the past, video editing required the use of special arrays of electronics designed specifically for the task of managing the video edits. Many studio-based systems—including some still in use today—are *linear* editing systems, which are more or less limited because video can be cut and spliced only as you move from frame to frame and sequence to sequence. For the most part, this sort of editing requires that you have recorded your elements mostly in sequence (or that you build a *rough cut* of that sequence, which is simply a pasting together of the main elements of your video or film in the sequence in which they'll appear) and that you then intercut, overlay, or otherwise edit your video and audio within the time constraints of your rough cut. Of course, some human editors are adept at linear editing and don't find it all that limiting.

Computer-based editing systems allow *nonlinear editing* (NLE). In this case, you don't necessarily need a physical rough cut of your presentation; instead, you can work with clips stored in various places. Once those clips are *digitized* (turned into digital computer files), you can apply a time-honored computing tradition to the world of video editing—cut and paste. In other words, with NLE, you've got a bunch of flexibility when it comes to how you shoot your video, how you arrange it after it's shot, and how you ultimately cut the video together and add titles, transitions, effects, and so on.

The editing process has become relatively less expensive over the past few years. Whereas professional-quality NLE systems were tens if not hundreds of thousands of dollars just a decade ago, the steady march of computing technology has changed that over time, so that even analog NLE systems can be acquired for perhaps only a few thousands dollars over the initial investment in your computer.

Digital video (DV) has changed that equation even more. By offering near-professional quality (some say it's perfectly fine for professional use) in a form that is already digitized, a DV camcorder makes it possible to do nonlinear editing for free with software that ships with many computer systems (using Windows MovieMaker and Apple's iMovie). You can edit at a prosumer or even professional level for well less than $1000 by adding software to a computer that's equipped with an IEEE 1394 port and enough processing power to run the editing software. That's just about all it takes.

PC Hardware and Software

Because of the breadth of options in the PC world, you'll find plenty of PC brands and models that are touted as being ideal for working with digital video—and, of course, you'll find just as many that aren't designed to

Mac or PC?

If you're looking for an argument to help you choose a Mac over a PC, it's fairly straightforward—the Mac offers integrated tools for digital video that can all be acquired directly from Apple, if you elect to go that route. Buy an iMac or eMac equipped with iMovie, iDVD, and a SuperDrive, and you can edit and burn DVD movies without ever leaving Apple's domain. Likewise, at the higher end, Final Cut Pro and DVD Pro can work together to help you accomplish even more.

If you're looking for an argument for PC over Mac, here's another easy one—speed. Intel-based PCs are capable of higher raw processing speeds that can, at times, result in faster rendering of titles, effects, animation, and so on. In head-to-head contests, for instance, the Power Macintosh G4 can come in second to some high-end, name-brand PC workstations when both run Adobe Premiere through the same battery of tests. This isn't true across the board and in every instance, but in the aggregate, PCs are a bit faster, at least as of this writing.

If speed doesn't sway you, you're joined by a good portion of the video editing community that remains a Macintosh stronghold. Mac hardware is often seen as "sexy," and Apple software programs such as iMovie and Final Cut Pro are generally category leaders, bringing in accolades for ease of use and integration and causing many professionals to swear by (and frequently at) the Macs they refuse to give up. That said, either platform is fully capable, and you're free to use whichever makes you more comfortable.

handle DV at all. (This is in contrast somewhat to Macs, as every current Mac model offers FireWire ports, iMovie, and the promise that you can accomplish some video editing.) A number of manufacturers are adding special video editing packages to their consumer computing offerings, bundling software, required cables, and even such extras as DVD burners and DVD label machines to sweeten the deal.

As for editing software, there's no doubt that the PC offers more video editing software packages than you'll find for Macintosh, although many of the major packages are available for both. In the case of the PC, however, the only movie editing software made by Microsoft is Windows MovieMaker, which is aimed strictly at the consumer rather than the professional. Seekers of high-end editors turn to third parties for editing software.

PC Hardware

You will find that the basic requirements for working with digital video are an *IEEE 1394* port and a processor capable of running the editing software of your choice. (At the time of writing, the general recommendation is a Pentium 4–based PC.) You'll also need a great deal of hard disk space. And if you intend to distribute your edited videos on any sort of optical disc, you'll need either a CD or DVD burner installed in your PC (or connected externally).

IEEE 1394 is the name of the international specification (from the International Institute of Electrical and Electronics Engineers) that describes the type of port and interface that most DV camcorders use to connect to a PC. The specification was originally developed by Apple, which calls the technology FireWire. (Other companies can call it FireWire, too, if they opt to license the name.) Sony, which uses the port on many of its computers and camcorders, calls the technology iLink.

Here are some general hardware specifications to consider:

- **Processor**   Should be a Pentium 4, although, for instance, Adobe Premiere currently lists its minimum system as a 500MHz Pentium III. The faster your system, the better.

- **RAM**   The minimum for video editing tends to be 128MB, and, again, the more the better. Consider 512MB a practical minimum if you're serious about video.

- **Hard disk space**   Video editing requires a great deal of hard disk space—about 2GB per 10 minutes of video. Remember that you may want to work with more footage than what will comprise your final project. For an hour-long video, that might mean upwards of 15–20GB just while you're working on that one project.

- **Hard disk speed**   To work with digital video, a PC's hard disk must be fast enough—generally most drives meet this requirement, particularly those that use either a SCSI (Small Computer System Interface, pronounced "scuzzy") or an Ultra ATA (Advanced Technology Attachment) interface of any type. Some earlier Integrated Device Electronics/Advanced Technology Attachment (IDE/ATA) drives may not be fast enough (about a 4Mbps sustained rate of data transfer is required) for video transfer and editing.

- **IEEE 1394 port**   If your PC doesn't have an IEEE 1394 port, you can add one with a PCI (Peripheral Component Interconnect) expansion card relatively easily. Many recent models offer built-in IEEE 1394 support that includes a port on the front of the PC's case, which can be handy for connecting your camera quickly.

If you've already got a PC that meets most of these requirements, you'll find that you can add an IEEE 1394 card, for instance, to give your PC the ability to communicate with a DV camcorder. Again, particularly if you're

upgrading to do some video editing, you should check your software's
requirements; some applications require certain versions of Windows
(Windows 98 Second Edition or later is necessary for IEEE 1394
compatibility) and may specifically recommend that you purchase a
DirectX-compatible IEEE 1394 expansion card and that your sound and
video cards be DirectX compatible as well. (DirectX is Microsoft's
multimedia application programming interface, or API, which enables
applications to access multimedia hardware via special DirectX drivers that
are managed by the operating system.) In fact, you might need to shop for
a more sophisticated sound and/or video card if your PC is somewhat aged.

focus

Another hardware add-on that's handy for editing speed is a real-time effects processor. These usually come in the form of a PCI expansion card and can range widely in price—the Canopus DVRaptor, for instance, is a $600 card that includes Adobe Premiere, boosting the software's ability to show edits and effects more quickly; prices range up to about $4500 for a professional package from Canopus (www.canopus.com). Other vendors of real-time processors include Matrox (www.matrox.com), Media 100 (www.media100.com), and Pinnacle Systems (www.pinnaclesys.com).

PC Software

As mentioned, many software packages for video editing are available for
the PC, although a handful stand out. Probably the most popular choice is
Adobe Premiere (see Figure 2.1), which has been the standard-bearer for
years. Premiere is a professional-level editing suite available for both PC
and Mac. The cross-platform nature gathers many fans, although Premiere
has moved more to the PC side of the equation thanks to Apple's direct
competition with Final Cut Pro.

Premiere comes heavily bundled with tools to help you create your
videos, such as the Adobe Title Designer for creating professional-looking
titles for your videos and an application called SmartSound QuickTracks,
which lets you create royalty-free soundtracks for your videos. (See
Chapter 10 for more details on audio editing tools.) The Windows version
of Premiere offers special sound-sweetening tools built as DirectX plug-ins
as well as support for Windows Media importing, editing, and optimized
exporting.

One of Premiere's strengths is its integration with other Adobe products,
not the least of which is Adobe After Effects, an application aimed specifically
at creating video effects. After Effects is popular with the *Star Wars* "fanfic"
(fan fiction) crowd, who always want to make parodies of their favorite
sci-fi epic. Of course, After Effects has many, many other fans, as well—it's
a wonderful application for adding all sorts of effects to your video. You'll

FIGURE 2.1

Premiere is the standard-bearer for desktop video editing in Windows.

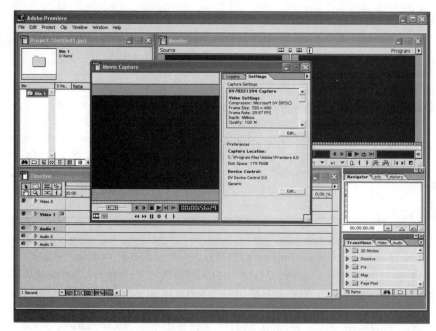

also find that Premiere works well with other Adobe products such as Adobe Photoshop and Adobe's library of fonts and type tools.

Of course, other options are available: another major player, Pinnacle Software, offers various titles for video editing and DVD burning—Pinnacle Studio is the home version that's focused on quick edits and DVD (or video CD) burning, and the Pinnacle Edition (see Figure 2.2) is the prosumer-level software for editing larger projects. Pinnacle is also the maker of Commotion, a popular digital effects tool.

Beyond those are some options at both the higher and lower ends of the spectrum. Avid (www.avid.com) is the norm for editing in most professional circles, particularly for film and network television, with prices to match—from $3000 for Avid Express DV to close to $200,000 for the high-end commercial tools. Other vendors of high-end systems include Media 100, NewTek (www.newtek.com), Incite (www.inciteonline.com), and DPS/Leitch (www.leitch.com). For lower cost options, check out Discreet Cinestream (www.discreet.com) or Vegas Video (www.sonicfoundry.com).

 zoom-in

Avid also offers a great price on one of its products—free. Avid Free DV wasn't yet released at press time, but is planned for mid-year 2003. The software is meant to compete with Apple's and Microsoft's free offerings, giving users a multi-track editor with some impressive capabilities (while, of course, giving them a taste of Avid's pricier options). Check http://www.avid.com/avidfreedv for information.

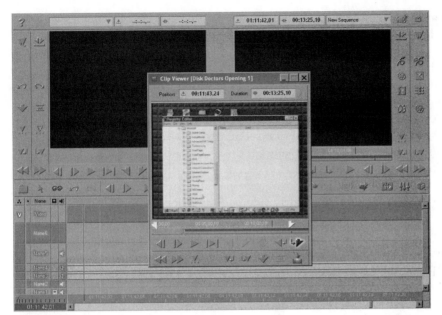

FIGURE 2.2

Pinnacle Edition is another pro-level editing tool available for PCs.

Mac Hardware and Software

The Macintosh portion of the video editing industry is a little different from that of the PC for two reasons. First, because Apple controls the operating system and hardware, it's much easier to recommend a specific model and vintage for video editing. Currently, any Macintosh on the market is capable of some level of video editing, and nearly all of the past few years' models have included a FireWire port and at least a copy of iMovie, Apple's consumer-level NLE package. And, of course, Apple has one of the more popular professional NLE packages, Final Cut Pro, which is appreciated both for its usefulness and its relatively low price. It's also Mac-only. Other solutions exist, as we'll discuss in a moment.

Mac Hardware

While all current Macintosh models support digital video editing on some level, the more powerful your Mac, the less you'll wait for your video editing software to catch up with you. The most powerful Mac models available are the Power Macintosh G4 line, which is recommended for video editing at the prosumer or professional level. A Power Mac G4 can be equipped with up to 2GB of RAM, it can handle hundreds of gigabytes of hard disk space, and it includes four PCI slots for adding expansion cards to upgrade the Mac to real-time editing and effects capabilities, to add computer displays to your Mac, and for other additions.

Another popular platform for Mac-based video editing is the PowerBook, which is often touted by Apple and video professionals as an ideal portable editing platform. The PowerBook G4, starting with the "Titanium" models, is generally powerful enough for professional-level editing, although some PowerBook G3 models are equipped with FireWire ports and are capable of running older versions of video editing software or iMovie with reasonable results. You can also equip any Cardbus-compatible PowerBook (all PowerBook G3 and G4 models except the original PowerBook G3 "Kanga" or "3500" model) with a FireWire expansion card, which would enable you to run iMovie or a third-party video editing package.

If you already have a Power Macintosh G3 or G4 or a PowerBook, you might be interested in comparing its specs against the requirements and recommendations that we would suggest for someone interested in running Apple's Final Cut Express or Pro versions (culled from both the side of the box and from our own experience):

- A 300MHz PowerPC G3 or G4 processor, with a 500MHz G4 processor required for real-time effects (a 667MHz PowerBook G4 is the suggested minimum for real-time effects in a portable setting)

- Mac OS X 10.2 or higher

- 256MB of RAM (with 384–512MB recommended as a minimum)

- 40GB or larger hard disk, with 100GB or larger recommended

Note also that the Power Macintosh G4 Cube models, the iMac DV model (and later), and any iBook equipped with FireWire can technically be used for digital editing, particularly with iMovie. However, as those models age, they become less likely candidates for prosumer-level editing.

The latest iMac G4 and eMac models, particularly those with DVD-R SuperDrives, are adequate for prosumer-level video editing, although even with some of those models you'll wait quite a while for digital effects rendering and so on. The iBook is probably the least equipped for video editing beyond the consumer level, with the double whammy of limited processor speeds (being the only new Macs that still sport a PowerPC G3 processor) and limited hard disk storage space. Still, they're handy for iMovie or the occasional higher-level task.

focus ————————————————————————————————————

The SuperDrive is Apple's name for a DVD-Recordable/CD-Recordable (DVD-R/CD-R) combo drive that the company includes in many of its Mac models. The SuperDrive is designed to work well with Apple's iDVD and DVD Pro software to create movie DVDs from edited DV video footage. The drives are generally Pioneer brand mechanisms and can be used with third-party DVD creation software, but Apple has made the integration of its NLE tools and its DVD creation tools a high priority, resulting in a near seamless integration between the software and the DVD-R hardware.

Macintosh Software

As mentioned, the big difference between Mac and PC is how much of the Mac experience is controlled by Apple. Not only does Apple make the computer hardware and the operating system, it also, in the case of digital video editing, makes some of the leading software application packages. Those include iMovie for consumer-level editing and the Final Cut lineup—Final Cut Express and Final Cut Pro—for prosumer and professional editing, respectively.

iMovie is easily the best consumer video editing package that we've seen, so much so that many iMovie users find a user manual superfluous. With iMovie 3, the feature set has been ratcheted up somewhat, so referring to a manual might be necessary. For basic editing tasks, however, the interface is streamlined and fairly straightforward (see Figure 2.3).

FIGURE 2.3

iMovie offers an attractive and fairly easy to grasp interface for video editing.

iMovie is suited, at first blush, to home video and consumer-level editing of organizational videos or event videos. The truth is, however, that iMovie gets used a lot by professionals, too, who sometimes find it useful for quickly cutting together a demo reel, a mock-up of a future project, or a quick in-the-field edit to show a client, put on the Internet, or burn to optical media. The interface makes it truly a simple matter to bring in digital video clips, arrange them on the timeline, drop in simple transitions, and even edit the audio. Then you can be back out to tape in a matter of minutes.

iMovie integrates closely with iDVD if you happen to have a DVD-R SuperDrive in your Mac. iMovie comes with FireWire-equipped Macs and can currently be downloaded for free or purchased as part of the iLife package. (iDVD comes with compatible Macs, but it can't be downloaded otherwise; it must be purchased to upgrade older models.)

While iMovie also can add titles, transitions, and special effects to a video—all of which would be high enough quality for the documentary video festival circuit—it leaves off for the prosumer and professional where Final Cut picks up. Final Cut Pro made quite a splash in its first few years on the market, thanks partly to the fact that it was less expensive than many of the systems with which it competed, while it promised professional-level video editing without requiring additional hardware, as many previous solutions had. That and an impressive interface that made editing familiar and somewhat more simple for video professionals helped make Final Cut Pro one of the cutting-edge tools when DV started to take off as an alternative to analog video.

Final Cut Pro offers capabilities that go beyond a consumer-level application such as iMovie, including professional-level transitions and effects, the ability to color correct video, support for chromakey compositing (putting your talent in front of a weather map, for instance), and the ability to skew and angle your video—lots and lots of features. The interface gives you access to 99 tracks of audio and virtually unlimited tracks of video, making serious productions much easier to manage than what's available with an interface such as iMovie's. Final Cut Pro also supports various formats, including traditional video formats, DV, DVCAM, and others. Final Cut Pro can also support the film and high-definition TV 16:9 aspect ratio, and it can be used at 24 frames per second to edit film, particularly when coupled with Apple's Cinema Tools for Final Cut Pro.

Is Final Cut Pro overkill for what you intend to do? Apple must have realized that somewhere between $999 professionals (Final Cut Pro) and $0 consumers (iMovie) are some prosumer and organizational customers who need to edit DV with a more sophisticated tool. Enter Final Cut Express (see Figure 2.4). Final Cut Express tosses out some of the high-end options— you can't edit film or nondigital video formats, you can't set up batch

FIGURE 2.4

Final Cut Express gives you the Final Cut interface and many of the tools, but without the high-end, high-dollar extras.

captures of clips, and you can't work with third-party expansion cards, for example—to offer the Final Cut interface and editing tools at a more palatable $299. For users who are sticking strictly with digital video, it's a great way to get access to professional-level titling and effects tools without spending quite as much money as the pros do.

We've talked a lot about Apple's tools, but they aren't the only tools available for the Mac. Adobe makes both Premiere and After Effects for Macintosh, which offer a cross-platform advantage of letting you use Macs and PCs together for larger projects. Premiere's interface is good—it's familiar to most folks who've done some editing in the past, and it offers many of the same strengths as Final Cut. Plus, Adobe offers both Premiere and After Effects together in the Digital Video Collection bundle, which also includes Adobe Photoshop and Adobe Illustrator for $1249 at the time of writing—an interesting way to negate the pricing advantage of Final Cut Express if you happen to need those other Adobe tools as well.

Some of the same names make Mac and PC solutions, so you'll find that Avid is a huge player in professional, broadcast-quality (and cinema-quality) Mac-based editing, as is Media 100, Pinnacle, and Canopus. On the low end of the market, iMovie has pretty much scared off any contenders, so you'll find few, if any, choices in the $50–$200 space.

Working with Digital Video

After you've put together your computer and software, you're ready to consider how you're going to get that video from the camera into your software, get it edited, and then get it back out of the software to an easily viewable format. Fortunately, all of that is relatively easy to do. Because digital video is stored as a computer file on the camcorder's tape (which is usually MiniDV tape but might be another format such as Digital8 or DVCAM), the process of *capturing* video from a digital camera is as simple as *copying* the file from your camera to the appropriate software program (see Figure 2.5).

After the digital video footage is captured (again, think *copied*) to the computer, you can edit it in your software. Digital video editing software will generally leave your original files intact, creating project files that rearrange the video into clips or on timelines, at least until a certain rendering phase takes place. At that point, the video data is collected and sometimes rewritten into new files, or "printed" back to videotape or to a similar media.

With many computer-based editing programs, that video will spend its entire time on the computer in the DV Stream format, which is the same format used by the camcorder and imported into the computer. Once the edits are complete, you can export back to your DV camcorder, which can then be used to play the video on a television, transfer it to an analog VCR

FIGURE 2.5

Here's an example of Adobe Premiere for Mac capturing video from the camcorder.

and so on. Or, you can leave the computer files stored on your computer for playback on-screen.

Sometimes, however, you may have good reason to not only store the video on your computer, but also to change the file format. And, in the process of editing your video, you may find that you've got other video clips to deal with that are already in a different format. In that case, you'll want to know a little something about the various video file formats, which are discussed next.

File Formats and Translation

Although the DV Stream format has some compression to it, its not nearly as compressed as many other video file formats, meaning the result is a fairly large file. In raw DV files, each minute of video takes more than 220MB of disk space, or about 13.2GB per 10 minutes of video. That's a lot of space, and, what's more, it's utterly impractical for just about any sort of playback or transfer aside from editing and moving from tape to hard disk and back again.

To use the video for different purposes, then, you'll likely translate it into another file format. Those formats can range from international standards such as the MPEG standards, to proprietary formats such as Apple's QuickTime or Microsoft's AVI or Windows Media formats. In many cases, that format is designed specifically for the targeted medium—if you're creating a DVD movie (or a video CD) from your DV Stream files, you'll edit them together and export them from your video editing software into an MPEG-2 file, a file with the standard compression and format for burning onto a DVD that can be played back in consumer equipment. MPEG-2, by way of comparison, requires about 2GB per hour, which means the files are a sixth the size of DV Stream files—that's part of what makes them work well for DVDs.

focus ————————————————————————————————

MPEG stands for the Motion Picture Experts Group (http://mpeg.telecomitalialab.com/), which is a working group, creates audio and video compression standards. Along with the MPEG-1 (compression that works for CD or hard disk storage), MPEG-2 (DVD-quality compression) and MPEG-4 (online streaming compression) video standards, MPEG also created the MPEG Audio Layer 3 (MP3) standard that's popular for music storage and online transfer.

Even so, the same file would be pretty close to useless for regular CDs or for hard-disk based movies—in that case, you'd choose an even more compressible format such as the MPEG-1 format, which requires about

1GB per hour. MPEG-1 is an older format that's less sophisticated, so you might begin to branch out to more proprietary formats such as the Windows Media format that's used on Microsoft Windows platforms or the QuickTime format used primarily on Macs, both of which can be used with various *codecs* (compressor/decompressors) to change their data rates and ultimate file sizes. (Both formats can also, in various capacities and with some limitations, be used on the opposite platform—you can play some Windows Media feeds on Macs and you can use QuickTime technology in Windows if the correct applications and support files are installed.) The more compressed a file (and the less sophisticated the codec), the less true it is to the original DV Stream file, perhaps introducing artifacts, color shifts, or blurred and blocky motion sequences.

At the other end of the spectrum are files small enough to be transferred or streamed over the Internet. These are highly compressed QuickTime or Windows Media movies; Real Media movies (www.real.com) for playback in the RealOne line of players (a popular but proprietary approach); or the MPEG-4 standard, which emerged relatively recently as a contender on the Internet streaming front. Using these formats, you can place a relatively small video file on a server and make it available to others over the Internet, or you can attach it to an e-mail, place it on a Zip disk, or otherwise make it accessible. The movie will probably be smaller in appearance and of much lower quality than the DV Stream file, but those technologies are getting better all the time, so that even relatively large movies can be streamed over an Internet broadband to a user with great results.

focus ——————————————————————————————

Video **streaming** is a process whereby small bits of a movie are sent over the Internet in packets and then reassembled on the receiving computer, so that the video can be displayed on that computer after only a short delay. The major advantages to streaming are that you can begin to watch a recorded video before the entire file arrives, and, for live events, you can view them nearly as they're happening. Certain file formats and codecs are better suited for streaming than others.

So how do you get from a DV Stream movie to one of these other digital movie formats? *Translation.* Generally you'll need either a video editing application that's capable of making the translation happen or you'll need to use a secondary application that's up to the task. With some video editing software (see Figure 2.6), such as Apple's applications or Adobe Premiere, you can output (usually via an Export command) directly to these other multimedia formats, choosing your codec and other options, such as the dimensions of the resulting digital movie in pixels and the throughput and/or number of frames per second in the digital movie, which can help to control the size of the movie file. (The smaller the image in pixel dimensions and the fewer frames, the smaller the file needs to be to store the entire movie.) In fact, it's not uncommon for computer-based multimedia movies to be half the resolution of DV and to show only 10 or 15 frames per second instead of the full 30 that NTSC (National Television Standards Committee) video generally uses.

For cases in which you can't easily translate to a particular format—or in which you need more efficient and effective translations—you'll turn to a utility program specifically designed for the task. One of the leaders in this area is Discreet (www.discreet.com), which make the Cleaner series of video encoding tools that enable you to translate to a variety of formats supported by Windows Media and QuickTime technologies. Canopus offers a fairly strong competitor in ProCorder, which is designed with much the same translation and encoding tasks in mind.

focus

In our experience, these tools can be handy to have, although they can also be expensive. The size and quality of files—particularly for use over the Internet and in other limited bandwidth situations—is clearly better from a dedicated utility than it is from a video-editing package, even in the tightly integrated world of Apple's QuickTime technology. If you're serious about Internet video in particular (or, more generally, in using your video in a variety of mediums), dedicated translation software is highly recommended.

Saving, Backing Up, Archiving

With the size of DV files comes a real problem for anyone interested in recording and editing more than a few minutes worth of video: How do

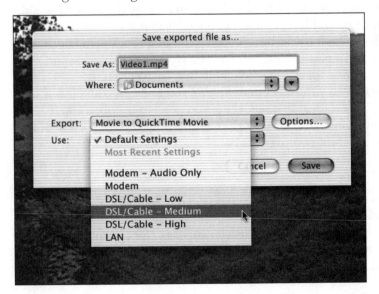

FIGURE 2.6

Using some video editing software, you can export directly to other movie formats.

you store that video, and, once you've got it in your computer, what do you do with it when you need to do something else? With that 13-plus GB of storage required per hour (and probably double to triple that amount necessary to edit a project *down to* an hour), even the most advanced computers are good for only a few projects before you need to start moving files around. Here are some thoughts on managing these huge files.

Archive Your Raw Footage

The DV tapes are relatively inexpensive compared to how much data they hold, so they can also be useful for archiving your files. In most cases, you can't export a video *project* file to tape, meaning you won't be able to back it up so that you can start immediately into your editing. Instead, you should consider two different points at which you archive your video. First, archive the *raw footage* tape, which is the one you used initially to get the shots that make up your video. You should use your raw footage tape as infrequently as possible, and once it's no longer necessary for getting the video into your computer, immediately store it in a safe, dry place where you can get at it again when necessary.

Archive a Rough Cut

One step that some amateur video editors skip is creating a *rough cut*— which is simply a series of shots that you plan to use in your video, set aside before you've done the detailed edits, titling, and transitions. When you have created that rough cut, drop in another DV tape and export that footage from your software to the tape. Again, this isn't quite the same as *saving* the project file—you would still need to re-import this footage and, probably, cut it apart with your video editing tools to restore it as individual clips. Still, that's much better than being forced to go back through all of your tapes to find a particular scene that you've chosen to use in your video. This is a great timesaving technique that enables you to reload the basic footage of your project without forcing you to dig into all of your raw footage tape. This is great in cases where you need to restore a clip that got cut too much in editing or rework an entire project (or a portion of the project) with different edits or effects.

Get a Big Drive

Serious video editors with multiple projects in development will need a large hard disk and potentially one that is dedicated to the purpose of storing video. If you use an external hard disk for this task (for instance a FireWire or USB 2.0 disk), it's easily transported or locked away for safekeeping. Today's standalone hard disks are getting larger and larger—approaching and surpassing the 500GB mark—and they can store a lot of video. If you're serious about storage, you can use RAID (redundant array of independent disks) technology to gather together terabytes of data storage that can be used to archive your videos. High-end storage still costs a little more, but it's nowhere near what it used to cost, and even small drives of only a few hundred gigabytes are worth every penny. With a hard disk, you can actually archive the project file, making it easier to dive back into it when necessary.

Burn It

Finally, if your projects are small enough, you can always consider burning the project data folders and other materials to DVD-R, which at 4.7GB is up to the task of storing about 20 minutes or so of raw DV video. It's not an ideal solution, but it's an option. (An even better option is looking into other removable options that enable you to store even more data, but most such options are pricey.)

focus

Using a lot of DV tapes? Don't forget to label them, and realize that DV tapes, just like VHS tapes, have a copy protection mechanism you can use to make sure you don't record over a tape that you've designated as a keeper. Look for a small switch that can be thrown back and forth on the tape to determine whether or not the tape is locked.

Adapting and Importing Analog Video

Before we finish this chapter, we should take note of a circumstance in which you may find yourself: You've got a great new (or fairly new) digital camcorder and you've got plenty of digital footage on little digital tapes. But what can you do about all that analog footage you took in VHS or Super8 or some other mode many moons ago? What will become of it?

The easiest answer is that if you want to edit it along with your DV footage, you'll need to *digitize* it. Indeed, turning analog footage into computer files used to be the norm for computer-based NLE tools—however, these days, it's becoming the exception. Still, a lot of analog tape out there needs to get into a computer for editing, and you have three options to accomplish the task: camcorder connections, a breakout box, and a PCI expansion card. Regardless of which option you choose, the net result is footage that you can get from the original analog format into DV, which can then be edited in your NLE application.

Camcorder Connections

The first option is to use the analog video input on your camcorder as a pass-through connection. With many camcorders—particularly those in the higher price brackets—you can connect S-video or composite cables to the camcorder, which then enables you to record the analog picture to digital tape just as if it were being viewed through the camera's lens. Once the analog images have been recorded to DV tape, the next step is to import from the camcorder to the computer just as you would any digital footage. (Nearly all camcorders have analog video *out*, so that you can watch the picture on TV and, therefore, record to an analog VHS VCR. But not all have an analog *in* that enables you to do the opposite.)

Breakout Box

Another fairly recent advance is the analog-to-IEEE 1394 (FireWire) breakout boxes offered by a number of companies such as SCM Microsystems (www.dazzle.com), which offers the Dazzle Hollywood DV Bridge (Figure 2.7) that enables connections from analog video devices directly to a PC's IEEE 1394 port. Other manufacturers that offer analog-to-digital breakout boxes include Synchrotech (www.synchrotech.com), Canopus, Formac (www.formac.com), and Sony Electronics (www.sel.sony.com).

PCI Expansion Card

The final solution is used less often these days, but it's still viable and a frequent choice for professionals. PCI expansion cards can take analog

FIGURE 2.7

The Dazzle Hollywood DV Bridge can be used for analog-to-DV conversions.

Photo courtesy SCM Microsystems, Inc.

inputs and digitize the picture into a DV-compatible format (or another digital movie format) that you can then edit on your computer. The cards are available from Pinnacle Systems, Matrox, Canopus, Dazzle, and many others.

And...Cut!

This chapter took a look at the computing resources needed and the optional equipment you can use for video editing. The discussion moved from computer hardware options to video editing software options and looked at the various video file formats, software that can be used to translate between those formats, and hardware that can be used to turn analog footage into digital footage that can be edited with NLE software. In the next chapter, we'll move on to suggestions and techniques for shooting good—or better—home movies.

Home Movies

WE'VE all been tortured by someone else's home movies—endless hours of driving from destination to destination, out of focus close-up shots of flowers and other wildlife, the shaky cam, the zoom in and out cam, boring and painstakingly bad piano recitals. You know what we're talking about.

Wouldn't it be cool if you could make a home video that you and your family actually wanted to watch every once in a while, for old times' sake? Producing a good home movie is difficult, in part because most people who don't work with a camera for a living don't know about the hard work—the planning and editing—that professionals do to make even a simple video entertaining and effective. The process of shooting home movies for most people generally involves turning the camera on and recording, with little attention to what and how it is being taped. But with some planning, you can avoid some of the pitfalls that lead to home movies that are more mind-numbing than the snow after a VHS movie ends.

Even badly shot material from any event would be more enjoyable to watch compressed down to 30, 10, or even 5 minutes—instead of hours. Of course, compressing hours of footage down to something watchable is a time-consuming task that you may not get around to if, say, you have a full-time job. That's why one of the keys to the successful home movie is to get *less* footage than you think you'll need.

On the flip side, since you're documenting real life as it happens, we realize it is sometimes difficult to decide what to shoot and when to turn off the camera. In this chapter, we'll look into how you can start to make those sorts of decisions, along with some other ideas and techniques for getting the footage you need in a manner that will be reasonably easy to edit down to something interesting enough to garner rave feedback at family reunions and neighborhood barbecues (or film festivals, pool parties, or whatever it is that goes on in your particular neighborhood).

What You'll Need

The essentials for a home movie are pretty basic: something to document, a camcorder to record it, and the desire to tell a story. Most boring home movies are that way only because they don't tell a story well. Truth is, *everything* has a story line; you just have to be willing to look for it. Take, for example, bathing a dog. Is there a story in there somewhere? It may not be a terribly complicated story—perhaps not quite the classic hero's story, with a sweeping crescendo, a fallen compatriot, and a false resolution before the final frames—but there is a story in it. To illustrate this concept, we will use a hypothetical story line about Nina's dog Monk—it's called "Monk's Bath Time."

Before we get too deep into finding the inner story, let's talk about the practical stuff. For a home movie, you'll generally want to be mobile, so of all the equipment we talked about in Chapter 2, you're going to go at it a little lean in this case. Most likely you'll be dealing with a lot of the stuff that's either part of your camera or attached to it. Because you're on the move, you probably can't clip a microphone to your subjects, and you'll most likely deal with natural light, room light, or perhaps a camera-mounted key light. Any more than that and you're probably straying from nonfiction.

Of course, the on-the-go nature of home video shooting means you'll likely want to have extra batteries and tapes on hand, as you'll be "in the wild" and may not have access to AC power or battery chargers.

How to Stay Organized

Successfully shot, whether it's documenting a dog's life or shooting the *Lord of the Rings* trilogy, is dependent on good *pre-production*. "Pre-production" may sound official, but it's just a term that's meant to suggest the planning; writing; and, of course, money-gathering stage of a video or film production process. The reason big movies sometimes go hundreds of thousands of dollars over budget usually is a result of poor pre-production. (Well, okay, sometimes budget overruns are due to acts of God—unexpected rain on days you're supposed to shoot outdoors—or acts of demigods, as in movie stars who storm off the set.)

What we're trying to say is that for whatever kind of shoot you're working on, pre-production planning is essential. Most of this is common sense. (Of course, it's common sense that's easily forgotten or ignored—we commit these sorts of bloopers on a regular basis. But it doesn't mean we don't try.) The classic shot-killers that planning can avoid include these:

- Forgetting to charge batteries
- Misplacing the lens cap
- Not locking down the camera on the tripod
- Forgetting the tripod or steadying device and getting a bad shot because your arm hurts and you move it as you're shooting
- Forgetting the tape or running out of tape during an important moment
- Not knowing that your subjects plan to turn off the lights in the room to give their presentation
- Not "checking your monitor"—meaning framing a shot poorly and shooting the segment without realizing there's a lighting problem, a distracting background object, or other problems
- Choosing a bad location for the camera that gets blocked by spectators or front-line subjects
- Assuming that your camera's microphone will suffice for the sound and not checking for ambient noise or accounting for chatter close to the camera

The most mundane tasks are easily forgotten, and generally these are things that can make or break shoots.

After dealing with the basics, make sure you have a clear idea of what you are going to shoot, where it will take place, and how long you intend on shooting. In our example, we know that "Monk's Bath Time" will start outside, when Monk is called in from the yard and then transitions into an interior shot in Nina's guest bathroom. Monk won't be terribly happy, and thus Nina won't be terribly happy, and lots of watery excitement is expected. In terms of shooting, this translates to the following:

- The different lighting circumstances of moving from outdoor to indoor illumination should be considered (she may not use lights inside, but she might need to white-balance the camcorder).

- Whoever is shooting will probably not need a tripod, because Monk will be a moving target that could knock over the tripod with the camera attached.

- An hour-long MiniDV tape should be more than enough, but a back-up tape is a good idea just in case.

- At least two hours of batteries would be ideal, as well as backups and a power adapter with extension cord—just in case.

focus ——————————————————————————————

Before she embarks on this escapade, Nina's camera operator should (**should** being the operative word here) label the tape before inserting it into the camera. That helps them avoid a common scenario: You're done shooting, you pop the tape out, put it in your pocket, pop in a new tape, and swear that you will label it and remember that the really funny footage is on the tape you put in your left pocket—and you promise to label both of them later. But you never do. So, once again, you are left with a stack of unlabeled memories never to be viewed. Label your tapes!

You can also prepare yourself creatively. If you want to get technical about it, draw up a storyboard or create a shot list. A storyboard is similar to a comic strip—it's a series of illustrations that tell a story (see Figure 3.1). A storyboard can help you visualize a story line for your event so that you're not just shooting random scenes. It doesn't need to be artistic at all (the illustration is a professional example); stick figure drawings or even still photographs will help you in your planning just as easily. Save the artistry for storyboards that you'll use to pitch an idea to a client if you're trying to sell video services.

You can also create a shot list that describes the shots you would like to get, preferably in the order in which you will shoot them, so that you can easily glance at your list while you are shooting. Both of these tools will help any shoot run more smoothly. For "Monk's Bath Time," Nina might write a list of some shots that will help tell the complete story:

Shot List for "Monk's Bath Time"

1. A wide shot of Monk frolicking in the yard

2. Nina gathering up all the bathing necessities

3. Nina leading a hesitant Monk inside

4. Shot of Nina and Monk entering the guest bathroom

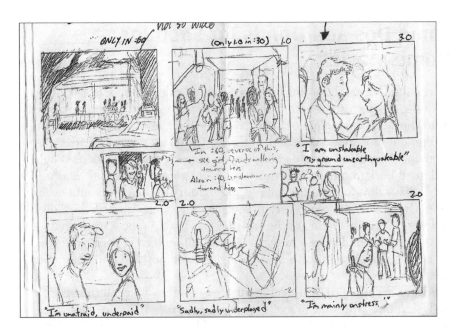

FIGURE 3.1

Here's a sample storyboard—another handy use for posterboard at the office supply store.

5. Close-up of the water coming out of the faucet

6. Close-ups of Monk's facial expressions during the bath

7. Close-ups of soapy hands

8. Shots of the struggling bather

9. Clean dog shaking self

10. A happy Nina

    Many opportunities for good footage will arise during the shooting process, but outlining a few essential shots will help you create a story with a beginning, middle, and end. Being prepared to tell a story before you begin shooting will help you stay focused during the event, and in the end it will help you create a much more enjoyable viewing experience for your family and friends. And, having said all that, be alert for spontaneous opportunities. A good videographer is generally ready to shoot on a few seconds' notice, when possible, to make sure candid shots get captured, along with one-time opportunities and other unscripted footage that might end up looking great in the final product. If you allow for some flexibility, good planning will actually allow for more spontaneity, because you'll have a good idea of how to keep the action moving forward.

Some Dos and Don'ts for Shooting Home Movies

As you'll see throughout this text, there are no rules for shooting digital video—only suggestions and techniques. Digital video is an interesting beast, because the technology has made high-quality cameras and editing equipment more accessible and, at the same time, the cameras are forgiving. While you should endeavor to get great shots with perfect light and great backgrounds, the primary goal is to get out there and shoot. You'll likely develop your technique and mastery of the equipment over time. (In fact, audiences in certain settings can watch video pictures of almost any quality as long as the *sound* is good; if they can't hear what's said or if the sound is too grating, a video is difficult to sit through. If the sound is good, however, sub-par lighting and composition don't hurt your video too much.)

Knowing some pro-level techniques can certainly help. In this section, we'll start out with some "Don'ts" and then move on to some "Dos" that serve as suggestions for better home video. Hopefully, these tips will keep you out of some of the classic potholes that home video producers fall into, while getting you some footage you'll be able to use in the editing bay.

Don't Narrate Constantly

It is not necessary to give us a play-by-play of every moment you shoot. One video we looked at in preparation for writing this chapter featured a family on a camping trip with the mother telling us every obvious detail of their trip. "Oh, we're getting out of the car now.... Dad's taking our stuff out of the car.... He's now taking the tent out of the bag.... Oh, look, there are some birds flying above.... Now we're walking to the river.... There's Lucy waving to me."

It was enough to make us want to shake the TV and scream, "Lady, you're not on the *radio!*"

For most types of documentary shooting, including home video, it's simply not necessary to tell the audience what they're seeing. Narration is a wonderful tool if the shooter is commenting on what is being shown, rather than stating the obvious. The woman in the family camping example could have had a much more enjoyable and informative home movie had her commentary been more like this: "Oh, I'm so glad to be out of that car! It's chilly out here tonight. As we drove in, the park ranger said it could get to freezing. But the air smells wonderful. It's crisp and clean.... It smells like someone already has a campfire going. Oh, those birds are gorgeous. They must be hawks of some kind!"

The trick to the best narration is to avoid telling people what they're seeing (unless it actually needs explaining). Instead, the best on-camera narration helps to create a bigger picture. How? Tell us what we *can't see*. What do you hear and smell? What's the weather like? How do you feel? Do these places remind you of things in your past? What do you like or dislike about the thing you are shooting?

That's not to say that all moments in your home movie need narration— far from it. The chirping crickets will give us more insight about your trip than a cameraperson rambling from behind the camera. Don't forget, if you say nothing at all, you can always add it in *post*. Ah, the beauty of computers.

focus

Post is shorthand for **post-production**, which is the process of editing a video; adding special effects, transitions, and titles; and outputting it to some sort of distribution medium. Saying you can "fix something in post" is common film-world banter that suggests you'll try to use narration, editing, and visual or sound effects tricks to overcome some problem you had (or some task you forgot to accomplish) while shooting.

zoom-in

Actually, using some of the documentary techniques presented in Chapters 5 and 6 might not be a bad idea in some home movies—in fact, those techniques may even prove funny and entertaining. Consider this possibility—steal a little "reality TV" technique for your home movies by interviewing the subjects after some silly action has taken place. Think "Real World" or "Survivor," where the shows cut between live action and the participant telling you what happened during a later interview. We could do that for "Monk's Bath Time"—interview Nina after the bath is complete and have her explain what happened and why. Then, you've got some great footage to help narrate the action. Plus, the juxtaposition of cutting between the calm interview and the lively dog washing would be amusing.

Don't Go Nuts With the Zoom Button

In Hollywood movies or on TV, when the director wants to mock the look of a bad home movie, he or she will have the cameraperson zoom in and out a lot. In our research, we had to watch 30 minutes of dress rehearsal footage for a wedding. In this footage, shot from a balcony, were approximately 32 billion zoom movements. The camera zoomed in and out over and over again with absolutely no *motivation* (film school terminology for "a reason for an action"). The person shooting was not zooming in because something important was happening—at least from what we could tell. We suspect he was just bored and felt that if he weren't pushing a button on the camera, he wasn't earning his keep.

Perhaps the first mistake was to put the camera on the balcony in the first place—after all, being right in the middle of the action would make for better shots and would have probably kept him off the zoom button because he'd be too busy getting in the action. With a camera on the scene, he might have caught more intimate conversations, mistakes made by the bride and groom to be, bickering between the wedding planner and the mother of the bride, and so on. Why zoom if you can be right there to catch the action?

Of course, being right on top of the action isn't always practical or *allowed*—Todd once got some successful "home video" footage using as much zoom as his digital camera could muster—he was shooting the film crew putting together a scene from an Adam Sandler movie that happened to be taking place across the block from Todd's New York apartment. To get the shot from a few hundred feet away (where about 300 other people were sitting on stoops eating ice cream and popcorn and watching the filming unfold), he clearly had to use zoom. Once there, however, he stayed off the zoom controls, held the camera as steady as possible, and panned back and forth to capture as much of the interesting action as he could (including one great shot of the director storming away from Sandler).

focus

Incidentally, Todd notes that for night-time shooting, even a small, one-chip DV camcorder can be sufficient if you have millions of dollars' worth of Hollywood lighting and technicians at your disposal. You know—just in case you were wondering.

We realize how tempting it is to toggle between T (telephoto) and W (wide) but, well, *don't* do it. Occasionally, perfect moments arise for zooming in and out, and by all means, zoom in for the kiss at the dress rehearsal. But don't zoom just to zoom. More than anything, it makes your viewers seasick and makes you look like an amateur.

The pros don't do a lot of zooming *during* a shot—particularly if that shot is a keeper. If at all possible, try to zoom between shots, when the camera is not recording. Then pick up and record again, and stop shooting before you change zoom settings, start recording again, and so on.

If you must use zoom, zoom in or out for a purpose. Purposeful zooming could include the following scenarios:

- To show a detail not visible from far away, such as Aunt Sue's flowery rhinestone pink pumps she wore at cousin Lhayla's bridal shower

- To catch the tears welling up in dad's eyes as he views the Grand Canyon
- To show your little league outfielder picking flowers and tasting them instead of watching the ball

A reason to zoom out might be to show an action not visible from a close-up. Sports shooting is a perfect scenario to illustrate this type of zooming. Suppose you're filming a sporting event and you're tight on the runner with the ball. Zooming in too close can cause the action to appear to be taking place in a vacuum. (It can also be a tough shot to hold, and fast action can seem exaggerated and shaky in a close-up, ending up in a picture that makes your audience queasy when you're showing the game in your living room.) If you're zoomed in to the ball and the audience starts cheering wildly, it's probably a good idea to zoom out, because the action between the players will be what you'll want to see later. Indeed, many sporting events are best shot in a medium-to-wide angle, with a second camera (if you have one available) used for close-ups.

 zoom-in

This is an example of how listening to what you're shooting is just as important as seeing the action. Use your ears as well as your eyes to help you decide what and how to shoot. Peeking through the viewfinder can seriously cut down on your ability to see all of the action around you, so you'll want to heighten your other senses to compensate. It helps to have someone working with you to spot the action, and, where appropriate, you can keep a schedule of events to help you make sure you're at the right places to get great shots.

A good reason to zoom in to a subject is to check your focus—again, you don't do this while you're recording. To guarantee something is in focus, you can zoom in on your subject all the way, set the focus (or allow your camera to do it automatically), and then zoom out to your desired shot size.

focus

Do not zoom in for a close-up shot while walking with or moving the camera. The seasickness level for the audience goes way up with camera movement in more than one place at once.

Don't "Step On" Each Other

Nina is a documentary filmmaker, and one of her big pet peeves is when she catches herself talking over the person she is interviewing—often called "stepping on" someone in the news-gathering/film business. On numerous occasions, someone might say something of great importance, only to be interrupted by another question by Nina or Nina's laughter or other people in the room talking. That footage becomes virtually unusable in her work at that point.

focus ──

Remember, even in home video, it's okay to suggest that everyone get a second or third **take**—a do-over. Tell dad to explain the recipe again, or ask mom to explain her coin collection a second or third time. You'll then have a better chance of capturing good footage to edit. (Our technical editor, Gene, notes that some professionals will pretend to shoot an amateur but won't press the Record button until they feel that the person in the shot has become more comfortable on camera. That's one way to save tape while "rehearsing" a subject who isn't used to being filmed.)

Of course, in a home video, it might not be as crucial to keep to a single loud voice as it is in a quality documentary film, but certainly it helps for everyone not to be talking at once. If grandma is reciting her prized recipe for the perfect apple cobbler, for goodness sake, go to a quiet room and wait to comment until after she finishes giving you the step-by-step. This may be your only opportunity to document this family heirloom.

focus ──

Sometimes it's impossible to keep people from talking over one another. We understand—especially if you come from a big, loud Italian/Jewish/Latino/Southern/fill-in-your-cultural-heritage family. Do your best.

Don't End Too Early

One of the more important rules in any kind of filmmaking is to start early and end late. (Unless you're dealing with union labor.) In this case, *ending late* means you need to keep your camcorder recording to allow your subjects to finish whatever it is they are doing, and you need to leave time to shoot *editing handles*, or footage at the beginning and end of a take that gives you more flexibility when editing. Try not to cut short a shot, because that cuts your story short in editing. It's worthwhile to shoot the entire moment during which the pie comes out of the oven, or to hold the camera on the dog during the final rinse of the bath, including the dog shaking out the water and running back out to the yard. You never know what will be good footage in the end.

focus ——

Excited new videographers make a common mistake—after getting a shot, they immediately drop the camcorder and point it at the ground, yelling out "That was great!" or something similar. Fight this instinct. Instead, quietly hold the camera for a few breaths after you think you've gotten what you wanted. That will give you a good **out handle** and keep you from seeing the dreaded, shot-ruining "whoosh" of the image that most of us have seen at some point in our career because of an overzealous desire to yell "Cut!"

Note that holding your shots for a few extra seconds is different from shooting *everything*—you should still make decisions about which shots you want to get. But once you're in a shot, stick with it until you're *past* the action. Then you'll have some extra footage to lop off when you're editing, which is a great position to be in. Think about it this way—it's much easier to cut away unimportant footage than it is to add footage that *isn't there*. The more options you have (within reason), the happier you'll be in the editing phase.

Do Use Multiple Angles and Vary Your Shots

Sometimes the reason you fall asleep watching your best friend's home movie of his kid's school play isn't because the play is dull (or it isn't *only* because the play is dull). The fact that your camera-wielding friend didn't vary his shots might have helped you find your way into dreamland. We have seen dozens of home videos of reasonably interesting events that were shot by someone who set the camera on a tripod and pushed record, never moving the camera or changing the size of the shot. We're all guilty of it at one time or another. But if you can help it, we recommend eschewing this approach in favor of one in which you get some different shots and angles on your action.

focus ——

Obviously, playing with angles can get a little dangerous, because you may need to record the event for posterity, for the official record, or for the scores of parents who are going to want a copy to use to torture their children when they're teenagers. In that case, you probably don't want to mess around by moving the camera too much—plant the tripod and let it roll. But if you can, get your hands on a second camera, or work with others—fellow parents or participants—who have video cameras, and conspire to use their footage in your editing. Use the other footage to interject some different angles, close-ups (staying out of camera no. 1's field), and audience reaction shots. Edit those back into the show, and other parents will be amazed by your brilliance.

If you are taping an outdoor barbecue, for example, try to position yourself in a location where you can easily get a good wide shot as well as some close-ups. Most of the time, you will want to begin with a wide shot, establishing the setting and how things relate to each other in the park. During the barbecue, you'll find reasons to vary your shots. Push in on Bob the nosy neighbor as he listens in on a conversation. Go tight on your mild-mannered librarian friend Susan as she chows down on a foot-long hotdog. During the softball game, make sure you get a tight shot of the angst on Eric's face when he swings for strike three. (One more word of advice: Walk around an area where you'll be shooting before the event takes place or at the beginning of the event so that you get a sense of the different angles, walkways, and obstructions you'll need to consider when shooting.)

Here's a quick rundown of the basic types of shots:

- **Wide shot (long, establishing, or master shot)**   If you have only one opportunity to shoot something, this most basic of all shots should probably be your chosen shot size; this shot includes everything in the scene relating your subject to its environment.

- **Medium shot**   The idea is to place the subject in the environment, with the subject as the main focal point. For a person, that might mean framing him full body with background elements in view, or framing him from the waist up.

- **Close-up** This shot concentrates on a person's face or on a detail of the subject, in a sense isolating the subject from the surroundings so that your audience is fixed on his expressions or emotions.

- **Extreme close-up** Highlights more detail than a close-up shot to the point that the item or person being shown is almost abstract and difficult to place, such as a human eye blinking or the stamen of a flower. Use this shot sparingly, as it can have a shocking effect.

- **Two-shot**   A shot in which two people are visible in the frame and within close proximity to one another, such as occurs during an interview, a newscast, or an exchange.

Do Be Decisive About What You Shoot

It isn't necessary that you shoot every single moment of an event. Unless you're documenting the mating rituals of the soon-to-be extinct *woozle* of southern Timbuktu, never to be seen again by anyone in the world, spare yourself and your former friends the hours of tape. We want just the highlights. You endured the event so we don't have to. If you shoot everything, it's likely we'll just fast-forward through the boring stuff—which may be upward of 75 percent of your footage. There's no reason to waste all that tape.

The decision to shoot is really the catch-22 of video production. You need to have the shot on tape if you're going to be able to put it in the video—that would seem to be a law of physics. But if you have too many shots, you may end up without any desire to watch that footage—let alone catalog it, find the good bits, get it all into a computer, and edit it into something interesting.

A friend of ours shot a wedding using two cameras, each following the bride and groom throughout their entire day. He ended up with nearly 24 hours of footage—which has been sitting in his living room for more than a year now, unedited. The bride and groom haven't even seen the footage. Indeed, even they have no desire to shuttle through 24 hour-long tapes.

In watching home movies, feature films, film festival material, documentaries, industrials, and so on, we have found that *less* is almost always *more* (as long as that *less* is pretty good). The best way to do this is to make as many shot decisions ahead of time as possible—know the shots you want to get and get them completely, starting as early in the action as possible and ending once the action is completely done. Of course, that planning means being prepared to get the "spontaneous" stuff, too. In other words, *plan* to get conversation shots at a party or reaction shots from the audience at an air show. Plan to get shots at the entrance of the zoo or the door to your kid's playroom if your toddler daughter is rounding it while taking her first steps in new shoes. Sit and think through what it is that you'd like to have available to you for editing, and then plan to shoot that. Keep a notebook and check off the shots as you get them, if that helps you remember.

Then, if you're at a live event and you're not getting a shot that you had planned, just keep your camera handy and your finger near the Record button. You'll get some spontaneous stuff that you hadn't thought of, and, more than likely, one of those shots will be your biggest laugh or your teariest tearjerker.

Do Keep the Camera Reasonably Steady

We considered writing this chapter in only 11 words. It would have read:

Watch *The Blair Witch Project,* and then do the exact opposite.

But our editors said that wouldn't fill enough pages, and they got a little snippy when we recommended using 1048-point type.

Of course, what was most notable about *The Blair Witch Project*—after you waded through the hype—was the jerky camera movement. Of course, it was shot that way on purpose in order to make it *appear* to have been shot by an amateur. That probably helped to make it a successful movie, although we're not sure how enjoyable it was, because we've never been able to sit through it completely because of *all the irritating camera movement.* (Seriously, *Blair Witch* certainly proves the rule about steadying the camera. It's also notable because it's a filmmaker's idea of what amateur home video looks like.)

The first rule of videography is to keep the camera as steady as possible by using a tripod or similar camera-steadying device. Obviously, a tripod necessitates that you keep the camera in a single location, which brings us to our *other first rule* of videography—as much as possible, keep the camera in the same place while getting each individual shot. You might think that you are walking steadily with the camera, but it's nearly impossible to prevent jarring movement in your moving shots without using the proper equipment and methods. Most of the time, the shaky cam is totally unnecessary, because it's often unnecessary to walk and shoot at the same time. (Likewise, regardless of how light your camera is, your arm will get tired, which will increase the shaking effect, particularly if you don't use stabilizing equipment.)

Instead, think in terms of panning the camera to follow action that takes place *past* the camera, ideally in a plane that brings the action to and from the camera's position in a series of shots. (In English, that translates as "Have your subject walk toward—and then past—the camera.") When the action moves out of your camera's field of vision, end the shot and move the camera.

focus

Remember that you don't have to follow the action all the time. Instead, if you can, set up a series of shots in which you get the action moving past the camera. You can let the action go out of the camera's frame and then move to another shot. If you can't quickly set up in different locations, plan to be where the most dramatic action will take place (the finish line, the judge's reviewing stand, the altar) and place your camera there.

We have seen countless home videos in which the cameraperson keeps the camera running while walking to another location or following behind someone. Often, though, there is no need to record your trip from point A to point B. You can easily allude to the fact that you are going to a different location, stop recording, move the camcorder, and start recording once you get where you're going. And you can always record something along the way (get to know your camera's Pause and Record buttons well) if something catches your eye.

If you *do* have to walk while shooting or think you'll miss something important if you don't, zoom out as far as you can, even completely, to your camera's widest angle. You may also have a digital steadying or "digital stabilization" feature that could help a bit—turn it on, if so. This will minimize the amount of shaky cam (a little) and give you a greater depth of field so that your subject will stay in focus.

As far as general steadiness of the camera, if you don't have a tripod (and certainly not everything you shoot requires a tripod, particularly for a home movie), find a way to stabilize yourself and the camera. If you're standing, find something to lean against. Grab a chair if you're able to shoot from a lower angle, or prop the camera on a table or other stable place. You will be comfortable and thus will have a more enjoyable time shooting, allowing you to be more creative with your technique.

 *zoom-in*

Chapter 7 discusses some steadying hardware you can add to your camcorder to get better results while moving around with the camera.

Do Remember that Lighting Is Important

Digital video technology handles most lighting conditions very well, but you should still abide by a few rules.

If it's dark, it's dark. Even we're guilty of shooting in complete darkness, thinking that technology will compensate for the lack of light. They're not x-ray cameras, after all—not yet, anyway. DV camcorders handle low-light situations very well, but as a rule, if you can't see anything through the viewfinder, your camera probably can't see it either. Consider using at least an on-camera light source. (See Chapter 6 for more discussion on lighting.)

More at issue, however, is where to position your light source relative to your talent. It's best not to shoot directly into the sun, for instance. Instead of a black screen from lack of light, you'll have an overexposed (white) screen due to too much light. Most people use the automatic settings on their cameras, so the camera is in charge of determining what exposure is appropriate for the shot. Generally, the camera will expose for the brightest (or hottest) area in the frame. If a bright light source is behind your subject, the subject will appear in silhouette. If you're not making a horror flick or trying to create a sense of mystery, you probably want properly exposed people in your video, so you may want to move your subject so that the light is shining on them rather than from behind them. Also, shadows on people's faces (which happens when the light source comes from the side at an abrupt angle, or directly below or above) may be exacerbated by the automatic exposure level that the camera uses.

Here are a few useful tips when you are shooting with natural or existing light sources:

- Try to shoot your subjects with light on their faces rather than with light coming from behind them or from any extreme angles (directly to the side or directly from above or below).

- A light coming slightly from the side is preferrable, so that the face doesn't look flat. It will allow for more definition of the face or subject matter and create subtle shadows for depth.

- If your subject is too bright (perhaps a landscape on a particularly sunny day), your camera may have an internal ND (neutral density) filter setting that will help bring down the exposure. Turn it on or try setting it to automatic.

- If your camera has a *zebra setting*, use it from time to time to see what the camera sees in terms of exposure. This will help train your eye.

focus —————————————————————————————

The zebra setting on camcorders works by placing lines (that look like zebra stripes) in portions of the frame that the camcorder believes are overexposed, allowing you to compensate by changing the exposure (or recomposing the shot). Check your camcorder's manual for discussion of a zebra feature and how to use it correctly.

- If you have to shoot in low light levels, you may be able to adjust the *gain* (a setting on your camcorder that changes the amount of light that your camcorder attempts to capture electronically) and shutter speed levels (how quickly the shutter opens and closes to allow in light). For home video, you'll likely find that the automatic settings are the best, but if you're the handy type, dig into your camcorder's manual and figure out some of these settings.

- If you're serious about what you're doing, buy and use screw-on filters for your camcorder, including those that can help in adverse lighting situations.

Do Get Good Sound

As you'll see emphasized in later chapters, one of the most important elements of any good video is good sound—which we'll define as *sound that you can hear crisply that also doesn't get in the way of your story*. For your home video sound, keep these things in mind:

- Wear headphones (a variety that covers your ears) when filming, as that will give you a decent idea of how things sound as they're being recorded.

- Consider using a strong directional microphone—your camcorder manufacturer probably has an accessory microphone that it calls a "shotgun," or directional microphone, or you can acquire other vendors' microphones that fit the accessory shoe of your camera. A directional mic picks up sound in one specific direction.

- If possible, wire people with *lavalier* mics (mics that clip to collars or other parts of clothing).

- At the least, get the person(s) to speak close to your camcorder, and as you're setting up the shot and listening through the camcorder, take into consideration how the ambient noises sound.

- Remember the wind—you should have wind screens for your microphones, and if wind is a persistent problem, find a location to talk with your subjects where the wind is not strong.

 zoom-in

One of the problems that filmmakers from our area (the American South) have with outdoors shots are extremely loud insects, which can be amplified by on-camera sound equipment. When you hear such sounds through your headphones, it's a good time to consider moving an interview or lengthy conversation inside so that you can get better sound—you can always use those outside shots later without sound or with the sound turned down on those clips.

Do Practice

Ultimately, you will decide what works for a particular shoot. Practice shooting as often as possible to get to know your camera and to determine what feels most comfortable for you. In addition, learn to use your camera's manual settings, if they exist, so that you will have more flexibility in the future. Shoot your husband cooking dinner for the kids, your grandmother gardening, the neighbors arranging their new lawn gizmos—just keep shooting until you feel comfortable. Once you get to know your equipment well, you'll be able to think about it less and use it more effectively as a tool or instrument, the same way you might use a paintbrush or piano (except you might not carry the piano around on your shoulder).

Watching movies, TV, and videos *for craft* will also be helpful in finding a style and technique that suits you. And don't forget other people's home videos. Sometimes you can learn more from bad examples than from good ones. At the least, maybe you'll be left with a strong sense of what not to do.

Approaches to Editing Your Home Movies

Most people never edit their home movies. Who has the time? Who has the patience? Who knows how?

If you're like us and you've ever spent time with a camcorder and a dream, you've probably got plenty of tapes lying around that you never watch, because they're just too long and monotonous. Or you might have tapes that you keep around to show friends and family, but you fast forward to get to the good stuff. That's what editing is for—getting to the good stuff!

Editing can be tedious, but it can be worth every minute of effort. It takes at least twice as long to edit as it does to shoot (probably more like 16 times as long), and editing involves an incredible amount of organization. Plus, you have to learn how to use the editing software. We empathize with your plight, but your friends and family would be much more respectful of your moviemaking if you showed them something enjoyable to watch. In fact, they may even encourage you to produce more work or help them edit their lengthy home videos to pass on your secrets. And what will do the convincing is good camerawork, decent sound, and great editing.

Finding the Beginning

Where do you begin editing? Probably where you begin your storytelling—at the beginning. Of course, that's easier said than done. Figuring out where to begin is one of the most important yet most difficult parts of the process, because there are many ways to tell a story. But is the beginning the beginning of the tape? If you haven't been labeling your tapes or keeping track of your shots, you may not even know where the beginning is without some research.

focus ───

Now you know what that ubiquitous "Scene 1, Take 27" clapboard is for in the movies! When you're shooting your own, consider using a similar system. Holding up your storyboard or a sheet of paper explaining the shot you're trying to get before you get it on tape will help you when you're reviewing your work before editing.

The best way to determine what is your story and where it begins is to *know your footage*. For example, you may think you got a certain shot, but you failed to press Record, and that part of the event was never captured. You may think something would make a brilliant shot but it actually ends up looking wrong through the viewfinder. You may find gems in footage that you thought were throwaways. Knowing your footage will help you find the story as well as let you know if you need to shoot additional material or come up with other ways to fill in with narration, still images, or music. On top of that, you can make notes on your shooting style so that you won't make the same mistakes again or so that you can pat yourself on the back for being a self-taught director of photography.

In practice, this means sitting down with a notepad and your tapes and going through them to catalog the stuff that you think might be useful. Use the tape labels (or label them now) and timecodes to get a sense of what you've got and when:

Monk's Bath Time

Tape 1, 00:12:12—Good shot of Monk sleeping
Tape 1, 00:15:01—Walk from inside to outside
Tape 1, 00:18:03—Starting the bath
Tape 1, 00:22:11—Good close-up of washing
Tape 1, 00:25:08—Good close-up of sponge
Tape 1, 00:30:12—Shake-off scene
Tape 1, 00:32:15—Exterior establishing shot
Tape 1, 00:35:04—Monk sleeping again
Tape 1, 00:40:02—Ambient sound and water splashing
Tape 1, 00:44:05—Happy Nina
Tape 1, 00:48:03—Nina getting out of car after work
Tape 1, 00:50:05—Reaction of Monk to car door

A professional-level catalog list might go even further than this, but this level of detail will work for a home video. This should help you once you get into the actual editing, as you'll have a sense of what footage you need and where it is. Notice from the sample list that not all of your shots are necessarily in order—those last two shots, for instance, might have been something we decided to do after thinking more about the project or after seeing the raw footage and deciding there still wasn't a good beginning. Knowing where those scenes are located on the tape is crucial, because you're going to need to find the footage to put it at the beginning of the video you are editing.

focus ───

As much as we'd like to say it ain't so, fact is that digital video takes up a lot of hard disk storage space on your PC, and many consumer-level computers can't handle hours and hours of it. As a result, cataloging becomes important even for short home movies so that you know fairly quickly what tape and at what timecode you'll find a particular shot before you pull it into the computer.

Another issue to keep in mind when planning your edit is how long you want the end product to be. If you're putting together a montage of shots of your dog, just for fun, you may want to pick out a song that fits the mood you're trying to set and allow the length of the song to dictate how long your video will be. Also keep in mind who will be viewing the final product. If you're making something for your four-year-old and his friends to watch, realize that 30 minutes can seem like an eternity for them unless those minutes are filled with action and laughs (and, usually, cloying little catchy tunes). Video of an anniversary dinner celebrating 50 years for your grandparents is probably not the place to test your epic filmmaking skills—although it might be a great time to drop in some old photographs, happy music, and a little cleverly narrated history. Be creative, and at the same time, be considerate of your audience.

The Middle

Once you've established a beginning, your next daunting task is to tell the story—now is the time to show the juicy parts and tell the story that you set up in the beginning, making people laugh and cry along the way. For a sporting or ceremonial event, this may include all of the best plays or moments in chronological order, while *intercutting* any audience shots, reactions shots, or other secondary footage you got to complement the time-based sequence. If you're editing a two-day hiking vacation through the mountains, you should probably follow the trip from point A to point

B, filling the middle with beautiful or interesting things you found along the way, with reactions from other hikers, and so on. (If you can do it, it's handy to do your reaction and cutaway shots with a second camcorder or at least a second tape. That's not always practical for home video, but it's something to try if you're serious about documenting an experience and/or you've got a friend with a camcorder and the desire to help out.)

focus

What's **intercutting?** That's when you take clips and cut them together to show action from different points of view and from different camera angles. Chapter 9 explains this in some detail, as well as how you can edit sound so that, for instance, you can show the video clips of something that your subject is talking about even when you're not showing your subject on camera.

The middle is where you should experiment with editing to compress time. We realize the comedic value in following along as your hikers ask one another "Are we there yet?" but it's important not to make the audience sit through many minutes between such jewels of wit. (And, remember, you're not supposed to be walking with the camera on—anyway, at least not much.) Instead, the editing bay gives you the option to compress time, as in the following:

- Show a bit of the beginning with everyone excited about the trek.
- Cut to five miles up the road, where a little tiredness is setting in.
- Cut into ten miles further into the trip with folks complaining vocally.
- Finally, end this sequence with the arrival and pathetic cheering (or the rescue helicopter and the daring heroics—remember to be flexible in your planning!).

A series of experiences like that from the two days cut together and condensed down would likely prove to be enjoyable to watch. An audience wants to see the meaningful moments of your experience. Keep in the juicy bits and cut out the fat.

The End

This is (usually) the easy part, particularly in home video production. Either the event will conclude or you'll run out of footage. If you had a story line in mind, here's your chance to wrap it all up and possibly even make a point. Most of the time, your ending will be obvious in a home movie, but if you're feeling creative and you want to spice it up a bit, maybe you'll create a cliffhanger and keep your audience waiting for your next masterpiece.

Let's take some examples of ways to end a home video that shouldn't take too much additional effort:

- **End on faces** If everything turned out well, a great way to end a home video is to focus on a smile—your child's cake-smudged face, your spouse's sigh of holiday contentment, your grandfather's self-satisfied head nod after a story well-told. Fade to black.

- **"The sunset"** End a vacation with a shot of the plane heading home or the Paris skyline through the airplane's window. A "riding off into the sunset" shot is a great way to go out.

- **The foreshadowed event** The ending can be effective if it's foreshadowed earlier in the film—for instance, if you have the family gathered around a window in the airplane discussing their excitement over a trip to Paris, you might have the video end with a very similar shot, but this time the family is asleep on the flight on the way home from the vacation.

- **Narration** Feel free to wrap it up by talking over images of the event as it ends and goes to black. If the story is true, you might even mention what happened "after" the video ("Bob is now doing two to four years in state prison for stealing that statue").

- **Montage** In your editing software, one fun option is to cut together small snippets of the scenes that the viewer has already seen and set them to narration and/or music. That's a great visual cue that things are wrapping up, and it gives the viewers the opportunity to recall the emotions they felt throughout the video.

- **The "Ferris effect"** People of a certain generation refer to the film *Ferris Bueller's Day Off* the way their parents refer to *Rebel Without a Cause*. Ferris (Matthew Broderick) narrates the film in asides to the audience, including a funny ending that tells people to "go home" because the movie is over. Something similar can be an okay way to end a home movie, particularly if the subjects have already endeared themselves to the audience. A young kid right in the camera saying "That's all!" can be an effective way to transition into your credit roll.

Post-Production

Once you have all your footage laid out on a timeline as you'd like it to be shown, you might want to consider adding sound effects, music, video effects, narration, or titles to enhance your work of art. As you'll see throughout the video projects discussed in this book, you can add some basic elements to a video to give it better production values, add to its overall professionalism, and bring your audience into the presentation. Here's a quick look—we'll elaborate a bit more in later chapters.

Music

Use music to set the mood of your video. Watch movies and television for long enough (as Todd has), and you'll see how the professionals use music to create a character's personality or to set up an action. Use your favorite songs on the radio to complement your high school graduation video or old love songs from your grandparent's swinging years for their anniversary video. Using music relevant to the event you've documented will make your project more meaningful and enjoyable, preserving your experience at a particular time and place not just visually, but also emotionally.

Sound Effects

Sound can be great little shortcuts to help better tell your story. If cousin Billy sits next to your best friend Monica at your family reunion and they have a love connection, you might add a cartoon siren sound to point out cupid's arrow just to be funny. Sound effects can sometimes say what you're thinking without narration.

Video Effects

Fades, dissolves, and other transitions will help to compress time and alleviate jump-cuts that can be awkward to watch, as will be discussed in Chapter 9. For "Monk's Bath Time," Nina dissolved from Monk trying to escape from the tub to the next time he tried to escape and then to the next, to indicate that time had passed without having to show the entire 10 minutes. If those shots were cut together back to back without dissolves, the viewer might get confused, thinking that Monk was impossible to wash. With the dissolves (see Figure 3.2), the audience is aware that you're compressing time, and viewers make an unconscious mental note that says "Hey, this has been edited just to show the funny bits; let's go along for the ride and see if we chuckle."

Narration

Spoken text can be helpful in expressing what is not seen on-screen. For example, if you want to give the history of a person or place that is not evident in the original video, you can add your thoughts in post to create a more complete story. This is a technique often found in documentary and

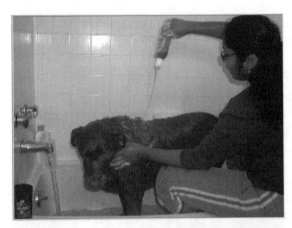

FIGURE 3.2

In this sequence, the dissolves cut between different moments of mirth.

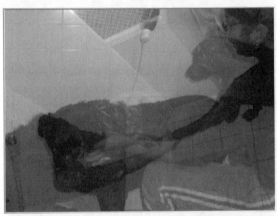

sometimes feature film work. It allows you to tell a more complete story by explaining footage that's on the screen or by explaining things that can't be seen in the pictures. Adding a narration track to your home video also allows you to watch the finished product with your audience rather than having to pause and explain everything as it happens.

Graphics

If you're feeling ambitious, you might want to throw in some graphics and titles to introduce a person if his or her name is not mentioned on-screen or to create a home movie reminiscent of reality TV or a documentary. You may also want to add a dedication, message, dates, credits, and other information at the beginning or end of your video. And if your friends and family don't mind a little bragging from the filmmaker, you can create crawling titles indicating director, editor, producer, craft service, and whatever else you'd like to give yourself (and others) credit for doing.

And...Cut!

The main point to keep in mind with home video is to keep things simple, but organized. You need to get the shots if you're going to show them to anyone. Once you've done that, watch and catalog the shots so that you get to know them and where they are. Then you can edit it together, keeping things trim and compressing time where possible while still telling your core story. Finally, add a little extra something in post—some dissolves to compress time or fades to start a new thought, and then add music and sound effects to set the mood. Add some titles or credits and send it out to tape. You've got a home movie that's in the top five percent of all home movies ever made—if your home movie had just taken a Mensa-qualifying exam, it would be a certifiable genius!

Next up: Take your home video skills to the next level by shooting events—speeches, weddings and other milestones or memories.

Wedding and Event Video

YOU get only one chance to catch the magic moments between a bride and groom at a wedding ceremony. Will you be in the right place to immortalize the kiss of death on video? (We couldn't resist.)

Weddings and other one-time events—such as speeches, award ceremonies, birthdays, retirements, or family reunions—can be tough to shoot for many reasons. But a major reason for their difficulty is the expectations of those involved. What the bride finds important will differ from what the mother-in-law wants, as well as what the mother of the bride, the maid of honor, the bride's sister, and of course the groom each wants.

For an award ceremony or retirement, you'll need to convey how the moment is special for the person or people you're covering. Your job should be to cover all the essential moments, and if there's time to spare, you can throw in a little something extra. You can't please everyone, but you can strive to be alert during the event so that you capture all the once-in-a-lifetime stuff on tape. That's the first step. Then you can spice up the footage in the editing room—particularly if helpers are shooting with additional camcorders.

In this chapter, we list the shots that can't be missed and offer tips on how to be one step ahead as the event unfolds, how to get everything covered without being in the way, and how to make something simple and straightforward meaningful for a lifetime.

What You'll Need

Unlike the usual home movie shoots, wedding and event videos call for much more attention in pre-production. In fact, this type of shooting is dependent on your being a great *producer*. What you'll need is organization.

Producing is an ambiguous term in the film and video industry, but essentially, a great producer knows what needs to be accomplished and how to do whatever that is efficiently and effectively. For example, a Hollywood movie producer might be responsible for acquiring the rights to a script, finding crew and resources, and—most important—getting the money. Once all of that is in place, the producer and the production team determine how to get the work accomplished within a certain time frame for the amount of money they have to spend.

For any project you put together that goes beyond a typical home video, you'll need to do some producing—similar to the Hollywood type, but probably with fewer pool parties and ritzy lunches. You may not have a huge special effects budget and actors clamoring for more money (or you may well have that, as you saw in Chapter 3), but you will have a set period of time to shoot, a cast of characters to keep up with, equipment and people to organize, and a story to tell.

The "What" of Your Production

The first question that needs to be answered when you're planning your event coverage is "*What* needs to be covered for the event?" For a wedding, does the couple want only the wedding ceremony filmed or do they want to include the rehearsal dinner, the bachelor party (well, maybe not), the bridesmaids' luncheon, and the reception? Does the couple want the video to be formal or personal? Do they expect you to capture the vows up close, or will they settle for an audience member's perspective?

focus

For weddings and other important life-moment events, it's important that you be honest with the subjects involved so that they know what to expect from you. Don't exaggerate your abilities. If you don't have much experience, tell them that you may make some mistakes and that you will be trying to get just the basics covered in terms of the look and coverage of the project. Then, if you happen to exceed their expectations, it'll be a wonderful surprise. At the same time, you should listen to **their** hopes and expectations, and be prepared to recommend that they use a different producer if you think you can't meet them.

If you're shooting the wedding or event as a gift, you could determine what is essential for the video based on how much you love them, we suppose. But if these lovely folks are paying you a fee, you need to know what they want, acknowledging specifically on paper what you will be responsible for, because there can be a gap between the couple's expectations and what can realistically be done on camera without requiring a full crew and/or being very interruptive during the wedding itself. We can't emphasize enough how important it is to *get the specifics down on paper* so that everyone is clear on what is expected—on both sides.

focus

A key issue for you as a videographer is how much to charge for an event. You could do a little investigating to determine the going rate for comparable wedding videos in your area. Professional videographers will have factored in the cost of tape stock, equipment rental (even if it is their own equipment, they would likely assign a cost to its use over the length of the shoot), time shooting, editing facilities (that also includes their own equipment, if applicable), editing time, videos and/or DVDs to be output for the client, as well as any essential pre-production time. You should also consider your own experience level—if you're shooting a single event, we hope to be able to help you with that in this chapter. If you're going into the event video business, you probably want to consider some time spent assisting an established event videographer to help learn the ropes and gain some wisdom.

Following are some of the considerations you must make clear to the subject(s) of your wedding or event video:

- *The finished product is unlikely to look like a soap opera or Hollywood feature movie.* Not only do you have only one take, but for most weddings and other events, you'll have less control over the ambient sound, lighting, and a host of other factors. In fact, you might want to show the participants any previous video work you've done to give them a sense of how theirs will turn out.

- *The more intimate the shot is supposed to be, the closer the camcorder will need to be.* If you can tell your subjects up front that the distance between them and the camcorder will affect the quality of the production—but a camcorder up close could affect the quality of the live event—you'll brace them for one of the more common pitfalls, where, for example, a couple expects you to catch every quivering lip and welled-up tear at a wedding, or a speaker expects to look like the president of the United States standing at his podium, even though the only place for a camera is well away from the action.

- *Using multiple camcorders is pricey and time consuming but can be worth the extra expense.* Using multiple camcorders might distract from the ceremony, and this is important to try to avoid. Still, using multiple camcorders is a great way to capture various perspectives for editing together a more professional looking product. It also means you've got backup shots in case your primary camcorder goes down for some reason. Remember that you've got only one chance to get this event on tape.

- *External microphones are ideal.* You may broach the possibility of asking your bride and groom or other event subject(s) to wear wireless mics (see Figure 4.1), if they're willing and if you can get a chance to rehearse the sound before the actual event. If that won't fly, you should try to arrange to record sound from the facility microphones where the event is taking place, if possible. Emphasize to the subjects that sound is one of the most important aspects of the shoot—*hearing* the quivering voices at a wedding, for instance, will be moving to the viewer, almost regardless of the images.

Other types of events—speeches, family reunions, and so forth—probably won't require such intense production. (After all, most of us have seen C-SPAN news, so we're accustomed to seeing speeches covered with one reasonably stationary camera and relatively few high-end special effects.) A single-camcorder setup will probably work fine unless you're looking for audience reaction shots or the ability to interact with several people, in which case you may want to set up several camcorders. Again, particularly

FIGURE 4.1
Wireless microphones can be handy for event shooting.

Photo courtesy Nady Systems

for speeches, reunions, religious services, funerals, and other such events, sound is crucial—getting the best sound should be as important, or more important, than getting the best images. Encourage your subjects to wear microphones or to remember to stand in front of the microphone for their entire speech.

The "Where" and "When"

After the "what" is in place, you need to lock down the *where* and *when*. Where does the event take place, and what's the time frame? When are you expected to start shooting, and how early do you need to be there before the event begins? Where can you park so you don't have to lug your equipment a mile down the road? Who can answer your questions after you arrive at the event location?

Confirm that you will have a direct connection to the wedding or event coordinator in case last-minute decisions need to be made when the bride and groom or other subjects are busy getting dressed or pacing backstage. Coordinate the when and the where, accounting for travel time, traffic, and natural disasters (at least weather). If you miss the father of the bride escorting his baby girl down the aisle, you can forget about that glass of champagne and the fat check at the end of the evening.

If you cover your pre-shoot details, you'll need only a camcorder and sound equipment, the energy to endure someone else's mushy lovefest—or a keynote about flat feet—and someone to help you tote all your gear and commiserate with about the exorbitant amount of money spent on flowers, bad organ music, and poofy bridesmaids' dresses. The first wedding Nina shot was much more than she had anticipated—14 hours on her feet with camcorder in hand the whole time. We hope your experience isn't like hers, but, just in case, be sure that you have a cold beverage waiting for you and a massage scheduled for the next day. Shooting a big event can be more difficult than you might expect. (And remember to drink the punch *after* you're done shooting. Keep your head clear until you are officially off duty that day!)

focus —————————————————————————————

Assistants are wonderful for shoots and easy enough to find if a college—or even a high school—in your immediate area can supply student aides. Many students will help out for free as unpaid interns for the opportunity to work with the equipment and techniques you'll be showing them. When you're in the field, an assistant is pretty much mandatory—you'll need someone to run for batteries, tape, cable wire, and so on, or someone to run a second camcorder at important moments.

Pre-production

If you are diligent in preparing yourself for the shoot, you will have much more time to solve problems when they arise. And we use *when* specifically—the job of a video producer is almost all problem solving after you arrive on the set.

Planning the Shoot

Looking back at our personal experiences, neither of us can recall a shoot—whether it was a big movie or a television show or personal documentary—that went perfectly well, no matter how much we prepared for it beforehand. Still, the better our pre-production work, the better we were able to deal with unexpected problems as they arose.

Before you head out to the shoot, do some planning. In fact, putting together a checklist of things to think about (and then a checklist of things to take with you) is a wonderful idea. Some of the silly things that can throw off your entire day include the following:

- *Imperfect technology* Be prepared, as you *will* encounter electrical outlets that don't work, no available parking, people showing up late, missing or forgotten tapes or batteries, or Mardi Gras parades blocking every single street in New Orleans (a recent occurrence for us).

- *Driver error* Leave early for the event (the event folks will be pleased if the videographer is checking out the site before guests arrive), and know exactly where you are going before you back out of your driveway. If that means securing a map from the event coordinator, using Mapquest to create a route for you based on the address, or driving there the day before, then just do it. This point is especially important if others working with you are driving separately. You may not have the presence of mind to give someone directions over the phone while you're trying to charge batteries, praying that you remembered to pack the headphones, and driving the car simultaneously.

- *Location management* Try to secure parking at every location through the event coordinator so that you know where and how to unload and park. If you have a significant amount of equipment, everyone will appreciate this. If you can't reserve a parking space, at least know the best place to unload your gear.

Good carrying bags or rolling cases can help make a long walk from the car lot much easier, as can a helpful assistant. Think through how you plan to move your equipment around if your event coordinator proves wrong or less than helpful about unloading arrangements.

Equipment Checklist

In addition to considering common problems, you need to consider a list of stuff you should take with you. What's on this list depends on your equipment, personal preferences, the type of shoot, and the number and quality of your assistants. We'll stick to some of the basics, reminding you of a simple rule in the meantime: Unless you designate an assistant specifically for the purpose of running errands, having something in your bag is always much better than hoping you can get it later at the drugstore.

Here are some of the items you'll want on that list:

- Tape stock and extra tape stock
- Charged batteries for the camcorder and sound gear
- AC adapter and battery chargers
- Secondary camcorder
- Headphones (ideally, closed-ear models enable you to cut out some ambient noise and hear exactly what the microphones are hearing)
- Tripod and other stabilization devices (see Chapter 6 for an in-depth discussion of stabilization devices)
- Lighting equipment and shiny/bounce cards (metallic colored or white reflective materials to bounce light on a subject; see Chapter 5 for a discussion on lighting and lighting kits)
- Tools (a multipurpose pocket tool can be handy for short-handed shoots)
- Pockets or a fanny pack
- Tape (gaffer or duct)
- White cards or paper (for white balancing the camcorder)
- Lens cleaner or towelettes
- Rain protection for both you and the equipment
- Directions and parking instructions

- Wireless mics or sound gathering devices
- Schedule of the event's proceedings
- Sharpies and pens
- Beer for your wrap-up party

Many of the professional producers we know use a checklist like this one—perhaps one even more extensive—for every shoot, much like a fighter pilot uses a checklist before firing up the jet engine.

 *zoom-in*

The pros suggest that you keep your cases loaded with most or all of these essentials all the time, so that you're prepared to head out and shoot events—or even something newsworthy—at a moment's notice. You should also check all of your batteries and equipment on a regular basis to make sure they're all operating and stored in one reliable place.

Scouting the Location

Location scouting and managing is an often forgotten job in film and video production. Obviously, multimillion-dollar movies employ a location manager to find and maintain the exotic, far-off island retreats for movies like *Castaway*, but smaller productions often forget how helpful it can be to know your location before you start shooting. A feature film locations department will supply maps, secure parking, let each department know where they can stage gear and equipment, and provide other important details. Locations staff will create a working relationship with the owners and property managers; they'll know what is and isn't permissible on the site; be aware of anything that might interrupt the production, such as being in a flight path or within proximity of a rail line; and be responsible for making sure the location is treated respectfully and returned to its original state (or better) after the film has wrapped.

For event-based shoots, you should try—at the least—to visit your location(s) before the day of shooting. This will help you determine where you will be able to place camcorders while shooting the event, and it will help you get an overall sense of the terrain. In fact, after a quick location scouting expedition, you might be ready to go back and storyboard based on what you've seen. (While you're scouting, you can always shoot some video or digital still photos so that you can look at it when you're back home or at the motel. You can even use photos of video captures to create a storyboard.)

Scouting will happen on two levels:

- You're looking at what and how you're going to shoot.

- You're going to need to know some of the basic, practical stuff—finding electrical outlets in case someone runs out of battery power, locating the restrooms, and determining where you can place equipment that is not being used so that it is safe from weather, curious kids, and moving traffic.

While you're scouting, you should also consider the sound for the video—if the subjects (bride and groom, event host, and so on) will be using microphones for the event, will you be able to get a direct feed from the soundboard to go straight to your camcorder? Or will you need to find another way of getting usable sound? Any decisions you can make before the day of the shoot leaves you in a better position for a successful shoot. (We have faith that you can pull off a completely problem-free shoot with a little planning!)

Finally, don't forget to consider the lighting. Try to visit the location at the same time of day that you'll be filming, and get a sense of the natural and artificial light. If necessary, ask event planners about the lighting possibilities, as the weather could change for the day of the shoot. Look at windows, ask about window coverings (will they be open or closed for the event?), and, if possible, shoot some video in many lighting conditions. You can check out the shots on a monitor or TV to see how the final product might look and whether you'll need to ask for any changes or choose different angles on the day of the event.

Stuff to Get from the Principals

Before we tackle the technical pre-production, you may want to secure a few things from the wedding party, the event planners, and others. This list might vary a bit depending on the type of event, but these items are generally worth gathering ahead of time:

- *Invitations* to the event (get the actual invitations, not just your name on a clipboard, so that you can include a shot of the printed invitation in the video).

- A *schedule* of activities at the event (for example, at a wedding reception, this could be cake cutting, toasts, couple's first dance, throwing the bouquet, and so on) so that you are ready to shoot.

- *Phone numbers* (particularly mobile phones and/or pagers) for all involved parties.

- Confirmed *access* to locations so that you can set up your equipment before the event. You might ask for or arrange to have an ID hanging on your neck that the ushers or security people are instructed to recognize as legit for the event.

Equipment Planning

Technically speaking, you need to determine what equipment will be necessary for your shoot based on many factors. How many camcorders will you need? How will you record sound—straight to a camcorder, DAT, or MP3 recorder? Will you need assistants? We can't answer those questions for you, because every shooting situation is different; but no matter what you're shooting, you will need to consider the following:

- Make sure you have more than enough batteries and that they are all fully charged.

- Purchase more than enough tape stock, and label each tape for each camcorder before you begin shooting (for example: Camera A, Tape 1, Date, Name of Event).

- Organize your equipment and accessories into easy-to-carry bags the night before.

- Remind your crew to wear clothing appropriate for the event (comfortable and nondescript black clothing usually works well for events such as weddings—and don't forget pockets).

- Make sure, if you plan on shooting all day, that you schedule a meal in there somewhere. No one works well when hungry.

Learn to think ahead, and keep lists. After you've finished a day of shooting, try to jot down notes about how it could go better next time, including what you forgot to bring or what you forgot to do. You can prevent many unnecessary incidents by preparing yourself for the inevitable. After the essentials are taken care of, you can spend more of your creative energy on shooting the subject rather than just solving problems as they come up.

Camcorder Placement and Techniques

How many licks does it take to get to the middle of a Tootsie Pop? How many camcorders does it take to shoot a wedding? There isn't only one answer for either of these questions. *As many as it takes* is the best answer we can give. How big a wedding or event will you be shooting? What can the client afford? Does the location call for multiple camcorders?

Choosing Camcorder Location

For the standard church wedding with a sanctuary full of guests, or for an event such as a speech in a ballroom filled with people, three camcorders would be adequate, five would be decadent, and one would be tough.

Using three camcorders allows you to use one camcorder to shoot from the back of the room, taping the entire view and catching the action from the audience's point of view. In fact, you might use this camcorder's shots a lot when you get into the editing bay, as it will give you a baseline against which you can cut to the other camcorders. The other two camcorders at a wedding (see Figure 4.2) might be placed on each side of the bride and groom to get good shots of their vows and tears and general wonderment. These camcorders would also be able to capture *2-shots* of the wedding couple, the audience, and any speakers, musicians, and special additions to the ceremony. At a speech, the secondary camcorders might be used to capture a medium shot of the speaker from a 45-degree side view and then pan the audience for reaction shots, questions, or comments.

Using more than three camcorders can make your work more difficult in the editing room. You will have lots of footage to choose from, but much

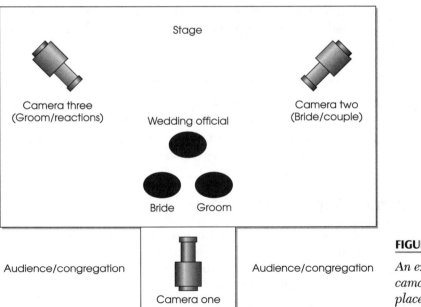

FIGURE 4.2

An example of camcorder placement for a typical wedding

of it will be redundant and tedious to log, unless you have the multicam editing feature that is included in higher end software. Save yourself the trouble and shoot using a reasonable number of camcorders, with a reasonable amount of shots.

When you're using multiple camcorders, try to make sure each is the same format camcorder, if possible, as well as the same brand. For example, a Sony Digital 8 camcorder will differ from a Cannon XL-1S as far as color temperature, exposure and gain levels, the way they handle black, and other factors. Even if the camcorders have the same type of settings and you match them, they will still handle color and light in different ways, because they were made by different companies and they use different optics.

focus

We realize that you may not have three of the same camcorder or even friends with the same camcorder to borrow from for the special occasion. That's okay. Just be aware that there might be a slight difference from one camcorder to the next, and try to plan for that.

If you must use several kinds of camcorder, try to make the most of an imperfect situation. If, for example, you have one Sony and two Panasonic camcorders to use in the project, use the Sony to get the wide shots from the back of the church and the two Panasonics for the shots closer to the bride and groom, so that when you cut back and forth between the close-ups of the bride and groom, at least that footage will look similar in quality. Sometimes your best work comes from improvising. Think of yourself as a jazz musician and just enjoy the process once you have all the equipment and logistics in place.

focus

If you use multiple camcorders and videographers, make sure that each of you is aware of the other camcorders in the area—by all means avoid getting the other camcorders and camerapeople in your shots, particularly for the "money" shots of the ceremony such as the bridal party walking down the aisle, or the moment when your subject receives her award from the president of the organization.

Sync Your Camcorders

If you are able to use several of the same type of camcorders for your shoot, be sure to synchronize all the camcorders' settings (make all the settings the same or as similar as possible) so that all the footage from the camcorders will look uniform. Set shutter speeds, gain levels, and color balance, and turn off any special effects (with the possible exception of an image stabilizer for camcorders that aren't mounted on tripods). You'll want to get the cleanest footage you can possibly get.

Remember that weddings, speeches, and other events are often of the once-in-a-lifetime variety for the principals. Your goal is to get good, clean footage of the entire event. You can play with the footage once it's in your computer, but if the clients want something straightforward and simple, you have to have good footage to provide that. If you shoot everything in sepia or at 1/15 shutter speed, the principals will never have the option of seeing their day through the eyes of the beholders. A rule of thumb is to shoot it clean, and play with it later.

 zoom-in ─────────────────────────────────

If you're lucky enough to be recording audio from a soundboard at the event, you may see no reason to use your camcorder's built-in mic. But be aware that it's best to get sound through the built-in mic anyway, as it can help you to cue the camcorders and sound to the same moment in time when you're viewing it later while logging your tapes and editing. In addition, if you can record quality sound on your camcorder, you may end up using it as a backup or for ambient sound in your final edited project. Chapters 6, 7, and 9 offer more advice on sound gathering.

More About Camcorder Settings

With some of the don'ts out of the way, here's a few dos in terms of camcorder settings (not all camcorders will have manual control of these settings):

- *Set shutter speed to 1/60 second.*   Note that if you have manual control of shutter speed, the reading may say *60* instead of *1/60*, which is the normal shutter speed for video.

- *White balance manually to the same white card, fabric, or surface— whatever is available.*   Better yet, white balance to a white item that is in the target area for the shot—at the podium or the altar, for instance. You generally white balance by zooming in all the way on a white item in the target lighting so that the white item fills your screen; then you press the white balance button on the camcorder.

- *Turn off digital zoom.*   This feature creates a zoomed picture by digitally enlarging the picture (instead of by changing the quality of a lens, which is called *optical zoom*). Generally the quality of the digitally zoomed image suffers, and you don't want this to happen in event video.

- *Set the focus on manual and use the manual focus controls.* One trick is to turn on automatic focus, let it focus on an object, and then turn it off. That keeps the camcorder from "focus hunting" (going in and out of focus when the electronics can't latch onto a moving item). Focus hunting looks amateurish in the final project.

- *Set exposure on manual.* Adjust the exposure based on your locations and subjects. If exposure is left on automatic, it may fluctuate as you pan or tilt the camera or if you are outdoors with clouds intermittently blocking the sun. Since you probably will not have control of the lighting situation at an event, you need to be able to at least control how your camera is seeing light. (The best place to learn more about your camcorder's exposure settings is in the camcorder's manual, which probably offers specifics about the camcorder's various semi-automatic and manual exposure modes.)

- *Set your audio settings according to how you will be recording sound.* Adjust the setting according to whether you're using the camcorder mic or an external mic.

- *For long shots, zoom in and focus.* Then zoom out, particularly if you plan to use any zoom motions during the ceremony.

 *zoom-in* ————————————————————————

Clearly, some camcorder setting issues are a bit advanced—we recommend that you read your camcorder's user manual for the exact instructions on using these settings.

Scouting and Setting

When you scout your location ahead of time, try to visit the location at the same time of day that the event will be happening if natural light will affect your shoot. If you see the site at 8 A.M. on your scouting trip, but you shoot at 2 P.M. during the event, you may be surprised that the sunlight you had planned for won't be illuminating what you had anticipated. Make sure that you bring your camcorder with you on the scout, so that you can make adjustments to your settings while you're there and not have to worry about it on the day of the shoot. You can set the other camcorders to match on the actual shoot day if those camcorders are not in your possession before the event.

Keep It Simple

In attempting to get clean footage, keep the steadiness of the camcorders in mind. All your camcorders should be mounted on a tripod during the wedding ceremony. Not only will that prevent the dreaded shaky cam, but it will also keep your hand from falling asleep and your shoulder from aching. If you have *at least* three camcorders, you can do a little experimenting with one or more camcorders, such as *rack focusing* (see the sidebar "What's Rack Focus?" for more info) from the unity candle to the groom slipping the wedding ring on his lovely lady's finger—or whatever tickles your artistic fancy.

You can save most of the fun, creative videography for the reception, and for in between the important ceremonial stuff, as that reflects the difference between the solemn ceremony and the party-atmosphere events. If you get daring and do a fancy pan-tilt combo, rack focusing on the cake sitting proudly in the middle of the reception hall (please *don't* do this), be sure that you have a static shot, too, just in case. Don't miss a crucial shot because you're trying to be creative. Focus your attention on getting the *important* shots, not on keeping yourself entertained throughout the event.

focus —————————————————————————————

A pan occurs when you move the camcorder on a horizontal axis, while a tilt suggests moving it up or down. Doing both at the same time would be pretty severe camcorder movement, but it's not unheard of in the music video industry.

As for tape—keep plenty on hand, all of the same brand and configuration. One little trick is not to bring *too* many tapes—for each camcorder, calculate the length of the event and then add in, say, two more tapes. That might actually help you keep the project inline and under budget, just by encouraging you not to get *too* much footage that you'll later need to catalog and edit.

What's Rack Focus?

Rack focus refers to the use of depth of field in a shot to pull your attention from one element of the framed image to another. Rack focus is an artistic way to change the focal point of a shot. For example, an object in the foreground will be in focus at the beginning of a shot, and then it will go out of focus as something in the background becomes in focus. Rack focus is easier to do with film because of the depth of field inherent in film—when you focus on something with a film camera, objects at different depths, either close to the camera or farther away from it, tend to be blurry. (If you watch movies carefully, you'll see this effect used often to put the focus on items—perhaps incriminating evidence—in the foreground.)

Because of the way video works, rack focused images are a bit flatter and there's less depth of field by default, although you can add depth of field to a shot. One way to increase depth of field is to move a foreground object away from a background object and then zoom in on the foreground object.

In event video, you may have a wonderful opportunity to work with depth of field and rack focus. For example, you could use two elements or objects, such as a candle and a podium, and place one in the foreground. Move your camcorder reasonably close to the candle, switch to manual focus, and then zoom in on the candle. Then manually focus on the candle. Once you've got it sharp, frame the shot so that you can see the background object, which should be a bit fuzzy. Now, instead of changing your zoom, manually refocus the camcorder so that the podium comes into focus.

One word of caution—with video, you'll find that it's easier to pull rack focus when items are far away from each other as well as from you. Experiment with different depths to get a sense of what your camcorder is capable of doing.

Getting the Shots

How exactly do you get these shots after you have the schedule of events nailed down in your head? Sometimes this is a no-brainer, because the bride and groom want the ceremony covered and let you shoot wherever you want afterward. The same might be true for a public speaker who is used to being on camera and knows you need access to get good shots. If you can, keep at least three camcorders stationary. If you must roam with one, that would be a luxury—and a distraction for the guests, so be mindful to stay out of the way.

Make sure all stationary camcorders have a good line of view to the bride and groom, or whatever is the main focal point. The camcorders should also have good vantage points of guests and other areas of focus when appropriate. Before the event begins, designate subjects of interest on which each camcorder will focus. For example, when a song is sung by the bride's sister in the ceremony, one of the camcorders should use the schedule to be prepared to get that shot. If for some reason the camcorders go unmanned, make sure the shots are set up so that they are wide enough to compensate for a shift of a foot or other movement. (If it's a lengthy Catholic ceremony, there's lots of time to drift.)

Regardless of the event type, you must consider many things when you're getting the shots:

- *Don't be obvious.* You may need to hide your camcorders behind plants and flower arrangements to be less distracting to the guests or audience. During the ceremony, especially, the camcorders should be virtually invisible.

- *Be anonymous.*   Wear black or another dark color of clothing of a nice enough quality that is respectful—that means, usually, leaving the jeans and t-shirts at home. (And don't do the tux t-shirt thing. That ain't cute.) Do what you can to avoid calling attention to yourself.

- *Don't be shy.*   At the same time you're being unobtrusive, don't be shy with your camcorder. When the ceremony is over and the fun begins, you can point a camcorder at someone and ask a question, or get right up front to catch the action. Always, try to recognize the difference between being proactive with your shooting and being a nuisance to your subjects. (Be wary of following people around—if you make them feel to0 self-conscious, you might end up keeping them from doing the exact things you want them to do.)

- *Use your time wisely.*   When waiting at a wedding reception for the bride and groom to arrive—or waiting at a dinner reception for the speaker to start—use one camcorder to roam through the guests and shoot candid interviews with friends and family, or grab images of the cake and food (cover what you can while they're not around)—stuff you know you'll need in editing to make the video more lively and meaningful.

 zoom-in ————————————————————

Gene, our technical editor, suggests using some of this time to record good wishes from the crew. It's a nice touch to add at the end of the video, after the credits, and it reminds your subjects of the enjoyable time they had working with you.

If it were your wedding day—or your graduation or anniversary—what would you want to remember for a lifetime? Because they're preoccupied with entertaining, schmoozing, or enjoying the party, the subjects in your videos won't always have an opportunity to admire the food adorning the tables, the decorations, or the hordes of anxious faces waiting to greet them. The whole day may be a blur for them. Your job is to record the event so they can experience it later and from vantage points that they weren't able to see during the experience.

Couples that come away from viewing their wedding video with a sense that they've seen another side of their own wedding will most likely be very pleased with your work.

For other types of events—particularly for speeches and rallies—you should strive to make your film look as if it was filmed by a professional crew. Often, that's as simple as getting reaction shots from the crowd and extra footage of the location from different vantage points—all of this is footage that you can edit into the final project. If the event is more laid back than a speech or ceremony—birthdays or family reunions and so on—get some candid shots, bloopers, and interviews, and toss them in where they are appropriate and make sense.

focus

One easy rule to remember is this—a major difference between an amateur and a professional videographer aside from skill with the camcorder is the pro's instinct for getting the footage that will be needed later when editing the project. If you have that extra footage, reaction shots, bloopers and so on, your time spent in the editing bay will be much more rewarding. Some of that comes with experience, but it also comes with planning and thinking ahead.

Shooting Outdoors

Shooting outdoors is an ideal situation for weddings and similar events, unless it rains (or sleets, gets cloudy, windy, hot, or cold). Of course, some events—such as football games and political protests—might continue on in the rain, in which case you'll just need to bear with it, perhaps taking off your camcorder's neutral density filter or adjusting the settings. And definitely take your camcorder out in the weather *only* if you have raingear for it.

The sun is an ideal compatriot in your videography, because it helps you get pretty footage. Nothing's better than natural sunlight—it's great for skin tones. Just hope the wedding planner accounted for where the sun would be during the ceremony, but remember that you can be flexible—especially if you are using three camcorders that you can move. In particular, keep a look out for shadows cast by trees and light filtered through leaves and branches that can create shadow patterns. Not only can those items cause an odd appearance on tape, but they can also affect your camcorder's exposure, particularly if you move through them.

When you're not busy recording the ceremony or event, try to capture the essence of the environment—the trees on the property, flowers in bloom, and the birds and bees. Capturing the setting for the wedding will mean a lot to the bride and groom, as they spent a significant amount of time deciding on that special place and making it picture perfect for their momentous day (see Figure 4.3).

It's important that you set your exposure on manual, particularly when you are shooting outside, so that you are properly exposing your subject—bride and groom, speaker or award recipient—not the sky, backdrop, or lights in the background. If your exposure is set automatically by the camcorder, it could expose for something brighter in the frame, which might improperly expose your subjects. The blushing couple won't be happy if their "I Dos"

FIGURE 4.3
*Here's a nice
wide shot
to set up a
wedding in a
downtown park.*

are shot in silhouette—or even worse, if the moment is overexposed on film. Pay attention to light changes during the ceremony, especially in the evening, as the light can change drastically within minutes as the sun goes down. (An automatic exposure setting can be particularly useful, however, if the lighting is going to change dramatically during the shoot—for instance, if you're moving between different lighting situations. The camcorder is slightly faster than you are at adjusting for changes in overall light.)

focus ————————————————————————————————

Many advanced camcorders have a zebra effect feature that helps you manually expose outdoor shots. In essence, the zebra effect will appear in the viewfinder or on the LCD on portions of the shot that are overexposed. Check your camcorder's manual for exact details. In our experience, the zebra effect can be a little touchy—if you're dealing with a contrasty shot (like a white wedding dress next to a black tuxedo), the camcorder may think the wedding dress is overexposed when it actually looks okay on tape. Experiment and get to know your equipment.

What about lighting issues for night shooting? It's likely that an evening or night wedding will have some lighting already set up so that the guests will be able to see what's happening down the aisle. If you are shooting an event lit by candlelight—where additional lighting for the camcorder would be obtrusive and ruin the mood, be clear to your principals that the footage will not be perfectly exposed and crisp. The images will be grainy and some parts may not even be visible. All you can do is boost your gain, set your exposure to allow the most amount of light in (most cameras have a setting around 2), and hope for the best. (Some camcorders have special night shooting modes; such features are relatively useless if you're looking to get a pretty picture, but they might be helpful if they represent your only choice.)

 *zoom-in*

For further comments on lighting, see Chapters 5 and 8.

Shooting Parties and Banquets

Banquets and parties are always a little awkward to shoot, because they're supposed to be fun, casual events, but they generally have a structure and some sort of focal point to keep up with as well. Take a wedding rehearsal dinner, for example. You have a seated audience, probably several if not dozens of speakers, and the bride and groom and their families. How do you cover all of them without the video seeming bland and stationary—or, conversely, like a home movie? Basically, you should use more than one camcorder. A stationary camcorder can document speakers at the podium or head table, and a roaming camcorder can catch the audience reactions, the brides' and grooms' reactions, as well as impromptu toasts and well wishing.

At a less structured party, roaming camcorders can move about freely to catch candid reactions and even interview guests. There's lots of room for improvisation. It's always a treat—at least, in the editing room—when you're dealing with a videographer who gets a little bold in casual situations. If you're feeling daring, get in the conga line with your camcorder, jump in the middle of the dance circle, or hold the camcorder above you looking down at the dance floor. Just make sure you get the most important stuff before you go roaming around the dance floor.

Consider the following if you'd like to maintain the essence of a party within your video rather than the standard point and shoot for most events:

- *Be adventurous.*   It's a party. Have fun with it. Talk to people. Make it interactive while also shooting behind-the-scenes as well as happenings across the room.

- *Vary your shots.*   Remember that you don't have to shoot everything as a close-up or in a wide shot.

- *Keep your eyes open.*   It's easy to get overwhelmed and unable to pay attention at a big event with many people. Don't let it intimidate you. Look around. What are people doing? What strikes you as interesting, informative, fun, touching, important, or unforgettable? Don't just point and record. Think about what you would like to see once you're in the editing bay, or if it were your event and you wanted to pop some popcorn and relive old times captured on tape.

- *Talk to everyone.* Interview the folks who are putting together the event—the caterers, bartenders, and organizers. What has been their experience? What do they think of the food? Of course, this may be unnecessary info for a banquet for a corporate event, but for a wedding reception, it might be fun footage to view later. What do the outsiders see? Is it the wildest party they've ever catered, or the happiest couple they've ever seen? Or did they all notice the brother-in-law who is a little touched in the head? Be creative. Use your best judgment.

- Grab some cake and champagne when the job is done.

Editing the Event

Like everything else you shoot, editing event video is really about compressing an experience to its essential moments of entertainment or poignancy. Fortunately, this is easily accomplished in the wedding video because you are guided by the event and not a story line—instead of coming up with too much in the way of transitional dialogue or narration, you can use effects, dissolves, and music to move from one point to the next.

You should begin by laying down a wide shot of the entire ceremony on your timeline so that you have something to guide you. You should be able to recognize when it is appropriate to cut from the wide shot to a more intimate shot, such as when the bride and groom are exchanging vows. Something that may be more tricky will be the procession of bridesmaids escorted by the groomsmen.

Nina watched a wedding video recently and appreciated the way the wedding videographer compressed the time of the procession. He simply dissolved from one shot of a walking couple to the next couple, holding long enough to get a good look at them both (see the Chapter 4 section of the included CD-ROM). It kept the video from becoming boring and stagnant by not showing everyone walking all the way down the aisle, one after the other. Unless something hysterical happens as someone is walking down the aisle, spare your audience all of that time and just show the pretty faces and clothes.

For other events, the editing cues will be reasonably straightforward, although your biggest problem may be defining what, exactly, is not *boring*, particularly for speeches and conventions. As the producer or editor, you may be falling asleep in front of your PC trying to find a logical place to offer some visual interest. For brainstorming, check out the way professional news camerapeople are able to maintain some interest during live-to-tape broadcasts by showing reaction shots, using slow camera movements, and using other tricks. Watch a little C-SPAN, and then incorporate some of those moves into your next production.

focus

With events, be careful with your cutaways and audience reaction shots. While news outfits are free to show a poor turnout or an audience full of yawners, your client or colleagues may not want to see those shots in a video of the CEO breakfast or the Homebuilders Association Quarterly Award Banquet. If your reaction shots aren't looking good, leave them on the virtual "cutting room floor" when you're editing.

After the ceremony and in the editing bay, you may want to create a montage of shots of the bride and groom from when they were children through adulthood and their courtship, and then use a dissolve effect to bring you to the historical wedding day. Or, if they have sparkling personalities, interview them to find out more about them. The interview might be useful in the final project, but it'll also help you get to know the couple better, which will serve as useful research for the project.

Basically, you need to create an introduction for the couple and the wedding ceremony. This would be a great place to use some of their favorite songs, poems, or stories as the audio track, making the video much more personal and memorable as well as creating a history between the couple. Take a look at shows like The Learning Channel's "A Wedding Story" to get ideas on how to utilize other documentary editing styles for your video, including pre- and post-wedding interviews with the bride and groom.

The reception can be approached much like the ceremony—lay down the essentials, such as cutting the cake and throwing the bouquet, before you start embellishing. Once the essentials are included, you can cut and paste as you wish to make the video fun and uplifting, featuring lots of happy, smiling people, laughter, toasts, people talking directly to the couple on camcorder—whatever footage you have that can make the bride and groom smile and laugh during viewing.

Ultimately, you're going for an emotional response from those who watch your video. Start with something sweet and cute, hope for tears of joy during the ceremony, and then go for smiles and gregarious laughter during the party. If you keep it short and sweet (preferably an hour, and longer only if you have priceless footage that will entertain and can't be left out), you'll be all the more loved. Don't forget the "Just Married" shot at the end, with the giddy couple waving goodbye to the crying moms—it gets them every time.

focus

Remember that the best videos (or films or TV shows) make you forget that they're videos—try not to overemphasize your technique and skill with the camcorder (or the editing software) so much so that this overshadows the importance of the moment and the emotion or experience for the participants.

Standard Wedding Shots

Here's a last list of the shots you're expected to get at a wedding:

- The rehearsal, folks decorating the car, and other activities, if you have the access and budget.
- "B-roll" (this refers to complimentary shots you get outside of the main action which give you options in the editing process) of all specialty items (dress and assorted accessories displayed, the church or location of the ceremony, the flowers, the cake, the invitations) and the ceremonial items (candles, rings, the ring-bearer's pillow, the flower girl's basket). This is all great stuff you can use when editing.

 zoom-in

In video production, you call the extra footage that you use to overlay interviews or speeches B-roll. You'll often hear professionals say they're going to go "shoot some B-roll," which means they're going to get shots of the location, general vicinity, and perhaps objects or scenes that were discussed in the piece. You'll often shoot B-roll after the interview, so that you can base the shots on what you hear in the interview. That isn't always the case, however—sometimes you'll shoot B-roll just because you can get a shot—many videographers will shoot something totally unrelated but interesting or unique if they think it might be handy to add to their library of footage for use in the future.

- The wedding party, pre-ceremony, getting ready.
- Folks arriving, seats filling up, and the arrival and seating of parents and grandparents.
- The entrance of the bridesmaids and groomsmen.
- The faces of the father and bride just before they walk down the aisle, and the bride's procession and crowd reaction shots.

- At the ceremony, the exchange of vows and rings, readings and recitations, the kiss, wedding songs, and everything else that happens up there.

- Get good sound.

- Try for a combination of 2-shots, medium shots, and close-ups of the bride and groom, ring-bearer, and flower girl.

- Musical performances and guest speakers.

- Throwing of rice, flower petals, bubbles.

- The reception: a chance to get plenty of B-roll that will make your video a hit—tipsy aunts, uncles going back for third and fourth helpings at the buffet table, friends pairing up, little kids running around.

- Entrance of guests greeting the new couple at the reception.

- Folks signing the registry book.

- Toasts

- Cutting of the cake and feeding.

- First dance, and dances with parents.

- More dancing.

- Garter and bouquet throw.

- Loading up in the car—Just Married.

- Tears of moms and sisters.

- Interviews or remarks from guests about the couple: predictions, well wishing, funny stories, advice.

Always think about what you won't get the opportunity to reshoot. Shoot those parts before you start roaming around and playing with other shots that may or may not make the final cut. Better yet, put yourself on *must shoot* duty and then get an assistant to shoot some entertaining B-roll.

▌And...Cut!

That's it for weddings and events. Next: getting up, close, and personal with interviews and studio setup.

Interviews

YOU'LL find that knowing something about interviewing and dealing with people on camera will help you with nearly all of the nonfiction video that you attempt to capture and edit, including documentaries. This knowledge will extend to event video, organizational video, weddings, home video, and other projects. Getting a good interview on tape takes coordination. You need to point the camcorder in the best spot; frame the shot; and maintain good light, picture, and sound quality. You need to put the person you're interviewing at ease by asking the "right" kinds of questions.

In this chapter, we talk about the equipment you'll want to have on hand for an interview. We also take a look at the art of the interview, including how to set up the interview and how to ask questions. We talk about using a studio and multiple camcorders to record a studio-based interview and editing your interview in your NLE software.

What You'll Need

The camcorder you use isn't as important as the approach you take to lighting and sound. (Of course, a three-chip camcorder is more desirable than a one-chip, and all the advantages and disadvantages outlined in Chapter 1 apply.)

For lighting, your budget will dictate your limits—if you've got some money to play with, you might consider a portable lighting kit (which can be acquired for as little as $500) that you can use to set up proper lighting in your interviewee's offices, boardrooms, or wherever you're interviewing. If you have the budget, you should also consider renting a studio or outfitting your own studio with sophisticated lights and the staff to run them. (We take a look at lighting later in this chapter.)

For good sound, you'll need some quality microphones—you may end up using slightly different types of microphones for interviewing versus other types of shooting, and we discuss these later in this chapter.

Finally, bring along your ears. A good interviewer is a good listener and someone who can focus well enough to ask appropriate questions at the appropriate moment while making the interviewee feel comfortable and talkative. That takes listening, respect for the person you're interviewing, and some confidence in what you're doing. It'll be fun.

The Art of the Interview

The interview is the foundation of nearly all documentary productions, and it's an important part of many other types of nonfiction video. You may think that the process of interviewing is as simple as setting up a camcorder and asking questions. But it can be much tougher than that—Nina likes to claim that there's a science to it, as well as some art. In fact, you may have to try interviewing a few times and then view the resulting footage critically before you get the sense of how tough a good video interview can be to pull off.

focus ————————————————————————————————

Chapter 4 discusses an equipment checklist for event video. This list is also handy for in-the-field interviews, with emphasis on two really important aspects of shooting—power and tape. An interview can be tough to schedule and even tougher to reschedule, so be sure you arrive ready to shoot as soon as you can get set up, and make sure that you've got enough battery power, an AC adapter, and enough tape for hours of taping. You never know how the shoot is going to go.

Choose the Appropriate Interviewee

One of the most important parts of your interview starts well before a camcorder rolls—you need to choose an interview subject who can provide the kind of shots and information that you need for the film. In some cases, you may not have a choice—if you're shooting video for a company or organization, you probably need to talk to the sales manager or CEO, even if that person isn't a whiz on camera. If you're doing on-the-spot journalism, you need to interview whoever is appropriate—and available—while you're on site.

If you're working on a documentary or similar project, you need to spend some time finding the right person to interview. That's not to say that you won't tape some people who you never use in your final project—that's inevitable.

Here's some advice that may help you make a potential interviewee a reasonably good interviewee on tape. When you're seeking a person to interview, look for someone who

- Is knowledgeable on the subject matter and, ideally, a confirmed expert

- Shows enthusiasm about the topic

- Is able to speak clearly without slurring words, mumbling, or speaking in hushed tones

- Can put ideas into words and formulate understandable metaphors or other descriptions of the subject matter

- Isn't camera shy

- Has some experience being interviewed, particularly on camera, and understands the process of sitting for a video interview

- Isn't overly volatile and will be willing to take some stage direction

- Isn't hostile to the process—unless it's warranted by the nature of the subject matter

You may find that you do quite a few interviews before you find the "right" person for the film—you may even shoot some of those interviews on camera, even if you're fairly sure you won't use them. That's okay—all that work is valuable research and, perhaps even more relevant, it's an excuse to practice your interviewing skills. You may come across people who simply won't do well in a formal video interview, but who still offer a great deal of information or insight about the topic at hand, and that can be a huge help.

Recognize that respecting your interviewees is crucial—you need to be able to establish that the interview is just as much about them as it is about making a video or building a project. Don't think of interviewees as mere cogs in your production machine, but remember that they have their own goals and desires that you may be helping to fulfill. Thinking in those terms will help you make them feel comfortable and welcome. It will also cause you to consider an interviewee's motivations and interests, which may help

Be Prepared

Research and interviews go hand in hand. While it may seem appropriate to walk into an interview with only a little knowledge of the topic, we'd go ahead and leave that to the younger talent at your local news station. It rarely makes an interview better if you know nothing about the subject at hand—most of the time the opposite is true. The more you know, the better you're able to guide an interview on camera to the more interesting, important, or relevant discussion points.

Before you interview someone, do some research regarding the topic and the interviewee's field of study or work. You may also want to learn more about the person you're interviewing, particularly if a biography or anything published by that person is available. This offers you the opportunity to show some respect for that person and her work as well as to get a sense of whether she has any particular agenda, additional interests, or conflicts that you might need to know about.

When you walk into an interview, you should have some questions planned, but you should also be prepared to deviate from those questions. The best thing about having something written down is that you can refer to it when necessary—such as when you've exhausted a particular topic and need to move on to another. Similarly, notes will help you make sure you've covered all of the topics you planned to cover before ending the interview. There's nothing worse than getting up, taking off the microphones, milling around a bit, and suddenly remembering another question you meant to ask.

you decide whether he or she is really the right person for your interview. One key to knowing that is research—see the sidebar, "Be Prepared."

Setting Up the Shot

Before you get started asking questions, you'll need to set up the shot. To do that, you've got a decision to make—who is going to be on camera and how will those people be arranged?

Following are some common approaches.

Focus on the Interviewee

For much of your documentary and organizational filming, you'll focus on the interviewee—in fact, you may not even use the audio of your questions, but just the audio of the interviewee's answers. In that case, you can focus your lights and your attention on the interviewee in a chair, at a desk, or, if appropriate, standing. He'll need a microphone, but you may be able to get away without one. Figure 5.1 shows an example setup.

FIGURE 5.1

Here's an example of a one-person interview shoot.

Two-Shot

A *two-shot* simply means that both you and the interviewee are in the picture; you may be facing one another, although most of the time it's best to "cheat" toward the camcorder a bit—place your chairs at 30- to 45-degree angles to the centerline between the two of you so that you can comfortably look at one another but your body language is oriented to the camcorder. See Figure 5.2 for an example.

Two-Camcorder Shooting

In this case, both the interviewee and the interviewer have camcorders pointed at them (see Figure 5.3), so that they can have a conversation and the editor is free to switch between the two shots. This is a great way to film a conversation, as you can get not only the give and take, but also the reaction shots of each participant.

FIGURE 5.2

In this example of a two-shot setup, the camera is positioned so that both participants are visible throughout the interview.

FIGURE 5.3

Using multiple camcorders, you can get more than one shot at a time and edit them later.

Three-Camcorder Shooting

Finally, a three-camcorder setup will generally allow you to combine both the two-shot approach and the two-camcorder approach by placing the two-shot camcorder *between* the two isolation camcorders (see Figure 5.4). This is how most nightly newscasts are filmed, as well as many talk shows, "how-to" shows and public affairs shows. It's best saved for a studio environment, as you're unlikely to be able to fit three camcorders and the crew far enough apart in someone's living room or office.

Location and Seating

Once you've chosen the type of shot you're going to use, you need to choose the location for the interview and the seating arrangements. Choose a location appropriate to the topic. For example, if you're filming a documentary about obsessive behavior and you are interviewing a bibliophile, you might arrange to shoot in the interviewee's favorite library. If you're interviewing a racecar mechanic, you might shoot in his shop. It can be ideal to shoot

FIGURE 5.4
Here's a sketch of how three-camcorder filming can work.

people in their favorite rooms in their house—with their photos, books, or even pets around them—as that may help them to feel at ease. Look for the most comfortable spot that still promotes good posture for the camera.

In any case, you want a relatively plain and unmoving background—a wall of books, a wall of tools, a picture, or similar items. You should do what you can to avoid distracting or overly busy backgrounds—you want to steer clear of motion in the background and keep the focal point on your interviewee.

focus

If you must shoot where people or cars are moving in the background, see Chapter 8 for tips on making your depth of field shallow so that the background is out of focus and less of a distraction.

Now you need to drop yourself into the scene according to the shooting arrangement. Here are some considerations that will help you get the best-looking shots for your interview:

Remember that your interviewee will be looking at you when you're sitting and chatting—that's how you want it. You need to sit in a place that allows the camcorder angle to look natural while that person looks at you. If it's a one-shot, you'll probably sit to one side of the camcorder, out of view. For a two shot, you'll both be on camera, but you'll cheat your chairs a bit (rotate them toward one another, but not face-to-face).

Place your chair close enough to the interviewee so that you can speak at a normal conversational volume, but realize that your interviewee may change the volume of his voice once the camcorder rolls, particularly if he becomes nervous.

If you're using a single camcorder that's focused on the interviewee exclusively, you should sit so that your eyes are at about the same level as the height of the camcorder's lens. This keeps the interviewee from looking above or below the camcorder, or too far off to the side. Most of the time, you don't want the person speaking on camera to look directly into the lens. Be sure to tell the interviewee to talk to you, not the camcorder.

Once you're in your seat, focus on staying upright and still. Instruct your crew to be as quiet and as still as possible. Make sure that nothing behind you is distracting the subject. This is called *maintaining the eyeline*; the eyeline is an imaginary line that follows the path of the interviewee's eyes. If she is looking way off camera or moving her eyes around the set, it can be distracting to the audience, as it pulls the viewers out of the moment and makes them think about the camcorder and crew behind the lens. Another reason an interviewee will move her eyes around is if you aren't organized with your questions or you aren't able to maintain eye contact during the interview because you're scrambling in your notes—again, it's another reason to be prepared.

Don't let the interviewee rock in a chair—choose a straight-backed chair that doesn't cause him to fidget or slump. We sat through a documentary recently that placed three different interview subjects in rocking chairs—it was a riveting story but very difficult to watch.

An eyeline sets up a visual relationship among the elements in a particular environment. Your purpose in sitting across from the interviewee is to help her maintain an eyeline by giving her someone to converse with actively. By providing a conversational setting, your interviewee will also be more comfortable, leaving you with footage that looks more natural (see Figure 5.5).

The closer the eyeline is to the lens without actually having the interviewee look directly in the camera, the more powerful your shot will be. Having the interviewee look close to the lens helps to keep the viewer involved in the discussion.

Get a Name

Always ask the people you are interviewing, while the camcorder is running but before the interview begins, to state their names and spell them. If relevant, you may also have them tell you what company or group they are affiliated with and their title. This serves two purposes:

- When you are in post-production, you will know who is speaking and, once you're editing, you'll easily be able to create a title effect for him or her.

- You or your assistant(s) can adjust your sound levels as the subject is spelling out his name. If you need more time to adjust your levels, ask him to spell his company name, too.

This second point is just a little trick—because most people will say "Testing, one, two, three" at a different volume level than they'd say their name or spell it, particularly if they're aware that the camcorder is rolling. Asking them to spell their name and company name gets them to speak in a normal voice. It also helps them relax by starting out with an easy question and suggesting that the interview needn't be rushed.

FIGURE 5.5

On the left, the interviewee has proper eyeline; on the right, the interviewee seems to be looking too far off camera.

Ask Open-Ended Questions

When the tape is rolling and after the names are spelled, you're ready to ask questions. Make them good ones! In particular, you want to avoid questions that have "yes" or "no" answers. Instead, ask questions that require some explanation. Plus, in interviews that you plan to run without the questions audible, you need to ask them in such a way that the interviewee will make the subject of the question clear in her response. Here are some examples of bad questions:

- *Do you like ice cream?* Probably a yes or no answer.

- *What is your favorite flavor?* You'll get a short answer, such as "I'm a fan of vanilla."

- *So your position is that Paul Revere never made that fateful ride?* Again, a "yes" or "no" answer is likely here. What's worse is that you may get something very non-specific, such as "That's right, I don't think he did. And I have research to prove it." Without hearing the question, the answer doesn't make much sense.

- *What was your favorite moment in baseball history?* You might get a decent answer to this one, but you've cut it close, because this could also be answered something like this: "Oh, that was July 28, 1994, the day Kenny Rogers threw a perfect game for the Rangers." The answer doesn't restate the question and doesn't elaborate.

A better way to ask questions is to steal a bit from the way a psychotherapist might ask questions—ask your interview subjects to describe things, to state their opinions, and to "tell you about" something. In particular, these questions—actually, many of them are statements—are well-suited to getting answers that will work on video *without* your audience hearing the question, which is the ideal approach both for on-location interviews (where you might not be able to manage sound as well as you can in a studio) and for many documentary-style interviews.

Here are some examples of good questions or interview prompts:

- *Tell me your favorite flavor of ice cream and why you like it.*   You might get "I don't have a favorite flavor," but for most people, you'll get an answer such as "My favorite flavor of ice cream is vanilla. I just like it because it's simple. Plain. A little like me, I guess."

- *You have an interesting opinion of Paul Revere's famous ride. Tell me about it.*   One of the key phrases in the arsenal is "Tell me about it," because it invites the interviewee to include whatever he thinks is important, while painting it in broad strokes.

- *You also have evidence regarding the breed of horse he rode. Please describe that for the viewer.*   In this example, you can direct someone who hasn't completely answered the question according to your research. (For instance, you happen to know that an important part of his story includes Paul Revere's horse, but he failed to mention it previously.) This question does two other things—it states the request, instead of asking it ("Can you describe…"), which cuts down on the possibility of the interviewee saying "Um, sure, I can describe that…" to begin his answer. Also, the phrase "for the viewer" makes it clear that the interviewee should tell the story as if he were addressing someone completely unfamiliar with it. Sometimes an interview subject won't go as deep into a topic as you'd like because he assumes that you, the filmmaker, already know about the topic and he doesn't want to insult your intelligence.

- *What happened on June 24, 1994, and what was going through your mind that day?*   Here's one way to ask a question when you already know the context—perhaps the entire interview is *about* baseball—and you already know that the date is likely to be significant to your interviewee. Asking the question in this way gets your interviewee not just to restate the date and the meaning of it, but to put himself back in that moment in time and reminisce instead of simply answering the question.

While you're asking questions, be sure you listen to the answers—not just to hear what you need or want to hear for your later editing purposes, but also to help your interviewee feel she's participating in a conversation. Whenever you hit on something that your interviewee is passionate about, you should try to follow it up by getting at that *emotion*.

If you're recording an interview in which the questions will be heard in the film, feel free to ask questions that guide the interviewee through her story. Try to be focused, but allow for the person to answer beyond "yes" and "no." And don't forget your therapist-like questions and prompts: *What do you remember from that time? Tell me about it. Tell us that story.* The questions can seem redundant, but they're all designed to peel the onion that is the emotion of a particular moment.

 zoom-in ─────────────────────────────

When you are finished asking the questions you had in mind, ask your interview subjects if there is anything she would like to add, something she had on her mind, or something you may have forgotten to ask. Nine times out of ten, she will say something important that you will use.

Changing Shots

Before we move on, we need to mention one little detail about camerawork. For the most part, your camcorder can remain stationary throughout an interview—there should be little movement if the interview is framed correctly. (Of course, this doesn't apply if the interview is a stand-up, where your cameraperson is holding the camcorder—but you'll still want to keep it as steady as possible, particularly during the answers.)

Remember that the interview itself, in most cases, doesn't need to be visually appealing—once you've gotten the answers from that interviewee, your next step will be to shoot interesting footage that you can overlay while your interviewee answers questions—it's those cutaways that will add the visual appeal in the final product.

If you or your cameraperson needs to reframe a shot, it's important that it happens during a *question,* not during an answer. That's because the question is less valuable footage—you can cut it, in most cases. The only time you should ever move the camcorder during an answer is if your interviewee goes out of sight of the camcorder and doesn't come back, forcing you to follow him. Occasionally (but rarely), you might also zoom in on a interviewee during a particularly emotional moment. At that point, a slow zoom is acceptable—but not essential. When in doubt, keep the same focal length and concentrate on getting a good, clean shot.

That said, you might want to frame confrontational or particularly poignant interviews as close-ups to begin with—again, the cameraperson can change focal lengths between answers. As the questions become more intense or probing, you can zoom in closer with the camcorder. (Remember, though, that the more you zoom, the shakier the image will appear if the camcorder isn't mounted on a tripod or stabilizing device. Go for stability over drama if you have to choose between the two.)

 *zoom-in*

It's also a good idea to record **ambient sound** after the interview is concluded. Take a few moments with a camcorder, and, with no one talking, record in the room where the interview took place—you can pan around and shoot trophies or books or artwork while, at the same time, recording the "sound" of the room. This can come in handy later in editing. Not only can you use this extra footage to give the viewer a sense of the surroundings for the interview (if those surroundings are important), but you also have some extra sound footage to use when you need to edit mistakes or delete questions.

Lighting, Sound, and Studios

Whether you're interviewing outside, in someone's home or office, or in your own studio space (or some rented studio space), you're going to need to consider some of the fundamentals when it comes to setting up your interviews. The more control you have over these elements, the better. Of course, it won't always work that way—if you're shooting documentary or organizational video, we guarantee you'll be shooting in a lot of people's offices and in conference rooms. The best option, though, is to control the lighting, control the sound, and, if you're lucky, control the environment by having the interview in your own studio.

Lighting for Interviews

The best lighting manages both to emulate real life and improve upon it somewhat, if only to exaggerate it slightly for the camera. When indoors, almost any type of purposeful lighting—even swivel lamps from a discount office store—is probably better than just shooting with the overhead lights in the room. If you don't have a choice but to work in office light, consider either moving the interview outside (on a sunny day, and assuming you have wind guards for your microphones) or turn up the lights as much as you can and try to place your interview subject so that no harsh shadows appear on his face.

The lighting can be simple, such as an on-camera light (a light that runs off the camcorder's power or off a battery and illuminates the area directly in front of the camcorder lens—see Figure 5.6). Such a light isn't ideal, but it helps a little in low-light situations. Most camcorder manufacturers offer models specific for their units (or built-in, in some cases), while

FIGURE 5.6

Todd's Canon GL1 sports this snazzy little key light for mobile lighting.

third-party lights are also available in all sorts of shapes and power ratings. Note that these lights usually don't do much for your interviewee's skin tones and appearance—they help you get the shot when the ambient light isn't good enough, but they aren't the all-around best solution.

If you're willing to lug around additional equipment, you might want to look into a portable lighting kit. The pros recommend tungsten or quartz lighting, because it's relatively easy to work with and is equipped with smaller lamps. You might also consider fluorescent lighting, particularly a new type called *daylight spectrum bulbs*, which do a good job of matching the color of daylight. Fluorescents have historically been bad lighting to use for video, but new fluorescent light technology makes it a viable alternative in professional video studios.

focus

If you're using your own portable lights, you'll probably want to close window shades and turn off other lights in the room. The reason for this is that different types of light have different **color temperatures**, which means they give off different casts of color. When they're mixed together, the result can be odd color problems in your video.

You can find kits and lights available at camera and video stores. Kits start around $400 and include cases for travel; professional-level kits can be a few thousand dollars, but they offer much more flexibility, including the ability to accept color gels, to focus the lights, and to alter their brightness and direction. Some manufacturers of inexpensive lighting kits include NRG Research (www.nrgresearch.com), Lowel (www.lowel.com), Photogenic Professional Lighting (www.photogenicpro.com), and Smith-Victor (www.smithvictor.com).

focus ————————————————————————————————————

When you're working with lighting, particularly on location, it's important that you try not to overload power circuits. Check the rating on your lights and other equipment, noting that typical household circuits can handle about 20 amperes of power per circuit—you may be getting close to that just with a simple lighting kit. Also remember that all the outlets in one room may be on that same circuit—in other words, don't forget to bring along a heavy gauge extension cord if you're bringing a lighting kit, as you'll probably need to use it to reach a second electrical circuit somewhere else in the building.

Once you've got your lights—whichever you opt to use—you're ready to focus on some key points.

When possible, avoid using light that emanates from one direction only. If the light is directly in your subject's face, the result will be bright but flat—it'll be tough to tell how far the person is from the background. If you have only one light way off to the side, you might create horror-movie effects that cast scary shadows on the subject's face. If you're stuck with one light on your camcorder, try shooting your interviewee at a *slight* angle to get a little definition in her face. Remember—the on-camera light will likely not flatter your interviewee's appearance, but it can be handy to supplement other lighting or when you need to shoot a stand-up interview in a darkened room or at night and have no other choice.

Some contrast and facial definition is good. You can encourage that by placing your main light (called the *key light*) over the camcorder and to one side (as if the light were looking over the cameraperson's shoulder). The key light off to the side will create some shadows on the interviewee. You can then use a *bounce* (a reflector, which is something you can buy from a photography store, or you can use white or foil-covered poster board) from the opposite side to fill in the shadows.

You can also use a *fill light*, if you have a second light along, which can be used to fill shadows without losing definition around the nose, mouth, eye sockets and so on. Using a key light and a fill light is called *two-point* lighting, and it's a common way to get good results. Figure 5.7 shows an example of a two-point lighting system.

 zoom-in

The fill light should use the same technology as your key light—quartz, fluorescent, flood light, and so on. Otherwise, you'll mix color temperatures and you might not get the results you intend. The fill light can, however, be a less **intense** light so that it doesn't overwhelm the subject with light, but just fills some shadows.

You can move up to a three-point lighting system by adding a *backlight*. A backlight, which should use the same technology as the other lights, should be positioned slightly above your interviewee and slightly off to one side—you then shine the light on the back of your interviewee, which adds a halo effect on the person's shoulders and head. What this does is help to add the appearance of depth to the shot—the light serves to separate the person from the background.

If you want to try for four-point lighting, shine a light on the background in your shot—whether it's a bookcase, a wall, or a painting. You can use a color gel on the light or a colored light—or, if the background is already interesting, just use a lower power version of the lights in your lighting kit. This is handy for adding a little background interest and pizzazz without requiring you to paint a wall. It isn't mandatory, but it can help the set look a little more professional.

If you're shooting outside, you can probably get away with using just reflectors and the sun, assuming it's a sunny day. (And if it's threatening rain, you probably don't want to use your pricey lights and electricity outside unless it's absolutely necessary.) Use your reflectors to fill in shadows that are caused by the sun. Don't place your interviewee directly in front of the sun or directly facing it, particularly if it makes him squint. Use the sun as a key light off to one side, and use a reflector to fill in shadows.

Shooting outside presents its own challenges—light can shift on cloudy days or if you opt to shoot beneath trees as the sun filters through branches. You should also keep a lookout for reflective surfaces, and you'll need to watch the humans and your equipment to make sure they aren't overheating in direct sunlight. Perhaps the biggest challenge that sunlight can present is the fact that it changes over time—if you have an interview that stretches for many hours, shooting outdoors can affect your ability to edit that interview out of sequence. Your audience may notice the difference between shadows on different parts of the same day if you cut back and forth between shots from different times. For that reason, it might be a good idea to shoot outside only for short durations and plan your longer interviews for indoors— ideally in a studio.

Sound for Interviews

Nearly any video production—but particularly an interview—is next to worthless without good sound. A richly recorded interview can be a wonderful thing, particularly if you've gotten good enough sound to hear the emotion— sadness, happiness, anger—in your interviewee's answers and comments. You'll get those, though, only if you have good microphones and you pay attention to sound.

Often when interviewing, you'll need more helpers than in some other types of video work—if you're holding the pad and asking the questions, you'll probably need a camera operator and, if space and budget permit, a sound recordist. Even if you can get only one helper, your cameraperson can wear headphones and keep tabs on the sound to make sure you're getting good audio.

Recording Choices

You can record directly to your camcorder—many camcorders have a mini-plug style microphone port that will accommodate one external microphone. We recommend that you work with XLR-balanced cabling, however, which will require an add-on converter box for your microphone connections. See Chapter 10 for more on those options. And if you do record sound to your camcorder and you're using multiple camcorders, you have an interesting decision to make—which camcorder do you choose? If you choose the most appropriate camcorder, it may make editing a little easier.

Here are some thoughts on audio:

- For documentary-style interviews that focus on the interviewee, we recommend getting your primary audio recorded to the same camcorder that you use to record the interview. That will make it a cinch to synchronize when editing.

- For news-magazine style interviews where the interviewer and interviewee each has a camcorder's focus, you'll probably want to record sound to the camcorder that's recording your interviewer. That's because he or she is likely to begin and end the segment, and having audio on that footage will be a little easier to synchronize in your editing software.

- For talk-show style interviews with three camcorders, we'd recommend recording your sound on the camcorder that gets the two-shot. This will be the foundation of the interview—when you go in tight on one of the interviewees, you'll be able to *overlay* the original video with video of the close-up shots.

Why is all this important? Editing interviews can be a bit touchy when you shot the interview with more than one camcorder, because you'll have a lot of footage to cut together and synchronize. When the audio is recorded on one clip and you're using video from another clip, you're going to need to make the lips of the talking person match the audio—that will take some practice. If you record to the camcorder that will be used most often in your editing, you'll cut down on how many little edits you have to sit through and tweak until you get it *exactly* right.

Microphone Choices

You'll also probably want to look into some particular types of microphone if you're interested in getting the best interview sound—each type of interview and location can benefit from a slightly different approach to sound gathering.

focus

Chapter 10 has more details on microphones and how you'll get them to record the best sound for you. At this point, we'll just say that if you can't hear the interview, it isn't a good interview—even if it comprises nothing but brilliant questions and brilliant answers. If you can't hear it, you'll have to scrap it or do it again. (We both speak from experience.)

Handheld Microphone   If you're working on camera in such a way that both you and your interviewee can be seen in the shot, you might as well use a handheld microphone and switch it between your mouth and your interviewee's mouth as you speak. This is the typical local news reporter's "stand-up" style interview. This type of microphone is usually a smaller handheld microphone, wired to the camera equipment and covered with a wind guard.

Boom Microphone   If you're asking your questions off-camera and only your interviewee is supposed to be seen and heard, you'll likely want to take the approach of using a directional microphone on a boom. (A boom is a long, usually telescoping pole that allows you to get the mic closer to the interviewee while keeping it out of the camcorder's view.) This is a standard setup that you'll see when people film documentaries. It requires two people—one handling the camcorder and one handling the microphone boom. It's a good way to get audio "in the field" when you're interviewing people while documenting events.

Lavalier Microphone   This type of microphone is for quieter, sit-down interviews (at least, usually you're sitting down) where you're spending some time with your interviewee. The lavalier, a tiny mic that attaches to a lapel or other part of a person's clothing, allows you to ensure that you're getting good sound and that it's consistent in quality. Lavalier microphones can be both wired and wireless—a wired mic guarantees the best sound for indoor shoots, but a wireless lavalier is perfect for interviewing while the interviewee walks around.

Working in the Studio

A studio doesn't have to cost a lot of money. A studio can be as simple as a room where you set up lighting and cameras and other elements that make it easy to get rolling with an interview. Or a studio can be a larger setup, perhaps designed for taping a public affairs show or some other type of chat show. It simply depends on your resources.

If you need to do a lot of interviews, having a windowless studio is a nice idea. Ideally, your studio has at least two walls that meet at right angles, where you can place some comfortable, nondescript furniture. Place that furniture so that you can look at your interview subject but you're not dead-on—instead, you're both tilted about 30 degrees toward the camcorder if you're using a two-shot. Otherwise, you can place a camcorder over your shoulder and look more directly at the interviewee. (See Figure 5.8.)

Your studio should provide space for your lighting, whether you use a portable kit that you can keep on light stands or more permanent lights mounted on ceiling brackets. You'll also need room for your camcorders—ideally, you'll have heavy rolling tripods that can be used to dolly the camcorders as necessary—in a low-budget studio, having your camcorders on regular field tripods should work fine.

If the room has an audible echo, you might consider using a rug or tightly-woven carpeting and, if necessary, some sound-deadening material on the walls such as sound-proofing foam. (We've seen sound-proofing

FIGURE 5.8

Setting up for a one-camcorder shoot.

foam cleverly mounted to a cardboard or wood backing that can be hung like a large piece of art, so it doesn't have to be placed on the wall permanently.) Finally, you should think about the backdrop—a dark color is probably ideal for most of your interviews, although you could consider painting different walls different colors. You might even paint a wall in a blue or green that can be used for chromakey effects (see Chapter 11) that are used for the integration of special effects.

A studio can give you the flexibility you need for your interviews while providing space for you to place your lights and camcorders in optimal configurations. If you end up with that sort of a setup, you can count yourself lucky.

focus

A lot of studios are set up for control-room management—instead of recording directly to tape, the studio camcorders feed their picture back to the control room, where the director can make decisions as to which camcorder will be recorded from at any given moment. With DV camcorders, things will work a little differently—all the camcorders will be taping and you'll need to import footage from each camcorder and edit it together to build the show.

Editing an Interview

Editing an interview isn't difficult, although it can be time-consuming, particularly if you're using multiple camcorders or you're interested in a lot of B-roll and cutaway footage. Using all that overlaid footage is the best way to edit an interview to keep it entertaining. If you're interviewing an artist about her art, for example, you need to show the art in question while she discusses it. If you're talking to a retired mayor about the way the city used to look, you should overlay his comments with B-roll footage of the city now as well as stock footage of the city in the past, if you can get it.

Technique

To make use of cutaways and multiple camcorders, you need to lay the foundation for the interview. You should begin by importing the entire interview footage from the camcorder that you used to record the audio. With this as the foundation track, you can layer on other clips—reaction shots from the interviewer, for instance, and B-roll footage that illustrates the subjects that were discussed in the interview.

For a basic one-camcorder interview, this is easy enough to do even with a consumer application such as iMovie:

1. Place the main footage of the interview on the timeline, and then choose Advanced | Extract Audio to extract audio from that footage. Now you'll have both video and audio on the timeline.

2. Locate a clip that will overlay the basic interview footage—a shot of something that's being discussed, for instance. Select that clip, and in the clip viewer, highlight the portion of the footage that you want to use, and then choose Edit | Copy.

3. Place the playhead on the timeline and choose Advanced | Paste Over At Playhead. The footage will be added to the timeline, but the audio from the original clip remains the same. Now you'll see different images while still hearing the same interview.

In more advanced editors, you'll do something slightly different—instead of pasting the video into a single video track, you can use multiple video tracks to overlay video. This is particularly useful for multiple-camcorder shoots and editing, because it gives you a finer level of control that iMovie doesn't offer.

For instance, if you used two camcorders to get footage of both the interviewer and interviewee, you'll have two different versions of the same interview that you'll need to edit together. First, you'll place the footage from the camcorder that you used to record the audio, and then you'll add in clips from the other camcorder. It's similar to adding B-roll, but there's a complication—you have to synchronize the speaking person's lips from the second clip to the original audio in the first clip. That's generally done by adding the clip—without audio—to the timeline on a video track that's above the original video.

In Final Cut, you place a clip without audio by first turning off all of the audio tracks in the timeline and then dragging the clip to the timeline. Only a video component will be placed, which you'll need to line up exactly to get the voice and lips to synchronize (you can highlight the clip and use the left and right arrow keys to move one frame at a time):

In Adobe Premiere, you can drag a clip to the timelime from the Project window—both the audio and video will be added:

Now, since you don't want to use the audio from the second clip, you can choose Clip | Unlink Audio And Video. Next, select the audio portion of the clip and delete it. That leaves you with just the video overlay but the original interview audio underneath it. Highlight the overlay clip and use the keyboard arrows to move it left or right by one frame, to line it up correctly.

Other Editing Tips

In interview editing, you're probably going to use a lot of straight cuts and few transitions—when you're cutting back and forth between interviewer and interviewee, for instance, you should use all straight cuts. As TV viewers, we're familiar with those cuts and they don't seem as jarring as you might think when you look at them in your editing software.

Likewise, you usually don't have to transition between B-roll and interview footage. Instead, you can save your transitions for when a particular interview segment ends or, for a long interview, you can use a fade-out transition to end one topic and begin another, particularly if you use titles on the screen for each of your interview segments. You can also use transitions if you need to cut between an interview with the same person that takes place on different days or in different locations—that keeps them from suddenly showing up with a different shirt on and no explanation.

On the CD-ROM   See the Chapter 5 movies on the included CD-ROM for examples of straight cuts versus examples where transitions make sense.

You'll spend a lot of time editing sound for your interviews. If you're doing documentary-style, one-camcorder interviews, you might want to edit your sound to remove the questions that you ask. One trick to doing this is to make sure you get some ambient sound of the room before or after you film the interview, as was mentioned earlier in the section "Changing Shots." You can then use that ambient sound to paste over portions of your audio where you need to remove a section that had you speaking. (More on audio editing in Chapter 10.)

And...Cut!

In this chapter, we discussed the art of interviewing, including a discussion of the equipment you'll need, the different ways to set up the shots, how to use multiple camcorders to greatest effect, and even how to ask questions so that you get the best answers. In the next chapter, we'll move on to documentary video, where you'll find that some of these interviewing techniques come in pretty handy.

Documentaries

THE term *documentary* can be deceiving. It conjures up memories of science videos in the sixth grade, do-it-yourself videos, or boring public television programming. *Narrative film*—fiction movies—has always seemed juicier, sexier, and more entertaining. But for those of us in the know, a documentary can range from a film shown on local public television to the Discovery Channel to HBO, which can be very different forms of the genre. In truth, most *docs* (short for *documentaries*) are made to educate and inform.

It's false to say that documentary cannot be entertaining. The good ones are informative and tell a story well, entertaining you as well as enlightening you about a topic that you may not have known much about. In fact, documentary film has enjoyed a renaissance, thanks to the ever-expanding number of cable television channels that carry short documentaries as well as feature-length documentaries, such as Michael Moore's Academy Award–winning *Bowling for Columbine*, that have garnered worldwide attention.

One reason why documentaries have a bad rap is because they don't always look as "good" as Hollywood fare. There are reasons for that—for one, documentaries tend to be shot on video. When you're documenting real life, it's hard to know beforehand what is essential to shoot and what isn't, so video is much more practical than film. Even though video is still inferior to film in certain ways (or, at least, video and film have different qualities), *tape stock* is much cheaper than film stock, which is why it has been the format of choice for most documentarians in the recent past.

focus —————————————————————————————————

Wondering **why** some folks think film is superior to video? Film has more grain to it (which equates to more resolution), and the process of its exposure is a chemical one, not a digital one, which results in an image that some people describe as "warmer" or "livelier." Film uses fewer frames per second than video (particularly NTSC [National Television Standards Committee] video), which results in some interesting blurring effects that we're all used to seeing in film but that we don't see in the same way in video. Perhaps most noticeable, however, is that film has a richness of color that video has trouble duplicating, and film can create a depth of field that's useful for making a scene seem a bit more three dimensional, as you're able to focus on different parts of the framed image.

Until the advent of digital video, filmmakers have never been able to shoot as freely as they can now; with broadcast-quality video camcorders now affordable, and major consumer companies producing prosumer camcorders—Canon, Panasonic, and Sony, for example—the genre has been revolutionized. The professional can more affordably create a product, and the amateur can easily pick up a camcorder and document granddad reciting his famous war stories from conception to finished product with archival footage and interviews *a la* the History Channel—in your own home. Plus, the digital video (DV) footage looks better than analog video footage, and available software tools can improve the look.

In this chapter, we discuss basic documentary styles, tip and tricks for better interviews, dealing with archival footage and photography, and telling a story. Ultimately, it all goes back to the *story*. If you don't have a story to tell, all the creative and technical guidance we can offer you will be worthless. Remember that even if you're documenting the mating rituals of your local waterfowl, there's a story to tell. In fact, there's *always* a story—you just have to find it.

What You Need

In terms of what you need to create a documentary, we already gave part of it away—you need a story to tell. Many times with any nonfiction story—but particularly in a 30-minute or longer documentary—your story will not be completely clear until the end of shooting, while you're editing. Still, you must start with an idea around which you can build the film.

focus ————————————————————————————————

Documentary is a standout among forms of video projects in that the quality of the images is not the most important concern—the story is. If you end up running after someone with the camcorder or your camcorder gets knocked around by an angry interviewer, that might be okay in a documentary, but it wouldn't necessarily work in other formats. Of course, having said that, you should do everything you can to get quality pictures when you're shooting and editing your documentary.

Documentary film isn't the first choice of many budding filmmakers—they sit around thinking of ideas and writing scripts for feature films or short fiction pieces. In fact, some people don't get into making a documentary until the need to tell some story becomes overwhelming—someone or something seems incredibly interesting and you have to tell the world about it. In other words, *few people make documentaries for the money*—particularly early in a career. That said, some people do make money selling documentaries to cable channels or getting them distributed as features—but that's a reasonably rare phenomenon. Stick to wedding videos if you're looking to pay the bills (see Chapter 4). Documentary is for videographers with a passion for telling someone or some thing's story.

Many methods can be used to shoot and tell the story of a documentary—in 24 hours or over a span of 10 years; with on-camera questions or without; following the subject in its natural course or re-creating that course—the variations are endless. We suggest you begin with this premise—you're going to shoot with *one* camcorder—and then plan accordingly. While a documentary can be shot with multiple camcorders and a large crew, you'll greatly simplify the project by using just one camcorder and a small crew. For most typical documentary projects, we recommend no more than three people: producer/director, cameraperson, and sound recordist. Because you're generally dealing with reality (not actors), it is important that you maintain intimacy and trust with your subject matter—thus, the smaller the crew, the more likely that will be accomplished (not to mention the project will be cheaper, more mobile, and easier to manage).

Any digital camcorder will likely do fine for your documentary filmmaking, but if you want to air your project someday on television or the big screen, it's important that you spend a little more to shoot broadcast-quality video, such as three-chip MiniDV, DVCAM, DVCPro, or DigiBeta—get the best you can afford. (See Chapter 1 for more in-depth discussion of equipment.) If you're self-distributing the film to your friends and family, format will be of little concern, as long as your camerawork is good and you tell a good story.

Easily more important than a clear image is clear *sound*. Sound is crucial to documentary film if you are recording an interview or the natural sounds of an environment. At times you will shoot MOS (which means without sound—see the following Zoom-In), but more often, sound will be an important element in your documentary work. If you don't get an audible interview with the prime minister or if you're following waterfowl but fail to get their mating sounds on tape, you have virtually useless footage. And, as with a lot of your documentary shooting, you'll get only one *take*—it's not like a feature film where you can reset the actors and try again. A fair amount of the time, getting good sound the first time is crucial.

 *zoom-in* ————————————————————

The term MOS supposedly comes from a German director who may have said, on the set, something to the effect of "We will shoot this mit out sound"—though we think this is likely a filmmaking urban legend. Our technical editor's best guess is that MOS is short for mute on sound, which we can live with.

While Nina was working on a music documentary, she unfortunately learned the hard way how important sound is for a project (particularly music-based projects). She initially approached the project as a guerilla filmmaker—a one-woman crew with a camcorder and using only on-camera microphones. During the editing process, she grew to appreciate the importance of good sound. Basically, if you can't clearly hear what someone is saying in an interview, you can't use the footage—or you'll need to narrate it or use it to overlay other audio that you've recorded. In such cases, you may have to go back to an interviewee or someone else who is featured in your documentary and ask them to repeat some of the things they said. If you have shot video that is out of focus, but the sound is flawless, you can at least use the sound under other images—or work to stylize the footage you have.

There's an adage in filmmaking that says whenever the audience for your film or video complains about the lighting or camerawork in a shot or sequence, it's because there's something wrong with the *sound*. Study your own viewing habits and note how willing you are to watch poorly lit shots, fuzzy sequences, or even relatively boring pictures—as long as the sound is good.

How do you get good sound? You can study that in depth in Chapter 10. The easy answer is to get the microphone as far away from the camcorder and as close to the subject as possible. Note that sometimes "as far away from the camcorder" is still *on* the camcorder—particularly if you are a one-person crew.

As you'll see in Chapter 10, you can use directional microphones, various mounting options, and other techniques to improve your sound gathering, even if you don't have a sound engineer running alongside you holding a boom mic (which is the most common way to ensure good sound, incidentally). A wireless, lavalier, microphone can be helpful for this sort of sound gathering as well, as it gives you the luxury of getting the mic close to your subject.

Along with the story, camcorder, and microphones, you'll need a tolerant and patient family. Documentary filmmaking is extremely time-consuming and not the cheapest hobby. Prepare those around you for the obsessive tendencies you may display when working on your baby. This is normal behavior—we promise.

Documentary Styles

After you have chosen a story to document and acquired the tools to accomplish the task, you have to decide *how* you want to tell the story. You can tell the story visually in any number of ways—much as you can vary a recipe and still create a savory dish when cooking a meal, or use the same ingredients in different ways to make several different dishes. Perhaps a dozen filmmakers could be documenting the same subject as you, but each filmmaker will have a unique approach. It's a good idea to define your particular approach to the story before you begin shooting.

If you're familiar with documentaries, you might already recognize the differences between the ways that filmmakers approach their subjects— Ken Burns (*Civil War, Baseball, Jazz*), Albert Maysles (*Gimme Shelter, Grey Gardens, Lalee's Kin*), and the typical hour-long piece for the Discovery Channel are all very different types of documentaries. Albert Maysles, along with his late brother, David, are innovators of the *cinéma vérité* style of filmmaking, in which the filmmaker tries to capture the subject in its natural environment, allowing the story to unfold itself. (*Cinéma vérité* means "truth cinema" in French.) Maysles Films continues to make films in this fashion as modern television, perhaps unfortunately, has manipulated the style and capitalized on it with today's "reality television" programs.

Along with reality styles come historic documentary, personal documentary, and what we're calling "educational reels" or more straightforward teaching films. We look at some of those styles in this section.

focus ──────────────────────────────────────

Documentary is not limited to what we mention here. Many documentary styles can be and are used, none of which have any particular rules to follow. Often, filmmakers mix styles. As the director, you are responsible for the overall vision of the project, creating a style that compliments both the subject and your personality.

Vérité Video

When shooting reality, you must consider many variables. Consider that your production values are governed by lighting, sound, and camcorder stability, and you can see that all three are challenged when you're not in complete control of your environment.

The *vérité* style can be worth the hassle, however, as it is one of the most powerful ways of telling a story. Generally, no verbal commentary is needed from the filmmaker since the story tells itself—thus, the filmmaker doesn't have to try to convince an audience of his or her point of view, since it simply presents itself. That said, the subject matter can, of course, still be manipulated when it is edited, so *vérité* lives up to its name only when the director has the goal of maintaining the integrity of the message. (One dramatic instance is the film *Blair Witch Project*, which used *vérité* style to tell a fictional story.)

Here's a look at some of the issues involved with using this style.

Lighting

Lighting will probably be compromised when you're shooting "reality," as you have little or no control over it, which, unfortunately, can sometimes give the impression that your project was poorly shot from a technical standpoint. (Reality television cheats because these shows usually use huge crews and their locations are generally pre-lit. For example, MTV's *The Real World* takes place mainly in the house where everyone lives; the production crew has control of the set before and during the shoot. When the subjects are away from the house, a crew follows with lights and bounce boards to manage the lighting as they go.

Sound

Sound will always be difficult, unless all of your subjects are wearing wireless mics—but that creates another issue, as you'll need a sound mixer to keep everyone's volume levels the same. Another option would be to have a sound recordist with very strong arms use a boom mic to move from one subject to another as necessary. (More on this sort of thing in Chapter 10.)

Camcorder Stabilizer

In many other styles of video and filmmaking, you can leave the camcorder in one place or use relatively sophisticated stabilizers (or multiple camcorders) to get your shots. In documentary, that's true when you're shooting interviews and background, but when you're in the field, you may need to look into other camcorder stabilization options, such as *steadicam* outfits.

Subject Whim

Another variable to consider is the subject itself (or himself or herself). You never know what's going to happen until it happens. Ideally, shooting reality could be easy—small crew, no lights, no actors—but it poses more problems than you might expect, because you have little control in real-life situations. You can be surprised by anything from the subject acting erratically on camera or deciding not to participate to the subject committing a crime on camera or leading you into a dangerous situation. At the least, you'll want to be mobile and able to move with a minimum of fuss when you're shooting reality—that's one reason that a good backpack, fanny pack, or field jacket/vest (the fisherman's style, with lots of pockets) can be handy to help you manage batteries, tapes, microphones, and anything else you need to be able to run with.

Practical Issues

The *vérité* approach can have some practical implications as well, not the least of which is getting permissions for using images of people and locations that you encounter. With a less hasty approach to documentary, you can handle the paperwork a little more easily, working within the proper permits and getting signed releases from anyone who appears on camera. If your filming is more in the *vérité* or "reality" style, you may not have the luxury of stopping to hand out forms and ask for permission from everyone you shoot. Instead, you might find yourself doing what the "cops" shows do—fuzzying out faces or adding quick edits to avoid potential legal problems. (See the bonus chapter, available on the Web at http://www.digitalvideoideas.com, for more discussion on getting proper permissions and some of the legal hurdles to consider if you plan to distribute your work.)

Historical Documentary

Most people are familiar with Ken Burns's style of filmmaking. Think old photographs, beautiful and haunting landscapes, soothing voice-overs by the likes of actor Morgan Freeman and radio personality/author Garrison Keillor, sweeping music—historical filmmaking at its best. Ken Burns is famous for his series of films on particular subjects such as baseball and jazz music. Like the Maysles, Burns seeks to preserve the reality of the subject, but since his subjects are generally past their time, he often has to re-create the drama or personify the subjects—for example, using letters read as voice-over, intercutting old photographs and footage, and shooting locations that are important to the story and that still exist.

For example, in *The Civil War*, although the landscape where battles were fought nearly 150 years ago has changed, it was purposely photographed at the same time of year and the same time of day when the battles would have occurred. This style of documentary requires heavy research before the shoot, but it's a great way to tell stories about past events. You might consider swiping Burns's style for telling your grandfather's war stories or the history of your home town. Historical filmmaking allows you to have complete control of your subject, unlike *cinéma vérité*, making it easier to create perfect looking and sounding footage if you desire.

Personal Documentary

The personal documentary is a style that seems to show up a lot at film festivals and in some reality television, as well as in the series "P.O.V." that airs on Public Broadcasting Service (PBS) in the United States. In this type of program, a person introduces himself (or herself) in some manner to the audience and will present his world to you. The film is a personal account of whatever the subject may be.

For example, Todd could make a video about how his biweekly newspaper comes together and his role in that process. In doing so, we (the audience) would get to know everyone he works with and how they communicate with each other and with him, and Todd would offer commentary about how things seem to be going from his perspective as the publisher of the paper. Todd's personal documentary might have a scene or two similar to the shot after the credits roll on *Ferris Bueller's Day Off*—Todd (a la Ferris) looking straight at the camcorder saying, "Go. Why are you still here? The movie's over! The paper's done!"

This style of documentary gives the filmmaker a tremendous amount of freedom, and it allows her to express a strong opinion. It's also an easy way to be humorous. Nina produced a documentary about the myth of the Southern belle (you know, the Scarlett O'Hara stereotype and how it influences today's Southern culture) entitled *Belles and Whistles*.

In that personal documentary, the director, Anita, becomes the butt of her own jokes on numerous occasions. She was able to poke fun at her subject because she made fun of herself as well, making the film lighthearted, even as some of the issues of Southern culture can raise rancor in an audience. For some directors, it is easier to tell a story from their own perspectives than from a more general voice found in historical documentary. If your subject matter doesn't easily dictate a style, your personality might.

 *zoom-in* ——————————————————————————————

Want to do a personal documentary from behind the camera? It's not unheard of. Ross McElwee's famous documentary "Sherman's March" was taped with Ross talking from behind his camcorder—you occasionally see him reflected in mirrors and windows. If you're an aspiring actor or simply have a lot to say, pick up your camcorder—or get a friend to—and document yourself!

Educational Reel

Another type of documentary is the kind you will often find on TV's Discovery Channel or Learning Channel—the type that simply informs and educates. For example, a program about hallucinogenic frogs, tornadoes, or cute baby animals would fit into this category. These docs simply present the subject. Someone shoots footage of the subject in its environment, the voice-over presents the audience with some factoids, an interview with an expert offers more details, some graphics of whatever is relevant provides the visuals, and then you're watching at the end—getting informed and satisfied.

An example of an educational reel might be a documentary that covers severe weather, such as hurricanes—how they form, when and how they create damage, how they can be predicted. Compare that to a personal documentary about a family that survived a hurricane and how they managed to rebuild their home, a historical documentary about the effects of Hurricane Andrew in 1992, or a reality style documentary that follows hurricane scientists as they take a boat into the eye of the storm.

Educational reels are generally not persuasive filmmaking—although some of them are cautionary tales. This style of documentary filmmaking is best saved for how-to projects or for documenting the 100 varieties of roses found in your great aunt's garden. That's not to say they can't be entertaining—they can and often are. It's the level of interest in the subject matter that's more important than the presentation or production values that can get in the way of informing the audience.

Writing and Planning Your Doc

At some point, all the ideas swimming in your head have to come together— that means moving to the next phase, which is *writing*. Writing is inevitable. Projects with a historical focus are dependent on a script, and even a personal documentary needs an outline or a game plan if you're going to complete the project. If voice-over is needed, some writing will definitely be necessary. For many of us, writing has been daunting since junior high, but if you're shooting any type of video, your ideas have to work together to create a product that other people will understand, which makes writing a crucial part of the process.

Two approaches can be taken when you're writing a documentary script. You can write a script and then shoot footage that is appropriate to fulfill that script's parameters. Or you can shoot a bunch of footage on a particular subject and build the story and script from what you have documented. The problem with the first approach is that it may not be flexible enough to tell the real story, instead of telling the story as you perceived it before filming began. The problem with the second approach is that it's easy to get lost when you don't have a roadmap of some sort—in documentary filmmaking, you can lose your way if you don't know the parameters of the story on which you want to focus.

To tell a cohesive story and intellectually inform a viewer, serious thought and effort must be placed on writing. Without that focus and direction, the editing process can be unnecessarily torturous.

If you learn nothing else from this book, at least know to *be prepared before you shoot and before you edit*. With other types of video production, that's a straightforward process; with documentary, that preparation may be possible at the outset or you may need to form it in stages as your research continues to reveal the story to you. In either case, documentary planning will require some flexibility—interviews can fall through, circumstances can change, and unforeseen problems can arise. When possible, be prepared and plan your documentary—and then prepare a backup plan.

You should start with a general outline of your project on paper. This will help you determine what you need to shoot, at least initially, to begin to learn about and tell the story. This process is similar to creating a shot list, such as the list described in Chapter 3 regarding home movies. Next, you'll want to note the names of people you may want to interview wherever it is appropriate and what point you need them to make. You don't need to put words in their mouth; you just need a general idea of how these people are relevant to the subject and what points they may be able to make to contribute to the story. Finally, after the idea is outlined and your research has pointed you toward your story, any narration you envision for the project should be written, which will help you to decide specifically what needs to be shot.

focus

Being prepared can help you with the inevitable, ever-changing tasks that you'll be required to manage when you're out on the shoot. If you have a small crew, you may be responsible for the camcorder, the sound, and/or the lighting along with being the interviewer and the director— or even the producer. If you have a good idea of what you need to do going into a shoot, you'll be better prepared to make all those other decisions along the way.

This simple task of building an outline will help you keep your focus when shooting. Overshooting is typical for documentary work, since for most subjects the information can be endless. You'll save money and time—and sanity—if you define your project before you begin your cinematic journey.

Although no standard script form exists for documentary films, writing in the style of a feature script or a stage play would be more than adequate (see Figure 6.1).

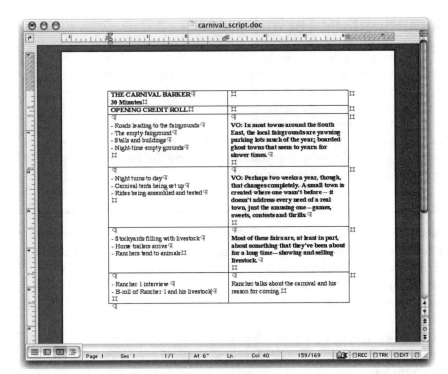

FIGURE 6.1

Example of a page from a documentary script

In addition to your outline script for the story behind your project, you'll probably want to write down any ideas you may have concerning music or sound effects. Music choices may initially be obvious to you, and you may not find it necessary to write them down, but it's never a bad idea to document your ideas. You can always change them later.

After you've done some shooting, you'll likely change your script somewhat—or, if you've been working from a broad outline until now, it might be time to write a more complete script. When you write a script after shooting, you're essentially doing a paper edit. You'll be considering your footage and deciding what story to tell and how to use your footage to tell that story.

 zoom-in _____

If you've got a good plan and a good sense of the story you need to tell in your documentary, you'll probably be better prepared to take advantage of golden opportunities, such as one-time shots that you can capture if you're on the ball. Every once in a while, you'll need to grab your camcorder and run—to a protest, a speech, or a special event. Part of being prepared is being able to gather your gear on a moment's notice and head off to a shoot. One of those slap-dash shots could prove to be a big moment in your documentary.

Documentary Techniques

Perhaps one of the most important techniques in documentary filmmaking is a *visualization* technique—always keep in mind that you are documenting a nonfiction subject; you're not fabricating a fictional story. When your efforts focus on *getting out of the way* of telling the story in documentary, many techniques will come naturally to you. A major point to remember is that you should be as unobtrusive as possible to your subject (unless you're shooting a personal doc) so that you can document the most natural state of your subject and its, or his or her, environment.

focus _____

Some filmmakers don't subscribe to the "get-out-of-the-way" school of documentary filmmaking, as they believe the filmmaker should be an instigator. (Michael Moore's *Roger and Me* and *Bowling for Columbine* vein of confrontational documentary comes to mind.) On the flip side, some believe that they should stay so far removed from their subjects that even in times of despair or danger, they will not intervene to assist.

However you decide to approach your subject—whether you're on camera and whether the camcorder is documenting the story in real-time—here are some techniques you can use for building a better documentary.

 *zoom-in* _____

Chapter 5 offers a more complete primer on interviewing, both in a technical and an interpersonal sense.

Interview Before You Shoot

When researching and planning your project, you may decide to conduct a series of interviews before you shoot any video. You may eventually end up putting those interviews or that research on tape for the final product, or you might simply use that information to continue your research. In either case, these *pre-interviews* will be important for your documentary. Not only do they give you a sense of what you'll present on camera, but they also help you learn more about the topic at hand, find new avenues of research, and discover additional people who you might want to interview.

Another interesting technique to consider is to record your pre-interviews, but not necessarily to the camcorder. With most of your new interview subjects, we encourage you to record these interviews at the *highest audio* quality that you can. This will be useful to you in a number of ways:

- You won't have to depend on your handwritten notes only, which can sometimes get in the way of holding a conversation if you're constantly asking the subject to wait on you to write everything down.

- You will be introducing your interview subject to the process of documenting his or her words, possibly making him or her a little more comfortable with the idea of a camcorder. Assure the subject that the on-camera interview will be conducted in a similar fashion, just with camcorder equipment.

- When reviewing the interviews, you will be able to determine who verbalizes ideas best, helping you decide who to get on camera so that you will not waste time and tape.

- Finally, you will have audio that you can use in the actual documentary if you record it using a high quality format. Many times, the person you're interviewing on film won't be able to duplicate what he or she told you in the initial interview with the same enthusiasm or level of detail. If you record your first interview, and you can't get the answer you want on camera, you can still plug in the audio (assuming you have the appropriate permissions to do so) when editing and lay down some B-roll for the video.

 zoom-in

Some pros recommend that you use a still camera on a pre-interview to take pictures of the location where you plan to interview the person—that can give you insight into the lighting and location issues you may face while shooting. It also provides a still image (or a number of images) that you could use with this interview audio if, for some reason, you aren't able to meet with that person in the future.

A little dancing is needed to make people comfortable with recordings. We suggest that you *not* give people too much time to think about the interview before you start—if you ask your subject if you can record the interview too far ahead of time, he or she might get too nervous and blow the interview. Here are some steps to help you get the best interviews:

1. Set up the interview and show up with recording equipment.

2. Ask the subject's permission to record when you're in front of him, with the suggestion being that it's routine. He will be less likely to say no if you ask in his presence and if you don't make a big deal about it.

3. Pull out your notepad at the same time you're recording and take notes throughout. This emphasizes that the recording is a backup to your note taking and doesn't make the subject feel as if he's on the hot seat at that moment.

It's important that you not lie about the recording or suggest that it won't be used in the documentary—you should be candid with your interviewees, saying that although this is a pre-interview, you want to get the best sound possible, in case you can't get to him or her at a later date or if for some reason the interview ends up being useful in the final production. In addition, particularly in your pre-interviews, be willing to back off of your request to record if your subject seems too anxious about it. More than likely this isn't a "hostile witness," so you'll be able to return to the subject for permission for the audio, or you'll be able to secure the permission for the audio when the person signs a permission form for video that you take at a later date.

focus

If you are "pulling a '60 Minutes'" and going after a hostile interviewee, get your permissions up front and get it on video tape the first time. Once your interviewee knows you'll be asking hard questions, the game may be up, so don't reveal that in a pre-interview. (You likely wouldn't even want to try a pre-interview with a hostile interviewee.)

Tricks for Nervous Interviewees

Here's something that happens all too often—a natural born talker gets in front of your camcorder, smiles throughout the process of turning on the lights and attaching the microphones, and then clams up on you when the camcorder rolls. Camcorders and cameras make all sorts of confident (and not so confident) people nervous.

One trick is to get people out of the "hot seat" and help them relax; consider moving them around a bit or giving them something to do while you're conducting the interview. It can be more of a challenge to your camcorder and sound operators, but it's a great way to break the ice for a difficult interview.

focus

A lavalier microphone—particularly a wireless variety—is ideal for helping people relax with a recording. It's less obtrusive than a boom mic or another type of handheld mic.

You might have the subject show you relevant pictures in a book or ask her about items in her office—anything to get her mind off the fact that she is talking and a camcorder is recording it.

When Nina interviews her father, she tries to shoot when he is preoccupied with his everyday tasks, such as gardening and cooking. He normally loves to tell stories, but when the focus is on him, particularly with a camcorder, he doesn't tell the stories in a natural way, so she distracts him (see Figure 6.2).

FIGURE 6.2

Nina, when interviewing her father, encourages him to move around.

This technique doesn't require any explanation—your subject will likely jump up and be happy to show you her pins for meritorious service or her trophies from sports victories, while at the same time telling you the stories associated with them. When you get back into comfortable chairs, you may find that your subject is able to open up a bit more on camera as a result.

This technique is also a clever way of giving your audience more information about your subject without having to tell them outright, borrowing from the *cinéma vérité* style. Nina's father loves to work in the garden, but it's not something she would have included in a voice-over, because it's not essential to the story she is trying to tell. However, the audience knowing that he loves to garden allows them to know him a little better and makes him a more interesting character in the film by showing him in his environment.

Finally, getting your subject out of the chair can get you some additional information. In a project Todd is developing on junkyards, he finds that the proprietors of those establishments are much more interested—and *interesting*—in being followed around showing him things than they are just talking in their offices. More can be revealed about the subject—what makes him laugh or what draws his eyes—than in a typical sit-down interview.

B-Roll, B-Roll, B-Roll

If you don't have tons and tons of B-roll, you will hate yourself in the editing process and so will your audience. No one wants to look at an hour of the same shot of the same person talking about the same subject. This goes for any type of video you shoot, but documentary can be a place where you end up craving good B-roll because a lot of your story may be told through interviews and voice-over.

If, during the interview, the person refers to something or someone else in the room, make sure that you film that item or person before you leave. (If you can get a shot of the object while continuing to get perfect sound, you might consider panning or tilting the camcorder—otherwise, don't lose the moment and the continuity of the shot on your subject.) In fact, noting potential B-roll may be one of the key reasons for having a notepad in front of you—or, if your cameraperson or an additional producer or production assistant has a free hand, encourage them to take notes on potential B-roll opportunities as well. If you end up using that part of the interview in your edit, you will be glad you had the B-roll so that your audience will understand to what the person on camera is referring.

Another trick to good B-roll is to be a good listener. If the subject refers to something that is not in the room, make a note to shoot it at a later time if it's important to the story. Cutting to something else more active or visually interesting during a "talking head" interview will make your video more enjoyable to watch and will give life to your subject matter. No one wants to hear a dozen people talk about how pretty rainbows are. They want to see the pretty rainbow; so show them the rainbow.

On the CD-ROM   See the Chapter 5 movies on the included CD-ROM for examples of video that includes B-roll intercuts.

Many documentaries are dependent on B-roll. For example, you can't interview animals, so you have to shoot all the B-roll you can if animals are important to the project. You might shoot that animal doing what it normally does, including what is unique to it, the foods it eats, the areas it builds its homes in, the land or water it roams, the animals that prey on it, and so on. Then you'll place that footage over a narrator talking about those (or similar) animals.

In terms of production budgets and planning, it's important that you get all of the B-roll you need at a given location before moving on. That means scheduling time for B-roll and keeping in mind your needs for shooting that B-roll—for example, wrap your interview while you still have light if you need to get B-roll outdoors at that location. If resources permit, use two camcorders during walking shots to get both B-roll and the main interview. Do what you can to make sure you don't have to go back to a location to get a shot that will be important months later when you're editing the project together.

Hold Your Shot and Get Handles

We've probably said this in every chapter on shooting, and we will continue to do so. It's better to have more footage than you need, rather than less—as long as it's not so much footage that you aren't willing to watch it and catalog it all.

If you're working the camcorder yourself or giving instructions to an inexperienced cameraperson, remember to keep shooting until your interview subjects finish their thoughts, and add some editing and breathing room at the end of the interview. Sometimes the subject will add to what he has already said and will give you better information because he will fall into a natural rhythm. (You should also warn him to try to wait a second before answering your questions, particularly if you are on mic or if you're using a mic that can pick up your questions as well as their answers.)

 *zoom-in*

This dovetails with an important interview technique, which is to allow a little silence at the end of your interviewee's response before you jump in with your next question. That gives you some dead air for editing, but it also gives the subject a chance to add anything else he might want to tack on—some of those periods get filled with interesting stuff.

Follow an action from start to finish. If you're shooting a bird flying down into the water, don't stop when it hits the waves. It'll have to come up sometime, so be there when it does. It might bring up a massively sized fish or garbage or something completely unexpected. Follow it until it is no longer necessary. A patient videographer captures better reality.

Protect Your Footage

Once you have shot the priceless footage, don't risk losing it. You may not have another opportunity to capture it again. Immediately after removing a tape from your camcorder, slide the safety tab over (usually a red or green tab, as shown in Figure 6.3) so that it's no longer recordable. If anyone accidentally tries to record on that tape in the future, an error message will pop up, and the cameraperson will not be allowed to record on that tape.

The next thing you should do is label that tape. Of course, we know you won't have to do that, because you labeled it before you put it in the camcorder—right? If not, give it a good name—we even recommend including the location, date, and time of day of the shoot. Every little bit of information can help you figure out where the important footage is when you're logging tapes and accessing them in the editing phase.

Store your tapes in a dry place away from sunlight at room temperature or slightly cooler. You should treat your tapes with the same respect you give your equipment.

FIGURE 6.3

The safety tab can be found here on most MiniDV tapes. (Shown in unlocked position.)

Getting the Footage You Need

You should be pretty well versed in the art of interviewing and gathering B-roll by now, but how do you insure that your footage is usable and pleasant to look at? Most audiences find it annoying—or at least off-putting—to watch footage that is wobbly and shaky, where heads are slightly cut off, people are framed too much in the center of the shot or too far to the side, things in the background are distracting. You can eliminate many of these issues when framing up your shot. To better understand the basic shots (wide shot, close-up, medium shot) refer to Chapters 3 and 9 for the basics and Chapter 10 for a deeper look.

The Rule of Thirds

The angle of the shot—wide, medium, or close—is not everything. The way you frame the shot can contribute to making your shot more powerful. Interviews that are shot dead center look unprofessional and are dull to the viewer. Try to avoid splitting your frame into halves (for example, placing your subject in the middle) because the effect is weak and static.

Instead, follow the concept called the "Rule of Thirds," in which the frame contents are ordered in thirds, vertically and horizontally. You should strive to frame your images with this concept in mind. For example, when shooting an interview, it is more pleasing to the eye to have the person framed to the left or right instead of smack in the middle of the frame (see Figure 6.4).

Likewise, your subject should look *across* the center of the frame to involve the audience—if the person is on the left side of the frame, she should be looking toward the right side and vice versa. If the person is looking off camera, to the audience, it seems like the person isn't participating or is distracted. By contrast, if you put the person in the middle of the frame, it

FIGURE 6.4

On the left is an example of a good shot using the rule of thirds; on the right, you can see how distracting it is when the subject appears to be looking off camera.

makes him look more like a newscaster who is speaking directly to the audience instead of to an interviewer.

You can see this difference by watching one of the talk shows on the 24-hour news channels versus watching a produced documentary or news magazine segment. On the talk shows, people are framed in the middle of the shot, and they look more like they're talking directly to you in the audience. On the produced piece, you're more likely to see the subject in the left or right third of the screen, looking across the center of the frame so as to involve the audience in the interview.

Be Aware of the Background

Always be aware of what is happening *behind* your subject. If people or objects are moving intermittently in the background, it can distract the viewer from the featured subject. Steady movement is less distracting, such as waves or a conveyor belt, for example, and are acceptable types of background movement. Try to avoid shooting in a restaurant or mall setting where people might be moving in and out of frame. The viewer will naturally become curious about the background when an occasional shift occurs, so try to avoid that scenario. Also, people in the background tend to look straight into the camcorder lens or feel compelled to scream "Hi, Mom!" while waving madly.

Get Serious About Camcorder Stabilizers

If you know you will be shooting from a fixed position, you should always try to stabilize the camcorder with a tripod or by another means, even if you have to improvise. When shopping for a tripod, you should consider three features: stability, smoothness of pan and tilt movements, and the ability to transport it easily, which we will call *tote-ability* (we had to make up a word somewhere in this book).

Tripods and steadying equipment come in varying shapes and sizes, as do camcorders and other equipment. If you are serious about your camerawork, you will definitely need to spend more than a couple hundred dollars for a worthwhile tripod. Some dependable brands to consider are Canon, Bogen, and Vinten. They offer tripods in a wide price range for the amateur and professional.

Table 6.1 offers additional descriptions of tripod equipment.

Get the Sound You Need

Every room in your house sounds different. The sounds in your backyard are different from the sounds in your front yard. The ocean and a river have different sounds. It is important for you to be aware of your aural space when you are shooting, because you will need to record it. Be prepared with an external microphone such as a lavalier mic or a microphone on a boom when shooting on location. (See Chapter 10 for in-depth discussion on sound equipment.)

Covering your sound is much like gathering B-roll. Sound can enhance your story greatly by creating a bigger sensory experience for the audience. After you finish an interview, make a point of recording a minute or two of *room tone*, the sound of the room. Have everyone stay where they are (because people in a room affect the tone of the room) and be silent for at least one full minute while you roll sound. You may never use this recording, but if you need it, you'll thank yourself. Instances where this might be usable is under B-roll that complements the interview (a ticking clock or the hum of the interviewee's computer); spots during which a car might honk in the background, which can be covered up with the room tone; or perhaps the sounds in that room are unique and essential to have.

 *zoom-in* ————————————————————————————

Want to hear how sound can set the stage? Listen to produced pieces on NPR in the U.S., such as lengthy interviews or sound features on the show "All Things Considered." You'll hear ambient sound often used very well to set the scene for an interview or news piece.

If you are shooting in a location with a number of unique background sounds, be sure to record them individually, if possible. When you're outside, record the birds chirping (these birds may be found only in that area and may have a unique call that will add to the personality of your location, for example), the ocean waves, the traffic (particularly if you heard traffic in the background of an interview), airplanes flying overhead, or whatever sounds are apparent.

TABLE 6.1

A Look at Tripod Options

TRIPOD	DESCRIPTION	EXAMPLE
	The standard tripod (legs or sticks is the terminology used by professionals).	Bogen 3405B (www.bogenphoto.com)
	The monopod—a single extendible leg used to support a handheld camcorder. This is a handy tool for shooting sports if you must run up and down a sideline.	Bogen 3425 (www.bogenphoto.com)

TABLE 6.1

A Look at Tripod Options (continued)

Tripod	Description	Example
	Baby tripod or high hat (not shown) for shooting low to the ground.	Cullmann Picollo (www.cullmann-foto.de)
	Saddlebag or beanbag—the best tool when improvising a shot.	Nalpack BeanieBag (www.nalpak.com/ detailsthebag.html)
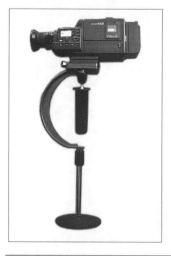	A counter-weighted steadying device; some attach to your forearm or shoulder and others are handheld.	Hollywood Lite "Ultralite" model (www.hollywoodlite.com)

If a constant interruptive noise occurs—take its effect on the interview into consideration—either get rid of it, move somewhere else, or shoot video of whatever makes the sound and get clear sound in case it becomes relevant to the story.

focus ——————————————————————————

Location scouting can help here. We've been in many situations in which a room that otherwise seemed perfect had overhead lights that buzzed or computer printers that made a ton of racket. If distracting sounds are going to show up on tape, you're better off choosing a better location as soon as possible. Even if you're on location and discover a sound problem, moving or rescheduling the interview is probably easier than having to reshoot it later because of bad sound.

Sound builds a story as much as the picture, yet we often forget that. Start paying attention to what goes on in your everyday spaces, so that you will be more aware when you are shooting.

Log and Work with Tapes

If you're going to convey your story effectively, you'll need to know your footage well. To know your footage, you will have to *log* every tape. This is the most grueling task in the entire documentary process, because it requires that you sit down and relive *every* moment you shot, paying close attention and taking copious notes as you go along. You should log your footage immediately after shooting, since it will be fresh on your mind.

As discussed in Chapter 4 (and in more detail in Chapter 9), you can log your footage using your computer before you import any footage into your editing software. Attach your camcorder to your computer via FireWire/ IEEE 1394 cable so that the two devices can talk to each other. As you play a tape in your editing software, you will be able to mark in and out points, indicating the beginning and end of a shot. That information will be saved along with whatever written description you give each shot.

You should describe each scene or shot with enough detail so that you know, without playing the tape, who is speaking, what is the topic discussed, what action is taking place, or for what scene the B-roll will be used. Each tape should have its own log. If you are a good logger, the editing process will be significantly simplified.

Learn to organize within your software. After every tape is logged, you can create folders (sometimes called *bins* in the software) for each person interviewed, each idea or performance, or for a particular time period (whatever the case may be) for the video, placing each tape in its respective folder. This will help you tremendously when you are editing.

Some software allows you to import an edit decision list as a text file or using special EDL (Edit Decision List) software to log the footage that you want to import. Using this technology, you can watch the video footage on a TV monitor and log it manually, and then type it in. Then, using the software's EDL import command, you import the EDL file. That tells the software which clips you want to import—specifically, it marks the beginning and ending timecode of each clip. With that information, the software can start rolling the tape in your camcorder at the beginning of the tape and then, noting the timecode, import each clip that you've decided you want to use.

After your logs are complete, you will easily be able to print them for easy reference. Strive to do an edit on paper so that once you are at the computer, it will be easy to drop shots into your timeline based on the work you have already done, saving you from having to open and close folders repeatedly to find what you need.

Historical and Stock Footage

If you are producing a historical documentary, you will inevitably need archival images and footage. How to obtain that footage may be a mystery to those not working in the film and video industry. Here are some resources that you might find useful in locating what you need for your project:

- **National, state, or local archives and history departments**
  These agencies generally have original footage and photos for use—government films are sometimes placed in the public domain and are therefore accessible. You will likely have to pay a fee only for the agency to duplicate it for you. If the footage you need is not in the public domain, you can expect to see a list of fees, depending on where you will be exhibiting your work. If your project will be theatrically distributed or broadcast on television, expect to spend thousands of dollars.

It's important not to assume that something is in the "public domain" or is "Fair Use" without consulting an attorney—particularly if you anticipate distributing your work to the public in any form. Just because footage is old doesn't necessarily mean it is public domain, as copyrights can be renewed and elements of a production can be copyrighted (such as music or images) even after another portion's copyright has expired. Likewise, Fair Use does not simply mean you can use clips of copyrighted work if they're "really short." Fair Use is a complicated issue—enough so that we'd recommend discussing it with an attorney.

- **Libraries and universities**   These institutions are often given original historical properties, much like archives and history departments. Once you have chosen what you need, copies can be made in whatever format you need and a fee will be assessed. Note that librarians and university curators can provide lots of information regarding the material, its relevance, and even its authenticity. Talk to professionals and see if they can help you.

- **Organizations or societies**   You may be able to locate non-profit organizations that have material for use. For example, the Daughters of the Confederacy may have Civil War materials available for use. If nothing else, they may be able to lead you in the right direction. As long as you are portraying the subject in a positive light, you should be able to request free use of footage they possess. It's likely they will agree to help if you offer to give them a copy of the finished product that they can use.

- **Families**   Families of famous folks often hold on to historical footage. Contact them directly. They may be open to donating the footage if you ask nicely.

- **Stock footage houses**   If all else fails, you can easily find online companies that can provide footage on whatever format you need for a fee. They will list their available footage, and you will be charged by the minute, generally, with exhibition considered in the price as well.

Using Still Photographs

Once upon a time, using photographs in a video was a time-consuming process. You had to find perfectly flat surfaces on which to lay or mount your pictures, being extremely careful not to damage them. Then you had to light the photograph with perfectly even coverage. And for every picture shot, you had to reposition the camcorder and framing. Photographers would sometimes spend hours and days shooting pictures for their videos. Certainly, you can still do it the old-fashioned way (which usually involves using special camera equipment that can pan a camcorder slowly past an image), but technology has made this process much easier—scanners and video editing software have revolutionized the process.

Almost any scanner will do, as digital video requires only 72 dots per inch (dpi) of resolution, and your image need only be 640 × 480 or, in some cases, 720 × 480 or a multiple thereof. Because of the oddity of DV resolution, it's important that you consult your nonlinear editing (NLE) software to see what images work best. Note, however, that images you intended to zoom on, particularly if the effect is a digital one, may need to be of higher resolution—300 dpi or better. If you want to use a picture that is too big to fit on your scanner, copy shops and some photo labs are usually able to scan images and burn them to a disk or CD for a nominal fee.

focus _____

Many video editing packages allow you to pan across a digital image just as if the camcorder were passing over a real-life photograph. In fact, such a feature was added to iMovie 3 recently and is called the "Ken Burns Effect," paying homage to the man who has familiarized the technique to many documentary watchers. In such cases, however, you may need to use fairly high-resolution images to keep the image quality impressive once it's been zoomed in on.

Editing Your Documentary

Editing your documentary is much like any other editing process. You'll have to know your story before you begin and then plug in the elements as you move along the timeline. The style in which you shot your project may play a huge role in the way you edit it. Do some homework by watching how the professionals do it. Go to your local video store and rent films made in a style that interests you or flip through the channels on your television—seems like some form of documentary is always on TV. Maybe you will be inspired if you don't already have something in mind.

The Sound Edit

As with most of your video projects, you'll probably begin your documentary with a rough cut, where you place each clip of video that's fundamental to your story in its basic sequence from the beginning of the project to the end. The difference with a documentary (as opposed to an event video or a feature) is that a lot of this footage will probably be rather long interviews. The rough cut may not be much to look at, but it will give you a good idea of where your documentary is headed.

The next step beyond the rough cut is to focus on your sound. This is called the *sound edit* stage, when you ensure the intercut images that you use make sense in reference to the interviews and narration audio that you have captured. If your documentary has defining narration or music, you should lay that down first in the rough cut. You will be able to simply drop in the shots you need according to where you are with the sound.

If you are working with interviews, the same process can be used. Your rough cut will lay out your key interviews. Then you fill in with B-roll, photos, or other footage when necessary. That way, you're able to start with the foundation of your story and then add visual interest as necessary to keep the viewer interested and engaged. (See Chapters 5 and 9 for editing tips that show you how to add intercuts and overlay video in your project.)

After you have finalized the timeline, you can begin embellishing the video with sound effects, music, graphics, and title cards for interviews. Once you've got your foundation interviews layered with your B-roll and photos, you can move on to adding effects such as fades and dissolves. Again, we recommend keeping these simple. You may also find you want to do your titling at this stage, so that you can use fades and wipes to remove some of your titles, if that look is desired.

focus —————————————————————————————

Keep your title graphics, using only the essential information and an easily legible font. With most documentaries, the more austere your special effects appear, the more seriously the audience is able to take your work. (Perhaps that's an oversimplification, but it's not a bad place to start.) See the Chapter 6 movies on the CD-ROM for more discussion of titling for documentaries.

The Sound Mix

The final step is the sound mix. This is different from the sound edit. Your goal in this part of the process is to make sure that everything can be heard well. Here are a few rules to that end:

- Music should not overpower an interview. Make sure that the speaker can be heard clearly above all other sounds.

- Take care to equalize sound levels, particularly as you move from one interview to the next. The sound from one person's interview cut right after another person should be manipulated so that one is not louder than the other, or it'll be jarring to the viewer. (See Chapter 10 for a little more on setting levels.)

- Any sound effects you add should be at a volume level appropriate for the picture. For example, if you want to add birds chirping to a woman being interviewed in a garden, make sure that the bird sounds are mixed well into the aural background and not louder than the person speaking. You are creating a soundscape and must find the harmonious balance between all of the elements.

focus —————————————————————————————

Adding sounds and effects that weren't in the original shoot can have ethical implications if you're trying to suggest that what the audience is seeing is a true story. You're better off mixing in some ambient audio from a location that you got when taking B-roll, so that you're at least mixing down audio that took place at the video site, even if it didn't take place at the exact moment that the interview questions did (or during whatever it is that the viewer is seeing).

And...Cut!

You should now be well prepared to take on any subject and educate the world around you. Good luck. Remember from both the last chapter and this one that the two keys are getting good sound and getting good interview answers. Remember—check your microphones and don't ask "yes" or "no" questions!

Business and Organization Video

YOU can probably come up with plenty of great reasons to shoot video for your small business, growing company, or organization. Video can be handy for sales, training, finding investments, or community outreach. Video can also be used for more mundane tasks, such as shooting video in the factory to evaluate quality control, taking video inventories of your products, or for shooting new locations for the widget plant (or a new office) and bringing it back to the board of directors. And, of course, there's the obligatory video for company and organizational parties, whether it's a day in the life of the president of the company or behind-the-scenes video showing the staff during the last big fundraising campaign for your non-profit.

The inexpensive nature of digital video and the ease with which it can be transferred to a computer should have the same positive effect on business and organizational video production that it has on home video and documentary. Indeed, the technological advantages are somewhat astonishing when you look at what is now possible with video; in the 1960s through the 1980s, it wasn't at all uncommon to find million-dollar television production studios in Fortune 500 companies—and many still have them— or to rely on outside production houses for all aspects of your video presentations. With inexpensive digital video camcorders and the relative simplicity of computer-based editing, those massive investments aren't necessary for producing in-house videos; creating videos for your small business or organization is a much more approachable process today, and video is a tool you can use regularly and under more circumstances than you might have just five or ten years ago.

In fact, creating video for your business or organization is so much cheaper these days that you should also consider how that video might be most efficiently delivered and used in other ways—such as video over the Internet or via CD or DVD. From producing training videos to adding video walkthroughs of your rental properties to distributing sales pitches or video product catalogs electronically, many interesting options and applications exist for producing video in a business setting. For other types of organizations, you can use video to document your banquets, for outreach and development purposes, or to train and motivate your volunteers.

What You Need

Organizational video requires a lot of the same equipment necessary for documentary videography (see Chapter 6)—although you're likely to do more stationary shots in organizational projects. It's common in an organizational setting to use a permanent studio (or a room that you can use as a studio set) with some fairly plain backgrounds and standard interview setups. It's also not uncommon to shoot those same types of interviews in and around the offices or buildings that house the organization or to put your talent in the appropriate setting—a warehouse, learning center, an atrium, at the site of a new project—so you may need to be prepared for that as well.

At the high end, a corporate video outfit might have most of the resources used by a local news affiliate in a mid-level market—a studio for interviews, editing suites, and mobile units that can accommodate a variety of setups. For small-business or startup projects, you can get away with a lot less. You may need to use only one camcorder for such a project, and you should be able to use a relatively simple stabilization platform for the camera—because you won't likely need many shots that require motion, a good tripod is all that's necessary. (Of course, a mobile stabilizing tool—such as a monopod or a steadying device—would be handy for some shots "in the wild" or for adding a little variety with moving shots. See Chapter 6 for a discussion of stabilization devices.)

You'll need to pay attention to lighting, sets, and sound gathering, according to the advice discussed in Chapter 6 in particular. In fact, you can make corporate or organizational video look great if you can keep a relatively simple set available for interviews, perhaps with a discreet logo or some other basic production design to make the set interesting, modern, and appropriate.

Some items to consider when you're tossing around ideas for sets for your organization or corporate video include the following.

Ideally, you should set aside a room or studio where you can build a set and control the lighting, as well as a place where you can safely leave cameras and tripods standing (see Figure 7.1). If you have control over the set, stick to neutral colors and opt for something that can be painted or changed fairly easily—stay away from "mahogany and brass" looks. If, however, that look is important to your company's image, you likely have plenty of offices already decorated in that fashion.

When planning a studio, consider how you can make the area flexible enough to accommodate a variety of furniture, sets, or situations. For instance, you might want a stand-up set for training videos—depending on what it is that you're teaching—and an intimate sit-down set for shooting product introduction or fundraising videos that include interviews with the CEO or production manager. Consider the space and how you can accommodate a variety of circumstances, as well as how you can store the furniture for the sets that aren't in use. And, of course, you'll need enough room for your cameras and light stands (unless you're fortunate enough to have the budget for ceiling-mounted lighting systems).

FIGURE 7.1

The ideal studio for small businesses and organizations offers flexibility.

 *zoom-in* ─────────────────────────

If you can secure a room for your studio that has a high ceiling, that feature could come in handy. Shooting down from a ladder or using a camera crane could be useful particularly for product demo or training shots where the camera needs to be able to see what your presenter is doing on a table or similar surface. It can also be handy to have lights mounted high on the ceiling.

One place to look for ideas is to turn on the TV and watch CNBC or other financial networks, where you'll find that a lot of investment houses have their own small sets for shooting their financial analysts. When the anchors on CNBC cut away to a financial analyst during the day, sometimes you'll see interesting little setups that would be good to emulate for use in business or organization video.

You can create a number of inexpensive backdrops in your studio that can be used for a variety of purposes—if you've ever had your portrait made in a professional studio (particularly the "glamour shots" type you find in many large malls), you've seen the rolled seamless-paper backdrops that can be used to change a scene. (Try your local photography store to find such backdrops.) You can also use creative lighting to change the background—for instance, shine a blue light up from the ground onto a white wall to give it some interest and separate the background from the people in the shot.

focus ─────────────────────────

What does "separate the background" mean? It's a common phrase with lighting pros that means trying to suggest the distance between a person and the wall behind them (or similar background). Using lighting and shading, it's possible to create a three-dimensional shot.

Another interesting possibility is to create a wall in your studio that's painted for *chromakey* use. Chromakey is the technique used to replace a single color in your video's background with another image—think of the way TV weather is done. (Chromakey is sometimes called "blue screen" effects, although most chromakey for video uses a bright green background.) While chromakey can sometimes be more of a distraction than an effective background, it can still be handy for certain types of shots—particularly for making product demonstrations or other PowerPoint-style presentations look visually interesting. You can also use chromakey with third-party digital backgrounds (see Figure 7.2) to add some pizzazz to your videos. (Chromakey effects are discussed in more detail in Chapter 11.)

Finally, you need to make sure the acoustics of the studio are appropriate. With your set in place, do some recording and see how it

FIGURE 7.2

Here's an example of a digital chromakey effect in use.

sounds. Is there too much of an echo? Can you hear sounds from other rooms? You might need to install some soundproofing or sound deadening foam or other solutions.

When you're not shooting on a set, you'll probably want to make sure you have a portable lighting kit and audio equipment similar to what you might use in a documentary setting. In fact, this may be all you need if you do most of your shooting in offices and buildings or in the field, following your talent on their appointed rounds or doing what you must to communicate the fundamental themes of the video presentation.

Ideas for the Small Studio

Interested in putting together your own budget-conscious studio or a studio for your organization? Here are a few hints to take you down the right path:

- The ideal studio is a fairly large room with high ceilings and no windows (or, at least, windows you can completely shut to light). Industrial carpet can be okay to use, because it can cut down on audible echoes.

- Paint the walls a neutral, soft color—no red, black, white, or overly bright primary colors.

- If the ceilings are high, mounting a cheap, medium-sized Chinese lantern or china ball above the set will create a nice, even soft light on your subjects so that your other lights will not necessarily have to be large light sources.

- Need two sets in your studio? You might want to consider draping textured, neutral-colored cloth from ceiling to floor to create a second set or a different look. (If you can roll up the cloth and store it by attaching it to the ceiling, so much the better.) Be creative with where you hang the cloth—it doesn't need to be one huge piece hung flat against the walls—you could hang several small pieces away from the walls, staggered or at an angle to create depth.

- Quality silk plants are a nice addition to give the set some color and items that can be in or out of focus to create a sense of depth. Stay away from real plants if you're not a green thumb, as someone has to water those plants when you're not shooting.

- Avoid mounting mirrors, framed pictures with glass, or anything else on the walls of your set that may bounce light and/or create reflections of the camcorders and crew.

- Bookshelves with movable shelves are a great choice that you can change to make the room look different. Use books for some interviews, and then use plates or pottery or anything—car parts—for other interviews if you need to make the set look different.

- Lamps (if they're seen by the camera they're called **practicals** to differentiate them from studio lighting) with bulbs from a camera store that are daylight-balanced or tungsten are useful on the set to provide more light as well as add interest to the set design.

- When selecting your furniture, choose chairs, not sofas—you don't want everyone sitting on the same side most of the time. If you like the look of a sofa, try a loveseat, which takes up less space.

- Barstool-style chairs (with backs) are ideal for on-camera talent if they're expected to stand and sit often (to greet a guest or demonstrate something).

- For training videos, you'll probably want a special table that's designed for people to use while standing—some office furniture is specifically designed to be useful at different heights, so you might opt for such a solution to get a surface that can be used as both a desk and a training table.

Planning and Writing the Video

As with any video project, business and organizational video requires some forethought and preparation. Unlike some other types of video, though, before you begin writing a script or blocking out scenes on a storyboard, you need to consider what is the purpose of your video and how you can best accomplish that purpose.

On a fundamental level, most of the organizational video we focused on in this chapter is designed to *teach* or *convince*. Arguably, teaching is a form of convincing, at least in the approach you take to setting up your shots—a good teacher convinces her students of the worth of the material and then convinces them to remember and/or implement the teachings. (Bad teachers skip some of these steps, which is why you sleep through their classes.) But however you slice it, most organizational video is about trying to convince someone of something.

Consider these examples:

- A sales video that is sent to prospective clients to show them the quality controls and the cleanliness of the plant where your circuit boards are manufactured

- A documentary about one particular family that was helped last year by your charitable organization

- A showroom video that is used to call out the important safety features of your company's products

- A video presentation for a press event to introduce a new line of products

- A tradeshow video loop that explains how to use your product in a particular field of scientific study

In all these examples, the core reason for making the video is to convince people of something and, in most cases, the end goal is to get some money to change hands. That said, each of these examples also *didn't* have something in common—the approach that you're likely to take to the writing and directing of the video. For each project, you might take a different tactic, from a documentary feel to a film that's more like a commercial to something that's much like event videography. Which tactic you choose will likely affect the outcome of the whole project, so it's important to choose wisely.

Choose Your Approach

How do you decide on the approach your video will take to do its convincing? Any number of factors could play into your decision, not the least of which is what your company or organization believes is appropriate and what your talent (whether hired actors or the president of your organization) is comfortable doing.

Consider the following pointers while you're trying to make that decision:

- *Maintain as much control as you can.* Often the people you're working with are important people who may outrank you in your organization, but they still need to listen to your direction on the set. You need to feel comfortable giving them direction while, at the same time, respecting their schedules and egos.

- *Consider documentary-style interviews.* It's inevitable that someone you're working with will feel strongly that he is a great TV talent, but he actually doesn't deliver lines well or doesn't communicate effectively when looking directly into the lens of a camcorder. To avoid such a situation, and to avoid bruising his ego, it's a good idea to set up your shots in a documentary style, with you off-camera asking leading questions. This also gives you considerable flexibility to leave your voice in for a more conversational tone or to use quicker cuts to pull sound bites out of the talent's answers. (See Chapter 5 for more advice on interviewing and interview setups.)

- *Use a strong talent if you have it.* If your director, CEO, or development officer happens to be very good when talking directly to the camera, consider using this to greatest effect, particularly to "ask for the sale" at the end of a video. Talking directly into the camera can be more authoritative and, if the talent is skilled, it can be effective and intimate. (Larry Jones of Feed the Children comes to mind—the organization's paid program is shown in many U.S. cities on Sunday mornings.) If the talent doesn't make those appeals well (think of, for instance, any owner or manager or a local car dealer or furniture store you've been forced to watch during your favorite "X-Files" reruns on the local Fox affiliate), you're better off getting them to state those goals and needs in a three-quarter shot, documentary style.

- *Take lessons from news producers.* As with most informational video projects, one of the biggest mistakes you can make is assuming that it's going to be interesting to watch someone talk. For corporate video or even for training video, you're going to need a lot of footage for cutaways, close-ups, and other matters that are discussed during the program. Be prepared to think in terms of that material, even if the core of your production is a speech or interview. For ideas, watch some of the heavily produced segments on television magazine programs produced by the major networks, such as "60 Minutes" and "Nightline." Also, check PBS ("Frontline," for example) and the BBC news programs for what tend to be slightly more austere, but well produced segments.

Consider the Location(s)

Part and parcel of planning and storyboarding your shots is to consider your locations. As detailed earlier, a studio is always an ideal controlled environment for shooting; if you're lucky enough to have an on-site studio, that's where you'll likely do your shooting. If not, you might try to requisition a room where you can set up a backdrop and lights and safely place and leave a camera on a tripod for the duration of the shoot.

Here are a few other items that you should consider *before* the production begins, particularly for when you need to shoot outside of a studio:

If you can't get a room for the shoot, the next best solution is probably a conference room or a similar large room with plenty of space to accommodate different camera angles and other necessities. It also needs to be an unoccupied conference room where you can shoot for a while.

One interesting phenomenon is that some people—workers, managers, or executives—can be shy on camera and may not want to be filmed in a public place, even if they are otherwise strong personalities. (Sometimes you won't know how a person will act until a camera is on him or her.) They may also not ask enough questions or not listen to your direction if their co-workers or underlings are watching, so a private location is often ideal, particularly for one-on-one interviews. Check your location for privacy—a CEO may know that her assistants can hear her every word uttered in her office, so you might suggest a conference room or other quiet place.

Putting an executive behind his or her desk might seem obvious, but it can be limiting during a shoot. Desks often look more cluttered on camera than they do in person, and the background of books or personal effects can be a distraction. It may also make the shot too formal and may separate the interviewer and subject if you're working in a documentary style. Unless you specifically need a "regal" look, opt instead for straight-back chairs and plain backgrounds.

Watch your windows and lights. If you have relatively little control over the location, you should still make sure you white balance your camera and be on the lookout for dramatically different light sources—the mixture of fluorescent lights and sunlight streaming into a window can be the kiss of death for an interview. (This causes a mix of *color temperatures* that can have unintended consequences when you record the scene—you can have trouble with odd blooms or streaks of color.) If you don't have your own lighting equipment with you, look for even, bright light and position your talent or subject to avoid deep shadows.

focus ───

Check your camcorder's user manual for instructions on white balancing. It's generally done by aiming the camcorder at a white wall or card, zooming in so that the lens sees nothing but white, and then pressing the white balance button. This gives the camcorder a sense of what color should be considered white in the current lighting conditions.

You'll need enough electrical outlets and a strong enough circuit for your shoot; with lights and cameras you can overload a typical 20-amp circuit, so see if you can use separate circuits for some of your lights. You'll also need to know something about the air conditioning and ventilation, as your lights may heat up a small room fairly quickly. Recommend that the room be cooled before the shoot starts and between takes or when adjustments need to be made.

Test the sound in the room, and see whether an echo that needs to be deadened (which you can do with rugs, sound insulating foam, and sometimes cubical walls or other portable walls). You should also check to make sure there isn't too much ambient noise—whining lights, air conditioners, and computer equipment—and make sure all phones in the room (or immediately outside the room) are turned off. Also check to see whether loud sounds can travel into the room from outside and, at the least, put up warning signs that ask people to be quiet near where you're filming.

If you need to leave your equipment overnight, make sure any special security requests are made in advance.

 zoom-in —————————————————————————

Something else to add to your arsenal of traveling video equipment are signs that say something like "Quiet Please, Video Production in Progress." You should also bring tape or a peg to hang them at eye level.

focus —————————————————————————

The more of these items you're able to broach with the people you're working with at the outset, the more professional they will perceive you to be and the more seriously they'll take your requests. If you start asking to resolve these issues after the shooting has already started, you'll end up with people who are much less helpful and much more annoyed by your presence and needs.

Communicate the Facts

Whether your organizational video is a presentation meant to convince or a training video designed to teach, you're going to need to do a lot of writing and planning. The core of that writing is going to be determining the facts of what needs to be presented and them moving on from there into outlining and storyboarding. With an outline—or even a rough script—you can begin to get a sense of the information you're going to communicate. Consider, for instance, a category of video that many organizations need—a fundraising video. You need to ask for money, but you need to tell your potential donor a little about the organization and its needs. How are you going to do that? Consider a sample outline:

```
Outline: The Student Video Project Development Video
I. Introduction
       A. What is the Student Video Project?
       B. What are the project's goals?
       C. Who is involved in the project?
II. This Year
       A. Overview of the projects this year
       B. In-depth with the fall documentary
       C. Preview of the spring documentary
III. The Pitch
       A. What are the reasons for donating?
       B. Donor testimonials from years past
       C. How much money do we want?
IV. Conclusion
       A. Why donating is a good idea
       B. Closing montage
```

This outline is rough and brief, but it also shows the way that an outline should get to the heart of the matter. One of the biggest problems that any writer can have—and, as of this moment, you're a writer, even if you're much more interested in camcorders than computer keyboards—is forgetting to get to the point of what they're writing about. This is particularly true of nonfiction writers, but it can happen to writers involved in any pursuit, from term papers to newspaper articles to industrial films. The key problem is maintaining the *scope* of your project as you write.

Usually, a writing project gets out of control when the writer (or writers) don't have confidence that they're communicating their video's fundamental purpose well. That's why, as you're outlining your nonfiction project, you need to keep asking yourself, "What is this video about?" Coming up with a truthful answer is the dilemma. Consider these two answers:

- "It's about how great our organization is, how it helps to educate and occupy at-risk kids who otherwise don't have after-school projects by putting a video camera in their hand and making them part of a documentary film production."

- "It's about our organization convincing potential donors to give us money."

The first one sounds a lot better, but the second one is probably going to help you focus your presentation. Yes, your organization does important things in the community and some of that will be translated in the video. But even if the video is entertaining it needs to be short and interesting, and it needs to lead the viewer toward the ultimate goal—*convincing* them of something (to give money). That means you'll probably leave some of the footage pertaining to your organization's mission on the proverbial cutting-room floor.

By the way, that doesn't mean there's no point in ever doing a video that promotes the image of your company or organization in the community—it might be a short video that you want to play at public events that you sponsor or to send to potential partners. In that case, the first bullet point ("It's about how great our organization is…") might be the better answer, since you're not asking for money in this video. That just shows how focusing on what your video is about can help change the approach you would take, even if the subject matter is similar.

Once your outline is done, you should consider storyboarding, at least the essential shots and angles you're going for while shooting. The storyboard helps you get a sense of how you're going to make the fundamental points in your video *visual*. That's why all three elements—an outline, a storyboard, and a script—are important and conceivably most important in corporate and organization projects. The outline helps you focus, the storyboard enables you to determine the visual elements that will fit with the outline, and the script will fill in the gaps in excruciating detail.

focus

For more on storyboarding, see Chapter 3; Chapter 6 also offers a lot of advice for planning a video production that's pertinent in this type of video.

That's the best way to succeed in your mission of convincing the viewer while, at the same time, best using the time of your talent and subjects. Having all of these professional tools at your disposal will also make it easier to sell your project to executives and, when the time comes, to give director's commands to those same executives or talent once you're on the set.

Make It Interesting

While you're covering all the bases in your outline and storyboard, you'll want to make sure you're making your presentation interesting, as well. That generally comes down to two things: planning for some interesting shots and writing some interesting material.

focus

This is a good time to stop and consider whether you need help on any part of this process. If you know you're strong with the camcorder but need help from a writer or reporter, now might be a good time to look into a partner or mentor who can help. Likewise, if you've got a good idea what to ask in the interview but you need help putting together good shots, talk to someone who knows about camcorders or photography and see whether he or she can help you with advice or come along on the job at a reasonable rate.

Interesting Shots

After you've got your outline together, your storyboard presents an opportunity to make your presentation interesting as you work to come up with ways to make the presentation more visual. Perhaps the most important consideration is to take any long presentations of information—particularly "talking head" interviews—and break those up with more interesting video, whether in intercuts, close-ups, product shots, or other types of B-roll.

So how do you come up with intercuts? The trick is to think about how to make your presentation as visual as possible. That means showing the action, not just talking about it. If you're creating a video that demonstrates the features of a product, for instance, you need to consider various product shots that can go along with the product manager's interview regarding the quality of the product and its careful creation.

Here's a shot list that might result from hearing a product manager's description of the product:

```
Shot List for Product Video
1.  Interview opening
2.  Product Shot (rotating platform)
3.  Interview shot
4.  Factory wide shot, robots in background
5.  Medium shot of factory workers in clean suits
6.  Close-up of precision manufacturing
7.  Interview shot
8.  R&D lab outside door
9.  Scientist at R&D table
10. Close-up of earlier product prototype
11. Interview shot
```

You'll end up with a lot of shots, but by focusing the shot list on visual interests, you'll do a better job of holding the audience's interest. Once you've created a list like this, you might find that it's easier to build your storyboard.

Interesting Words

Of course, another way to keep the audience's interest is to entertain them with an interesting script. Even product demo reels and development videos need some good writing to keep them moving along and at least not boring for the viewer. This starts with a good outline—if your project is focused tightly on having a clearly defined "being about something" mission, you're on the right track.

With the writing, you need to think about how the most important information can be presented in a way that's most memorable, and then you need to consider some opportunities where you can inject some humor, lightheartedness, or some level of creativity into the video. If humor isn't appropriate, another approach is to add some human factors to the video— anything that helps evoke an emotional reaction or otherwise helps your audience identify with the presentation.

Here are a few ideas:

- *Involve the viewer visually.* One reason people will sit down to watch something on television is to experience something they don't experience in their own lives. Keeping that in mind can be helpful while you're creating organizational video. If you have something unique to show, don't just talk about it—show it. For charities, that might be footage of your volunteers participating in a project or helping the needy. The more you can "put" your audience in the circumstances, the more they'll identify with it. (That's the same thing a good sales video does—it convinces the viewers that this is a product they can personally relate to and truly appreciate.)

- *Be funny, if it's appropriate.* If you're not funny, give the script to someone who is. Don't allow humor to muddle your message, but find a moment or two where something lighthearted can help bridge the gap from one sequence to the next. Often, this humor can come from real things that you catch on tape—kids waving, CEO bloopers, and so on—and they can really help set the tone. Of course, if you're making a promotional film for a funeral parlor, funny isn't a good way to go. While lighthearted or heartwarming moments can be important when you're creating a project about a serious topic such as a non-profit's fundraising drive for AIDS awareness or cancer research, jokes and pratfalls may not be the right choice. Ask the people you're working with or test some of the ideas (with footage or a storyboard) to see if the organizational leaders are comfortable with the concept.

- *Show warmth.* Where outright humor may not be appropriate, warmly emotional scenes may be. Depending on the purpose of your video, you can capture some of these emotions by including real-life scenes with animals, children, and families, or you can follow the organization's workers as they do their jobs. You may even find cause to hire actors or bring in your own (or your subject's) family members. Be careful, though, because manufactured or acted warmth isn't as good as the real thing.

- *Alternate emotions.* Most movies you see these days will masterfully take you from one emotion to the next; a painful moment where mom is going to have to go under the surgeon's knife is almost always relieved with a humorous or lighthearted moment in a subsequent scene. (Filmmakers, writers, playwrights, and others use this technique all the time to provide emotional *contrast*.) Use those possibilities where they seem appropriate by moving from darker or sadder subject matter to happier or more hopeful scenes.

Directing and Editing the Shoot

For business and organizational video, the mantra is *professionalism, professionalism, professionalism....* Even in documentary and feature film, you can get away with wearing a T-shirt and jeans and—sometimes—a slipped budget or a schedule change for the sake of art. Not so in business and non-profit video, however, particularly if you've been hired for the job. With your planning materials backing you up, you need to go in ready to place microphones on or near executives or donors, give them clear and respectful direction, and then coax the best possible performance from them. Next you'll look at some of the specifics of getting the job done.

Use Video Only for Visuals in Training

Some of the best advice Todd has ever heard came from a television producer he worked with on a cable TV show. When asked about producing industrial training videos, this producer advised that you should actually shoot **as little video as possible** for training materials. Why? Because video is, in some cases, the worst medium for training—at least, it's not good for entire classes' worth of training, because it's boring and can be tedious to watch a teacher lecturing in front of a classroom and a camera. It's also sometimes difficult to get a teacher— even a good one—to translate his or her lessons from a room, to which they may be good at speaking, to the confines of the camera, with which they may have less experience.

Perhaps the biggest problem with using a video for training is that it's difficult to bookmark— particularly if it's distributed on VHS tape. When you're studying for an important exam or to take a professional licensing test, the last thing you want to do is watch an entire lecture again or fast forward to the parts you need. While multimedia presentations that include video or DVDs separated into chapters can be great for presenting lessons, it's still true that it's easier to refer to a book for a quick reference or refresher versus trying to "refer" to video.

The advice with training is to consider the elements of the training that **must** be shown on video and then write a booklet or a multimedia presentation for the rest of the material. The best training packets use the best medium for the job—even a complex course might be able to get away with only 30 minutes of video clips instead of four or eight hours of dry lectures. By substituting a book, the student can learn at his or her own pace and then refer to the video for important visual lessons.

Using Multiple Techniques

Getting a business or organizational video *in the can* is generally a matter of putting together a collection of the techniques that you'll find covered in this book. Like a documentary, corporate video productions can be time-consuming to shoot and can require planning to get all of the ancillary shots you need to put together an impressive production.

Here's a quick look at some of the different setups and techniques and how they apply in corporate video.

Interviews and Studio Setups

The most basic element of a great deal of your corporate videos will be either an interview or a presentation by a single individual or a collection of such interviews with a few individuals. In the example of a corporate product rollout, you'll likely interview the product manager, vice president of development, and CEO or president of the company, among others. For a non-profit development video, you might interview past donors and the president or chairperson of the organization. In a training video, you'll likely have a presentation by a teacher or expert on the subject matter. For these shots, you'll want to concentrate on your lighting and visual interest within the interview shots, as you'll be relying on this quite heavily. (See Chapter 5 for more discussion on interviews.)

Documentary

Secondary to your main interview will likely be quite a bit of documentary footage gathered "in the field." For a product rollout, these might include shots of the manufacturing plant or shots of customers using the product. Depending on the length of your project, you may need to get a good deal of this sort of footage, meaning you'll need a field package for stabilizing your camera and, when interviewing, getting good sound. (See Chapter 6 for documentary tips and techniques.)

Event Video

The last component will be live event coverage that might be rolled into the corporate video project or events that you'll need to cover for a corporate or organizational client. For instance, in a development video, you might need to shoot a fundraising dinner or a speech by the director of your charity so that a few moments can be edited into the final development video. On the other hand, you may need to cover an entire press conference or dinner event or product rollout for your corporate/organizational client, requiring many of the same preparations as those discussed in Chapter 4.

In particular you'll need to consider the use of multiple cameras and you'll need to decide how best to gather your sound and take advantage of the crowd for cutaways and reaction shots, if appropriate.

Shooting Meetings

Whether you're documenting Steve Jobs (CEO of Apple, Inc.) at Macworld Expo or the town meeting at home in Smallville, your goal is to shoot what is *said*. Shooting meetings is a lot like shooting weddings (Chapter 4) in that you need to keep focused on the event itself and leave the creative camerawork as a secondary pursuit, if it's considered at all. You have been summoned to shoot the meeting because someone in the future may want to see what happened on that historic day. It's possible no one will ever see the video, but if someone does decide to take it off the shelf, you'd better hope that you shot everything they need to see. If you need to run to the restroom, make sure someone is running the camera for you, or hold it until the meeting adjourns. You're on their schedule.

Here are some things to keep in mind when shooting.

Get a Schedule

Before the meeting begins, meet with whomever is in charge of running the show and go over the schedule with them. Get a brief summary of what will be discussed and ask them to point out the folks scheduled to speak. You never know what interesting B-roll you'll get of the speakers during breaks. Remember that this type of shooting is dependent on content only.

 zoom-in ———————————————————

You should also ask ahead of time what sort of B-roll the company is comfortable with. Explain that informal shots can sometimes make a presentation more entertaining and human, but then give them the opportunity to opt out if they want you to shoot them only at the podium.

Find a Good Shooting Spot

It's likely you will have only one camcorder shooting the meeting. (Even though a second camcorder and operator is a good idea, both for a second angle and for backup in case you have trouble with the first camera.) Put yourself at a location where you have a good shot of the podium or everyone who will be speaking, whatever the case may be. If one person will be speaking at a time, use a medium shot or close-up (as long as you have a tripod—otherwise, the footage will be shaky if you're trying to hold a close-up using a handheld camcorder). When a group of people are speaking during a panel discussion, don't try to follow each one. Discussions should be shot wide, including all panelists in one shot so that you can see who is speaking to another.

focus ───────────────────────────────

If you have a second cameraperson for an event shoot, position her close to the action to get close-ups of panelists or reaction shots that you can cut in later. Shooting with two camcorders is also a great way to add some spice and variety to a training video, as you'll be able to have one camcorder shooting a steady medium shot of the teacher and another available for reaction shots, for getting a different angle (from the other side of the room, for instance) or for close-ups of the items being discussed. Of course, you can also use a single camcorder to get both the medium shot and the close-up, but you'll have to do it in two "takes." See Chapter 7's section on this book's CD-ROM for an example of a training video that includes medium shots and close-ups.

Get Good Sound

As emphasized in earlier chapters, this is a crucial point. In most cases, the sound will be more important than the video during a meeting. If a sound system is being used during the meeting, try to get a direct feed into your camera from the room's soundboard for the clearest sound. But be prepared with your own microphones, just in case. If you don't have external mics available to you, shoot close to the subject so your on-camera microphone will be able to pick up better sound. And, as always, test your sound before the event starts—that's the only way to know whether it's working!

Shooting B-Roll

From a combination of your interviews and your research will come ample opportunities and ideas for B-roll footage. You'll just need to go out and get it. One way to get a good sense of how to get this footage is to turn on the TV and start surfing for well-produced news and documentary pieces. You might even sit through some high-quality infomercials if you come across them.

One thing you'll see fairly often is the progressive sequence, from different angles, moving from an establishing shot to a medium shot to a close-up, even of inanimate objects. (This is a common technique on local news stories that don't feature a fire or wrecked car.) For instance, if your subject is a bank president talking about the security of the bank's vault, you might start with an establishing shot from outside the bank, followed by a medium shot panning the interior of the bank, and then a closer shot that focuses on the bank vault door clanging closed. All of these shots could be cut together into a B-roll sequence that is shown while the audience listens to the bank president speak.

On the CD-ROM See Chapter 7's section on the enclosed CD-ROM for an example of a B-roll sequence of shots.

What may surprise you—and you'll notice this if you watch TV critically—is how *many* of these shots you'll see even in a simple news piece on a 24-hour cable network. Often, you're watching file footage—the roll of the tanks, the march of the soldiers, the earnest nod of the leader's head—that aren't particularly timely or don't directly relate to the story at hand. You can do that, too, using stock footage or footage that you've got in your own library. It's best to get B-roll that's directly relevant, however, and usually that means getting out with your camera and taking appropriate shots.

Here are some notes:

- *Hold the shot.* Once it's edited down, your clip may end up being only a few seconds of B-roll of the outside of a building or the deep blue of the ocean. Still, when you're out getting the shot, you'll want a few minutes of each short shot so that you can pick and choose from different light quality or other minor imperfections.

- *Get different angles.* Remember that you'll often be cutting these shots together in a fairly quick montage—if the angles don't vary enough from shot to shot, they may end up looking like jump cuts, which are more jarring than interesting. For your wide shot, get a completely different angle on the bank than for your medium shot, which might be closer to the door or inside the bank. (Just do what you can with the camcorder and filters to equalize the lighting for the two shots so that the outside isn't *too* harsh compared to the inside shots.)

- *Get some sound.* You may not intend to use it, but you'll never know what you'll get unless you record ambient sound. Picture this piece—it's the end of a local news broadcast and the last piece is a little bit of puffery on how spring is coming. After the report signs off "This is Tony, saying, Happy Spring…" then the sound comes up from the B-roll and you hear the birds singing and bugs chirping. That's the kind of sound you'll need to get when shooting B-roll, just in case it's useful. It means paying attention to your microphones, keeping your camcorder (or external mics) steady, and not talking through the entire shot.

Pulling it Together in Editing

With all of this raw material, you'll find that you're spending a lot of time with your editing software putting together the final product, particularly for an important product rollout or development video. You'll also probably spend some time on other organizational projects as well, including your live event coverage and training videos. The key in the editing bay is to return to your core—what is this piece about—and then pull together the different bits toward that goal.

With this type of video project, you'll likely be doing a lot of *intercutting*, where various video clips are laid over a consistent audio track, as was detailed earlier in our shot list. One thing you'll likely need to do is put together a reasonably sophisticated "Edit Decision List" that you can use to manage this production. To get to that point, start by going through each of your tapes and locating the clips that seem appropriate to use for your video. That might include long clips from one batch of tapes—your interviews or training explanations—and many shorter clips from other tapes of B-roll, events, and so on.

With all of that logging done (which is discussed in more detail in Chapter 6) you can move on to an informal EDL (Edit Decision List), like the one shown in Figure 7.3. The EDL enables you to detail the tape, *timecode* (see Chapter 2), and specifics of a particular clip, including whether or not you'll be using the audio from that clip or whether it's an intercut of video over an existing audio track. With this sort of planning accomplished, you'll find that the actual edit is much easier to accomplish.

 *zoom-in* ————————————————————

Some software, such as Final Cut Pro, is designed specifically to work with a text-based EDL file to make it easier to automate the process of pulling in all of these video clips. As you move to larger projects such as these, you might consider exploring those features.

Once you've gotten the project into your editing program (see Chapter 3), you should take a few other considerations into account:

- *Keep transitions simple.* It's a good rule for almost any project, but the more serious the subject matter, the more sincere you want to be with your transitions and effects. A simple cut or wipe is good to move to the next idea; a fade is useful to end an idea or to move to another moment in time (see Chapter 9).

- *Use documentary-style titles.* Sometimes organization video producers will assume the audience knows the person you're seeing

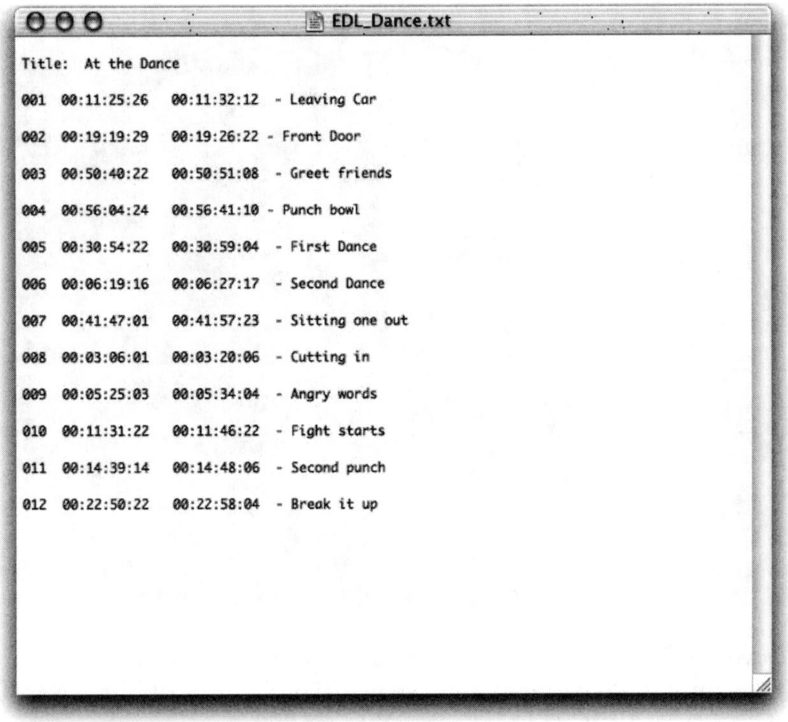

```
○ ○ ○                    📄 EDL_Dance.txt
Title:  At the Dance

001  00:11:25:26   00:11:32:12  - Leaving Car

002  00:19:19:29   00:19:26:22  - Front Door

003  00:50:40:22   00:50:51:08  - Greet friends

004  00:56:04:24   00:56:41:10  - Punch bowl

005  00:30:54:22   00:30:59:04  - First Dance

006  00:06:19:16   00:06:27:17  - Second Dance

007  00:41:47:01   00:41:57:23  - Sitting one out

008  00:03:06:01   00:03:20:06  - Cutting in

009  00:05:25:03   00:05:34:04  - Angry words

010  00:11:31:22   00:11:46:22  - Fight starts

011  00:14:39:14   00:14:48:06  - Second punch

012  00:22:50:22   00:22:58:04  - Break it up
```

FIGURE 7.3

An informal Edit Decision List can be used to track the clips you want to capture when you begin using your editing software with the footage you've shot.

on-screen, or perhaps the audience won't care who it is. We suggest you use documentary-style *lower-third* titles (titles that appear on the lower-third of the screen) to remind your audience who is the speaker and what is his or her job or title or significance (see Figure 7.4). You should also consider *where* this video will be shown—if it will be projected to large crowds on a smallish screen (which is often the case for fundraising videos), remember to make your titles larger than you might for other projects.

• *Use still images and graphics.* The magic of digital editing is that it's fairly simple to overlay slide-style computer graphics during the editing phase. You may even want to consider building these slides after the fact if you glean information from an interview or unscripted piece that can be communicated using a slide or similar graphical approach. Just make sure you don't present too much information in this way, as it can get tedious and you want it easy to read. A simple fade between the slide and the interview shot can be effective, as the interviewee continues to talk through the numbers or issues (see Figure 7.5).

FIGURE 7.4

Documentary-style titling works well for business and organizational video.

If your software doesn't format slides automatically (or if it can't work directly with PowerPoint, for instance), you can probably get away with TIF or JPEG format images that are 720 × 480 in dimensions

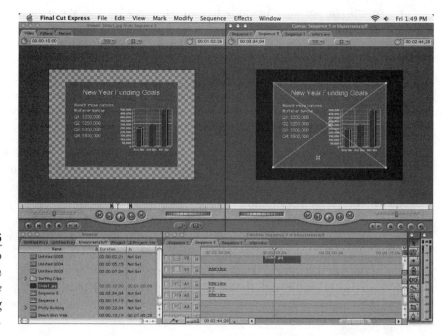

FIGURE 7.5

You can add to the value of an informative video using slides.

and 72 dots per inch (dpi). Some editing software can deal with 640 ×
480 slides, which is a bit more common a resolution for such images.
(720 × 480 is the technical resolution of DV, while 640 × 480 is a
common aspect ratio for computer video.)

Once you've gotten all of these elements in place, there's one last kicker—
if your organization or corporation has a sense of humor at all, put together
a "blooper" reel and either add it at the end of the video (with permission,
even if it's a sneaky permission from the PR folks) or hand it to your customer
separately. You'll have to be the judge of whether your client will go for it,
but a blooper reel is a ton of fun to edit and might be appreciated and
enjoyed by the folks involved.

And...Cut!

That's it for business and organizational video. In this chapter, you saw
some suggestions for how you should plan, write, shoot, and edit video for
teaching, selling, informing, or asking for money. In the next chapter, we'll
move on to a discussion of digital features.

DV Feature (or Short)

AH, the feature film—the most glamorous kind of filmmaking, filled with celebrities, glitz, and fame; million-dollar deals; luxury accommodations; and the best food, catered to your doorstep three—no, four—times a day. Sound familiar?

Probably not. But don't worry—it doesn't sound familiar to us, either. In this chapter, we help you get beyond some of those collective delusions we have about Hollywood filmmaking and, instead, introduce you to a world of meticulous planning, taming the wilds, and spending long hours patiently at work. We won't hold it against you if you insist on having your own monogrammed director's chair on set, but don't blame us for the eye-rolling you'll encounter, Mr. DeMille.

Making a fiction film can be a blast, whether it's *feature length* (a film of more than one hour in length), a *short feature* (a film of less than one hour, but usually closer to 45 minutes or less), or a *short* film (a film of less than 30, and often less than 10 minutes). At most film festivals, you'll encounter two categories—*feature* (over 45 minutes) and *short* (under 45 minutes). We like the three categories because they suggest different budgets and markets—shorts that are around 10 minutes are great for Internet distribution, for instance, whereas 30-45 minute shorts haven't quite found an audience on the Internet yet, for the most part.

focus ───

We'll call it **filmmaking** and **film** in this chapter even though we're referring to digital video (DV). Otherwise, we'd have to call it "videomaking" and "feature video" and that doesn't seem to be where the industry is headed—it looks like we'll be using terms with film in them well after the bulk of productions have moved to digital technologies. Also realize that we'll use the term feature as a stand-in for most any type of fiction film, including short films, unless we need to talk specifically about shorter forms.

In the past few years, feature filmmaking has been revolutionized with the accessibility and affordability of DV and editing software. Film festivals across the world are receiving entries on DV from both professional and amateur filmmakers. Film commissions now receive requests from needy filmmakers shooting DV projects in search of the perfect location, additional equipment, actors, and crew.

focus ───

Nina—who is the deputy director for the Mississippi Film Office and programming director for the Crossroads Film Festival in Jackson, Mississippi—can attest to the increase of requests and submissions from people with films shot on DV. This year marks the first year that the festival has had to provide a DV deck for projection during the festival due to the number of digital entries coming from both first-timers and seasoned professionals.

In this chapter, we take a general look at some of the planning you may need before you take on your first fiction film project, including how to turn an idea into a script, how to turn your script into a movie, and how to muddle through all the ups and downs you'll experience along the way. We also touch on some of the camerawork and editing techniques that can make your low-budget DV feature a possibility.

What You Need

Prior to DV, fiction films were shot in one of two ways: either on analog video or using a film camera of some sort, whether 8mm, 16mm, or 35mm. Most filmmakers agree that affordable analog video technologies (VHS, Super8, and even BetaSP) have a picture quality that doesn't look quite good enough for fiction and feature films. Although many filmmakers will shoot video for their short films because it's what their budget allows, few features are shot using analog video.

 *zoom-in* —————————————————————————

8mm, 16mm, or 35mm: these measurements refer to the size of the film itself, which equates to both the cost of the film and how big the projected image can be. 8mm is usually used for student films and was popular decades ago for home movies. A lot of documentary and festival fare is shot in 16mm; professional film is shot in 35mm, and the occasional blockbuster or Imax film is shot—or blown up to—70mm.

The costs of film can quickly skyrocket. Even a short film on 16mm has to budget hundreds or thousands of dollars for filmstock, sometimes (on a very tight budget) piecing together film by buying *short ends* or *recans*— unexposed film that was partially used by another client before being resold. Still, it can run hundreds of dollars to buy an hour's worth of film. And while some enterprising filmmakers own 8mm or 16mm equipment, a 35mm camera can easily cost $1000 a day just to rent the camera body and some lenses.

Going digital, then, can make a lot of sense for most of us, and as the quality approaches 16mm in some respects, you can use some tricks to make DV look more like film at dramatically lower costs. Of course, even digital filmmaking isn't exactly *dirt cheap*, as you'll see.

Equipment Needs

A digital camcorder lowers the costs of filming and gives you immediate access to the raw footage, which enables you to work with the final images quite a bit. This instant access also enables you to review the footage immediately after it's been shot, so that you can see what worked and what didn't and correct mistakes in sound, lighting, placement of actors or camcorders, and so on. That luxury can be invaluable, particularly when you're working at a location that was tough—or expensive—to get.

Many DV features go through quite a long editing stage, not only to get the story told correctly, but also to render many of the frames with special filters that make the video signal look more "filmic." A lot of programming thought has gone into creating software routines and packages that can make digital look more like film—at the outset, you might not worry about much of that, although we'll talk through some of the possibilities in Chapter 11.

We'd recommend getting your hands on at least one three-chip digital camcorder for your fiction filming and realize that feature filming can go a lot faster by using two or three camcorders, depending on the approach you take to directing the film. With multiple camcorders, you can get wide shots and reaction shots in the same *take*. With a single camcorder, you may need to get your actors to reproduce their performances in multiple takes, filming each actor individually to make up the different shots. The ideal situation is to use multiple camcorders and multiple takes, which allows you to choose among the best of them all.

 *zoom-in*

For the record, many huge-budget Hollywood movies shoot with just one camera, so that actors are asked to reproduce their performances again and again in order to get all the different angles necessary for editing. Some features shoot with two cameras; three is rare. In television, particularly sitcoms, using two or three cameras is more common.

Along with your camcorders, you need a significant investment in camcorder stabilization. If you must, you can get away with using a tripod for each camcorder, as long as each is relatively stationary. If you need to move the camcorder(s), you'll want to get some specialized stabilization equipment—shoulder mounts or counterweighted monopods—such as the setups discussed in Chapter 7.

For feature filming, you might even go a step further and look into a *crane, jib,* or *camera boom* that's designed to give your camcorder fluid movement in three dimensions, allowing it to stay perfectly still at different heights and angles for as long as necessary (see Figure 8.1). A number of these devices are made to mimic pricier setups that are used in moviemaking. A few of the makers are shown in the following table; note that most inexpensive camcorder jibs are designed to mount on a fairly sturdy tripod.

FIGURE 8.1

The CobraCrane (www .steadytracker .com/crane.html) is an example of a low-cost crane solution for shooting digital video.

Products	Web Site
Micro jib and full jib	www.habbycam.com/products.html
CobraCrane	www.steadytracker.com/crane.html
SkyCrane	www.skycrane.com/
Super jib arm	www.studio1productions.com/

You're going to need to get high-end audio for your feature as well—in most fiction filming, that means using a microphone boom and a directional mic, as it's sometimes too dangerous to wire your actors. (For example, if you get in a close-up and see the microphone, you'll ruin the illusion. In a documentary, that isn't as much of a problem, but in fiction, it's a big no-no. If you can wire under their clothes and get good sound, that's an option.) For good audio, you'll likely want to record to a device other than your camcorder, if you can help it—a lot of professionals use Digital Audio Tape (DAT) recorders to get the best sound, although you may also opt for a miniDisc recorder or something similar.

The idea is to record to some digital medium so that the audio can be imported easily to your computer and then synchronized with the video. That's not absolutely mandatory, however—as is discussed in Chapter 10, you can get good sound using external microphones in conjunction with your camcorder and a balanced audio breakout box. (As we discuss later in this chapter in the section "Post-Production and Editing" as well as in Chapter 10, you can also have your actors dub in their dialog in a studio later in the process, which can be a handy, though expensive, way to deal with shots where getting sound isn't easy or feasible.)

Finally, your fiction film is going to need some studio lighting for interior shots—you just can't get away with standard-issue home or office lighting, because you'll lose a lot of detail in people's faces and skin tones. You want your actors' faces to look warm and inviting—they've got to engage the audience, so it helps if it doesn't seem like you're looking at the actors in a darkened room. Lighting kits are described in Chapter 6.

Although three-point lighting may not work in exactly the same way for your film, particularly if your actors are moving quite a bit, you'll want to use at least key and fill lights to get as much light and as few odd shadows on your set as possible—unless creepy (high contrast and dark) shadows are called for. Of course, you can also shoot outside, which means you are at the whim of nature, but at least you're not responsible for turning on the lights.

Other Needs

In addition to the camera equipment, three other things are necessary for the making of a feature film: a good story, endurance, and flexibility. Without a good story, no one will care to watch your feature film—or, for that matter, your home movie, or documentary. For your feature, all the celebrities and special effects you can assemble won't bring a thumbs-up from your critics without a good story as the basis. Second, the making of a feature film is long and tedious, with problems arising every step of the way. Prepare yourself mentally and emotionally for a roller coaster ride. After shooting your first feature or short, you'll understand why so many stars end up in rehab. (We're kidding—a little.)

These problems are why you need to be flexible, both in your handling of management issues and in your storytelling vision; sometimes you'll have to compromise an idealized vision and instead go with the shot you can pull off before nightfall or before the actor quits or your crew walks out on you. And, who knows, it may be a better shot in the long run.

Unless you're really good at soliciting favors and non-monetary donations, you'll need to have money on hand to pay for items such as tape stock, food for the crew and cast, equipment rental, transportation, insurance, permits, supplies, and beer (or better) for the wrap party. You might need to pay a writer, cameraperson, or assistant as well. It's likely that if you are shooting your feature on video, you might not have much cash to begin with—but keep in mind that a well-fed crew is a happy crew, especially if they're not getting paid. Make sure you are able to feed your crew if they are putting in long hours, particularly at their own expense.

 *zoom-in* ————————————————————————

A friend of ours got around the issue of feeding people by stretching his shoot over several months. Once a week, our friend, Tom, and his buddies would get together for what they called "Poker Night," but they shot a scene of his movie instead of playing cards. It took a while to finish the project, but it was completed for little money, and they had a good time. His volunteer crew didn't get burnt out and tired from consecutively long shoot days, and the element of fun was maintained. Look for creative solutions to augment your lack of funds.

Writing Your Feature

One of the most difficult parts of making a feature is coming up with a good idea. Thousands of movies exist, but where did all those stories come from? When you're still brainstorming or thinking about how great it would be to make a feature, it seems easy as pie to come up with a story to tell. If you're lucky, you'll feel inspiration to tell a fictional story that comes from your experiences or your observations—or simply from a deep well of creativity. People who have a story so good or so important that it has to be told are among the most fortunate writers. (Of course, tons of bad movies started as good stories, which is evidence of how difficult it is to make a good movie.)

Adaptation

Story ideas don't have to be once-in-a-lifetime inspirations. Story ideas also come from existing works, such as novels, short stories, articles in the newspaper, real-life experiences, poems, songs, and even other movies. In such cases, you're looking at creating an *adaptation*—creating your film's story based on another work. Believe it or not, this isn't completely out of the realm of the possible, even for the aspiring filmmaker—you just have to choose the right story to adapt, making sure it's in your league financially and otherwise.

The most important element in adaptation is gaining permission to use another person's idea. For example, the producer for *The English Patient* paid for the rights to use the existing novel as the basis for a script. You probably can't afford to do that; however, you might be able to convince a friend who is writing a short story for his university extension class to sell you the movie rights to his work or partner with you to get the story told on film. You might find that you can collaborate to produce a film that a friend of yours has kicked around, or a film about something that was featured in your local paper that the principals are willing to share. You may end up borrowing from your best friend's notebook of stories, and something as inexpensive as a sushi dinner will suffice as payment. Whatever the case, you'll need permission to use the idea, you'll want to get it in writing, and, most likely, at least a little money should change hands.

focus —————————————————————————————

You've probably heard the term optioning a story or script. A producer offers a relatively small amount of money—perhaps $10,000 to $50,000 for a Hollywood story or, in our case, maybe $100 to a local writer—to keep it off the market for a certain amount of time. You might, for instance, offer a writer $500 to option her story for 18 months, and then promise $5000 for the writing of a script contingent on getting some financing, or a percentage of the gross receipts once the movie is made. All sorts of deals can be made, and, quite frankly, they can be made even on the local level if you think a story is good enough that you want to pay a little money to use it.

The Treatment

After you have a story, it's important to get it down on paper. The story is step one—not the script. *The story.* In Hollywood, movies are often sold based on a one-page *treatment* (although finished scripts are sold as well, of course). A treatment is a general description of the story told from beginning to end, introducing the main characters within that storyline as well as how the writer "sees" the film visually. All you're doing is writing out what's going to happen in narrative form, without camera angles and stage direction or too much detail about locations and sets. You want to communicate to the reader what the story of this project will be in less than three pages. A description might begin like so:

Amy Rogers, a pilot and lieutenant in the U.S. Navy, sets out early one morning (at "Oh Dark Thirty") from an aircraft carrier in the Caribbean Sea on a routine recon mission with a young ensign, Bob Adamson, who is a promising Academy graduate, pilot-qualified with a top gun attitude. The mission is a high-speed flyover of Venezuela to check on the status of civil tensions in that region. Adamson, in his vigor, takes the plane lower than is appropriate, when their electronics note an anomalous anti-aircraft battery. They get too close, however, and their aircraft becomes the target for a missile. To their shock, the missile is launched, and, although they dive to get away from it, it takes out their plane as they eject.

That's just the first paragraph, which might represent, at the most, the first 10 minutes of your feature. You then continue with the basic characters, plot lines, subplots, and anything else that you think is significant in the story. (This example, by the way, is already too expensive to make, which brings us to another bit of advice: remember your budget as you write.)

The Script

After you have a firm grasp on the story line, you can begin writing the script. Writing the script should feel like filling in the blanks, since you already have the story outlined. A feature-length script normally runs anywhere from 90 to 120 pages in the proper scripting format—which is important in scriptwriting. If written in proper script format, one page is equivalent to approximately one minute of screen time. (Indeed, one reason that the industry is such a stickler for the script format is that it's a reasonable gauge of the running time of the film as it's being written.)

The script format was also designed to be reasonably simple to accomplish on a typewriter—in a word processing application, it isn't impossible, but it can be helpful to use a special template or even a special application to write your script, depending on how serious you are about it. Applications that help you with scripting include Final Draft (www.finaldraft.com), Scriptware (www.scriptware.com), and Screenwriter 2000 (www.screenplay.com—see Figure 8.2).

focus ──

A great site that offers an in-depth look at script formatting and other screenwriting issues is Breaking Into Screenwriting (**http://breakingin.net/format_tutorial.htm**). You might also find it handy to look at professional scripts—check out Daily Scripts (**www.dailyscript.com**) for links to a number of scripts online.

Along with allowing you to judge the length of your feature, script formatting is important because it is the format with which your actors, producers, and crew are likely to be familiar if they have any filmmaking experience (or if they've been to film school or taken a screenwriting class).

A script format includes the following basics:

- **Scenes**   Scripts are broken into *scenes,* with each scene representing a stretch of unbroken action or dialog. In most scripts, a scene is between half a page and three pages long; scenes much longer than that might need to be broken up into smaller scenes. (For instance, a five-minute scene with two friends in a diner might need to be intercut with that scene you wrote showing one friend's apartment being broken into across town.)

- **Locations**   Locations are written in capital letters, as in "EXT. BARN—NIGHT" or "INT. HOUSE—DAY," followed by enough detail to provide a general idea of the place, but not so much detail

FIGURE 8.2

Here's an example of a script being written in Screenwriter 2000. Notice the distinctive formatting.

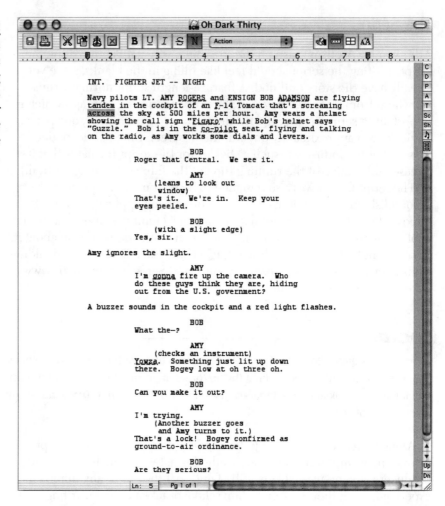

```
INT.   FIGHTER JET -- NIGHT

Navy pilots LT. AMY ROGERS and ENSIGN BOB ADAMSON are flying
tandem in the cockpit of an F-14 Tomcat that's screaming
across the sky at 500 miles per hour.  Amy wears a helmet
showing the call sign "Figaro" while Bob's helmet says
"Guzzle."  Bob is in the co-pilot seat, flying and talking
on the radio, as Amy works some dials and levers.

                    BOB
          Roger that Central.  We see it.

                    AMY
               (leans to look out
               window)
          That's it.  We're in.  Keep your
          eyes peeled.

                    BOB
               (with a slight edge)
          Yes, sir.

Amy ignores the slight.

                    AMY
          I'm gonna fire up the camera.  Who
          do these guys think they are, hiding
          out from the U.S. government?

A buzzer sounds in the cockpit and a red light flashes.

                    BOB
          What the-?

                    AMY
               (checks an instrument)
          Yowza.  Something just lit up down
          there.  Bogey low at oh three oh.

                    BOB
          Can you make it out?

                    AMY
          I'm trying.
               (Another buzzer goes
               and Amy turns to it.)
          That's a lock!  Bogey confirmed as
          ground-to-air ordinance.

                    BOB
          Are they serious?
```

that it keeps the set designer (or whoever pitches in to help) from being creative. Nearly every scene in your script begins with a location line.

- **Characters**   A brief description of the characters, including how they look and hold themselves, but not a lot about their background. (By convention, you use all-caps for a person's name when the character is first introduced in the screenplay, as in "ANDREW, a tall Frenchman in his early 30s....")

- **Actions**   The actions that take place in the film, but only in a general sense. Not "he flourished his left hand in disgust," but rather, "Bob walks into the room looking extremely angry." In the early scriptwriting phase, as you get closer to filming a scene, you'll find that you'll take notes and want to plan both your direction to your actors and where you'll be placing the camcorder in a scene.

- **Props**   Props that are necessary for the story line should be discussed, and, when first introduced, they should appear in all caps. ("Bob walks into the room looking extremely angry, with a PISTOL in his hand.")
- **Dialog**   The dialogue that will be spoken by the actors.

A fiction screenplay must be written in a very specific way to succeed: everything about the story should be *visual* and can be communicated on the screen or in the dialogue. Your screenplay should not read like a novel with the tiniest detail of a person or place described. Those details *will* need to be apparent on screen in a movie, however, or they won't be communicated to the audience.

For instance, if you begin by describing one of your characters as "ANDREW, a felon who was wrongly imprisoned for embezzlement," that's not going to do the audience much good because that description won't be written on Andrew's shirt when they're watching the film. Instead, you would need to introduce that information through action and dialogue in the story itself—perhaps with a scene in which Andrew's parole officer tracks him down at his tennis club and embarrasses him.

Also, although the characters' actions and important incidents that further the plot can be described ("The plane crashes through the terminal building, ripping it open like a tin can"), it's not necessary to describe the movement of the *camera* at any length. If camera movement is essential to a particular part of the story, you can include direction in the script; otherwise, just tell the story. As for the actual camera placement and movement on a shot-by-shot basis, those details are generally left to the director and her crew to make in the form of a *shooting script* (a script that describes actor placement and camcorder movement).

Build a Story

A formulaic approach to your screenplay is to create a "situational drama," in which you choose a situation, place characters in that situation, add some conflict, and then entertain your audience on the way to the resolution of that conflict. Here's an example:

- Will, an undersized punk-rock guitarist, meets Julie, a sorority girl at a college fraternity party where his band is playing. They notice some romantic chemistry.

- Julie already has an arrogant jock boyfriend, Cal, but she's attracted to Will and the dangerous life she thinks he represents.

- Will is also attracted to Julie, so he works to impress her with both boyish charm and affected machismo.

- Julie laughs a lot when she's with Will and feels alive with him, so she breaks up with Cal to be with Will.

- Cal sets out, in increasingly devious and dangerous ways, to destroy Will and his band's burgeoning career and to win Julie back.

- Will foils Cal at every turn, but he has to feign bravery in the face of mounting fear.

- Cal decides that violence is the only answer, and he comes after Will with the intent of hurting—maybe killing—him.

- Julie tries to stop Cal, and Cal ends up kidnapping her.

- Will, believing that Julie has gone back to Cal, descends into an angry depression until he stumbles upon evidence of the kidnapping.

- With renewed faith in Julie, Will sets out to find and stop Cal, which he'll have to do with brains, not brawn.

No, it's not the most original or compelling story—it's said that there are no truly *original* stories—but it illustrates the point. To get a better sense of this process, grab a pencil and paper while watching a movie and write down what you see as the significant plot points. Watch the progression of the story, and you'll see most features follow a basic structure—we learn the goal of the main character (or characters), we see stumbling blocks and challenges tossed at the character to keep her from her goal, and then we see her eventual triumph or (rarely in Hollywood) failure.

Of course, most movies also have some unique elements—a foreign locale, an accident, an expert in alien horticulture—tossed in to keep you entertained. Then, you need to alternate somewhat between funny, serious, and sad moments while building to a dramatic crescendo—and you'll have a story.

Your story is easily the most important component of your fiction film, so you'll want to spend some time on it—in fact, you might want to work on it in a class or writer's group so that you can get feedback from others on the story you're putting together. For many writers, getting the dialogue to sound natural is tough—aside from reading it aloud and studying the way the characters talk in the films you admire—a teacher, actor friends, or a writer's group can help you with that, as well. You'll want to spend a great deal of time trying to put together an interesting story and writing interesting, realistic dialogue.

focus _____

After you have some idea where you're going with the story, try to write a little every day. Don't be discouraged if you write ten pages one day and only one page the next. It's not likely that you'll produce consistently, but if you're able to self motivate, you're more likely to see through the writing phase of the project. If you have trouble with the writing, look to friends or partners who can brainstorm with you and get it rolling. Most important, remember that you've got to show the action visually and move the plot forward with action and dialogue—you can't tell a feature film; you've got to show it. (That's why voice-over, or having a character narrate throughout, is usually considered a last resort in screenwriting.)

 zoom-in _____

If your local community college or university doesn't offer evening classes in screenwriting, you might consider taking a class online. One option is Gotham Writers' Workshop (www.writingclasses.com) that offers online classes in screenwriting. (Todd has taken these classes in the past and enjoyed the process.)

Producing and Directing

When you're happy with your story and script, you're ready to turn it into a movie. First you've got to take off your writer hat and put on a producer hat. (You may need a hardhat for this job.)

Producing, as mentioned in Chapter 4, is all about being a good organizer. Producing a feature film is where you get to show off your skills. Once you've got a script in your hands—whether you've written it or commissioned it— you're going to need to manage two important elements of any production:

- The budget
- Everything that the budget buys

You'll be juggling locations, actors, time and money constraints, a hungry crew, equipment and resources, props, wardrobe, stage moms, animals, special effects, and your own life in the midst of it all. How will you keep up and make it work together?

Breaking Down the Script, and Delegating

First, you need to know *what* you'll be planning. Fortunately, that's fairly simple. In feature production, you need to plan the *scenes* in your script.

Each uninterrupted dialogue sequence that takes place in a single location is a scene; even if you return to that same locale and continue the action later in the movie after cutting away, you're in a different scene, at least as far as the script is concerned. In fact, if you use computer scriptwriting software, you'll likely find that each scene is numbered automatically by the software. Those reference numbers can come in handy, so if you're using a different word processing template, consider numbering each scene at its location line (like this, for example: 45 EXT. BAR PARKING LOT, NIGHT).

Next, you can treat the planning of a movie (the *pre-production* phase) like planning a big party or event. Make a list, divide the list into parts, delegate a great deal of the tasks, set a deadline for each task, and then make sure each item on that list gets accomplished before its deadline. That deadline is the moment in time when you've planned to shoot a particular scene.

An experienced film producer might refer to the initial list-making process as a *script breakdown*. This entails making a list of the scenes in the film and then listing everything that corresponds to that scene. Here's an example:

- The location

- Which characters will be used

- Costumes and props

- Special effects and equipment

- Extras (actors with little or no dialog)

- Makeup and sound necessities

- Extra crew, safety equipment, or stunts

After you've created the master list (it might actually be more of a spreadsheet or a table—see Figure 8.3), each line item for each scene will need to be delegated to the appropriate crew members—assuming you have crew members. If you happen to be filling most of the crew roles yourself, the breakdown will be especially helpful to you. It's much easier to keep up with the steps you need to take to film a scene if you can look at it in an organized manner on a piece of paper.

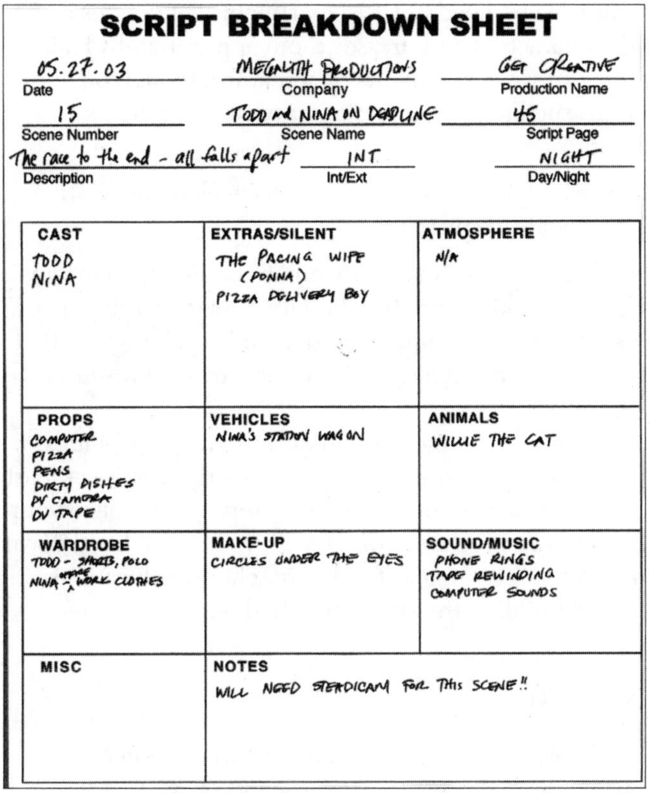

SCRIPT BREAKDOWN SHEET

05.27.03	MEGALITH PRODUCTIONS	GET CREATIVE
Date	Company	Production Name
15	TODD and NINA ON DEADLINE	45
Scene Number	Scene Name	Script Page
The race to the end - all falls apart	INT	NIGHT
Description	Int/Ext	Day/Night

CAST	EXTRAS/SILENT	ATMOSPHERE
TODD NINA	THE PACING WIFE (DONNA) PIZZA DELIVERY BOY	N/A

PROPS	VEHICLES	ANIMALS
COMPUTER PIZZA PENS DIRTY DISHES DV CAMERA DV TAPE	NINA'S STATION WAGON	WILLIE THE CAT

WARDROBE	MAKE-UP	SOUND/MUSIC
TODD - SHIRTS, POLO NINA - WORK CLOTHES	CIRCLES UNDER THE EYES	PHONE RINGS TAPE REWINDING COMPUTER SOUNDS

MISC	NOTES
	WILL NEED STEADICAM FOR THIS SCENE!!

FIGURE 8.3

An example of a basic script breakdown form

On big-budget movie productions, each department has a head. Here are some examples of a typical film crew:

- **Director of photography**   The head of the camera department, which includes the people who handle the camera as well as the crew overseeing the lighting.

- **Line producer**   Ultimately responsible for making sure that everything that everyone needs shows up when it's supposed to. Need tape? Food? Gum? Lights? Trucks? Plane tickets? Ask the line producer.

- **Production designer**   Responsible for the visual style of the locations used in the film (sort of like an interior designer—but for exteriors, as well). He or she is the head of the art department, which is responsible for designing the sets, arranging them according to the script, and supplying props handled by the actors.

- **Costume designer** The head of the department that creates a visual style for the characters and dresses them appropriately. Hair and make-up are separate departments on a feature, though on smaller productions such as a commercial, a stylist might handle wardrobe, hair, and makeup.

- **Director** Has the big picture of how all of these elements work together to create a cohesive product.

- **The mighty producer** The "man (or woman) behind the curtain," who is responsible for making sure the director gets everything he or she wants and needs (money), while simultaneously making sure that the director doesn't take advantage of his or her crew and resources.

On your set, you may have some, most, or all of these responsibilities. Since you're reading this chapter, however, we'll assume that you're at least taking on the role of the producer—you're going to step up and make your feature happen. To do that, you need to move on with your script breakdown and head on to the next jobs—creating a storyboard, choosing locations, planning your scenes, and building the shooting schedule.

Creating a Storyboard

Soon after creating your script breakdown, you'll want to put together a storyboard, which is useful for getting a visual sense of how your feature is coming together and how the scenes will work. Chapter 3 discusses storyboarding in some detail, but here are some slight nuances important for a feature:

- *Your storyboard should be as detailed as possible.* The drawings don't have to be fine art, but you should attempt to convey the major action in each scene.

- *Try to give a sense of the locations and atmosphere in your storyboard.* This will illustrate your ideas of the locations for the people working with you.

- *Use your storyboard to experiment with camcorder angles and placement.* Sketch out where you might want the camcorder to be positioned and where the actors stand. It's useful both for visualizing the shot and for brainstorming some of the direction that you can give the actors once you're on the set.

Don't let drawing talent (whether you've got too much or none at all) get in the way of your quickly outlining the action in your story. Even if you use stick figures, a storyboard will help you with the planning, which is really what's important at this point. Leave the gorgeous storyboards to the art directors who need to sell advertising concepts to clients.

Choosing Locations

Locations are one of the key elements in moviemaking. Bad locations immediately make a movie seem less professional and not nearly as enjoyable to watch. Think about it: the house and maze in *The Shining*, New York City in all of Woody Allen's movies, the field in *Field of Dreams* (which consequently became one of the most visited sites in Iowa, and it wasn't even a real baseball field—the movie built it), the library in *The Breakfast Club*, the New Zealand vistas in *Lord of the Rings*, and even the closet under the stairs in *Harry Potter* and *Signs* (not the same closet, of course). Movies call for numerous locations, unless we're talking about *My Dinner with André*, which takes place at a table in a restaurant, so be prepared to hire or designate someone—or spend a lot of your time to locate, make connections, and secure permission for your locations. Even movies such as *Star Wars* that take place in fictional locations need some real shooting locations.

If you opt to be your own location manager, step one is to break down your script and create a list of necessary locations, even if some of the sites are as simple as a driveway or a bedroom. Those types of locations seem like easy areas to go out and shoot, but oftentimes, your own bedroom or driveway won't work because of lighting, trees, electricity, space, or the way they look on film. In such cases, you need to find a location that looks good to the camera and that offers you all the support amenities you need for your cameras and crew. That takes some research and planning.

focus ⎯⎯⎯⎯⎯⎯⎯⎯⎯⎯⎯⎯⎯⎯⎯⎯⎯⎯⎯⎯⎯⎯⎯⎯⎯⎯⎯⎯⎯

Look for flexibility in your locations, and beware of locations that require significant changes to make them work for the film. One example is a location that is meant to be used in a period piece—for instance, a movie about the 1950s. If you use a street near your house, it might have appropriate architecture and trees, but newer cars will be parked on the street, and street signs and perhaps even satellite dishes won't look appropriate. Instead, you might need to set the scene on a more rural street, or inside, or in some more controllable environment. (Even better is to realize that period pieces are tough for a low-budget feature and avoid them.)

Go through the script and make a note of every location that's called for. Then read the script carefully (unless you have it largely committed to memory) to see if the script mentions any important particulars about those locations. As a director, some ideas may pop into your head as you're reading: What kind of bedroom do you envision—is it frilly and girly, does a single businessman sleep there, is it a room for a teenage boy, or one for a couple married for 35 years?

Remember that video and film are primarily visual mediums—unlike a novel, we can't just read the characters' thoughts or get a few pages' worth of background and childhood. Instead, the images, including the locations you choose, define the characters in the story. That's why locations need serious consideration—you can't shoot your own bedroom just because it's easy to shoot. If it works, that's great! But if your style isn't representative of the character and the script, find something more appropriate or plan on *re-dressing* your room (redecorating for the camcorder) so it fits the story and the character.

Eventually, you'll have to do some *location scouting*. Try contacting film commissions and offices, which are located in nearly 300 locations around the globe, including in most of the United States. They can help make your search more manageable by narrowing your options in an area and pointing you to locations that are friendly to filming and that offer the facilities and amenities you need. These offices might also help you bypass some of the red tape it takes to clear a location. If you need a red barn in the middle of a field or an office with a view, for example, they can help you find it—usually at no charge, at least for the help in securing the location.

The Association of Film Commissioners International has a list of offices around the world (www.afci.org). These offices exist to help any film or video production in their areas, so don't hold a grudge if you're not at the top of their priority list, as million-dollar flicks tend to garner more attention. (We can't imagine why.) A lot of people who work in this industry have a soft spot for small productions, however, so you should be able to get help when they have time to give it.

Why would someone agree to allow total strangers to shoot video on their property? Most of the time, people are willing to let you use a location because you pay them. Some people may be excited at the prospect of participating in a film, but you should realize that their enthusiasm can wane—particularly as your crew, camcorders, lights, actors, trucks, and vans start showing up and making a fuss. (The smaller your production, the more likely you'll encounter friendly location owners.)

In cases where you need to grease the wheels, if you don't have cash to pay them, find creative ways to make it worth their while—such as showcasing their business on screen, putting their friends and family in the film, giving them a "thank you" credit to encourage tourism, or even making improvements—mowing the lawn or painting or similar—to the location.

Taking care of a location is just as important as finding the perfect place to shoot. As you read the script, you may not envision having a large crew on site—but even a small production can start to look like a big deal if you show up with two or three vans, actors, a makeup artist, a script supervisor, and a boom mic operator. Even though you may not be paying any of these crew members, to outsiders it looks like a big production.

That means two things—they'll assume you have millions of dollars (because people assume that about all filmmakers, even when all evidence is to the contrary), and they'll be upset if you trounce their flowerbeds. Be respectful of the property by not damaging or mistreating it, and stick to the shooting schedule you give the owners. You could ruin the chances of another person shooting at that location or in the community if the property owners have a bad experience with you. They could also make sure that you never shoot in that town again if you treat them badly enough, so keep your crew on their toes and pick up after yourselves, treating each location as if it were your next-door neighbor's front yard.

focus ——————————————————————————————————————

While a cavalier approach to getting locations might work for your first small-budget feature, realize that working on location on a film can take a lot more forethought than is described here—in particular, you might want to consider liability insurance that would cover accidents or damage that your crew does to the surroundings. Likewise, written contracts or letters stating the terms of any agreement between you and the owner or manager of a location are recommended— and, yes, you may need to consult an attorney.

Planning Your Scenes

A good producer is a master at defining priorities. In planning the *shooting schedule*—a schedule that determines which scenes will be shot in which order—the first thing to consider is the availability of locations and actors. Those two elements will dictate the schedule, which is why big-budget movies are almost never shot in the order of scenes as they fall in the script. The goal is to shoot, all at once, every scene that requires a particular location as long as your actors are available. For example, if scenes 1, 13, 21, and the last scene of the movie take place in Miller's Grocery Store, you should try to shoot all of those scenes back to back so that you will not have to inconvenience the store owner more than once (or to minimize the rent he's charging you).

In addition, you may want to shoot the scenes in order if the sunlight and time of day is important for those scenes. Likewise, for interior locations, the fewer times you have to set up lights and sound, move furniture around, and so forth, the better. If you can shoot all the scenes you need by going through the setup process once, that's ideal. You can see how a storyboard can be convenient for this step, as it can help you to determine visually which scenes are similar and which shoots might benefit from being scheduled together.

focus ——————————————————————————————————————

Within a location, you will also want to break down your scenes by camcorder placement—wide shots, first, if possible. For instance, if scenes 1, 3, and 8 all need wide shots of your character entering the same bar, but they represent three different moments in the script (once with friends, once alone, and once wearing a tuxedo, for example), you should still shoot the scenes back to back to back as long as the time of day and lighting agree. It may seem like crazy Hollywood trickery, but seasoned producers know that it's easier to change your actor's clothing and shoot the same scenery at the same time than it is to move and re-move a bunch of lights and accessories to the same location.

After you have a sense of how many scenes you can shoot in each of your locations, you need to take into consideration when your actors are available. This can be a pressing matter for a low-budget feature, because your actors are probably working for little or no money—meaning that you need to be flexible with their schedules. If your lead actor is available for only five days, try to schedule all the scenes that require her within those five days, booking locations appropriately.

Of course, you'll probably have other actors to consider. In fact, you will constantly be deciding what's most important (the actor? the location? the time of day?) and then scheduling accordingly. At times you will not be able to make it work for everyone—even though you may have the perfect location or the perfect actor for a role chosen, something or someone might have to be sacrificed. It's a game of priorities.

And just to add to your scheduling headache, you should know that the process is going to take time. As you'll see in the "Directing" section coming up, you'll need about five good shots per scene. Professionals go on the assumption that a good day is about 30 shots—at most, that's six scenes per day. If your 120-page script has 60 scenes, that's 10 days, optimistically—15 or more days is likely. You'll probably want to schedule three, six-day weeks if you've got them; or schedule two, seven-day weeks; or one, ten-day span for your production. Then do everything you can to get your team to stick to those schedules.

focus ————————————————————————————

Realize that we're not covering a fair amount in this chapter—costumes, building sets, preparing for stunts—all of which can take a huge amount of time, expertise, and budget. Again, you can control these things in the scripting phase of your feature, by not including them in the movie. When you're making a feature on a budget, your best plan is to work with locations that can be used untouched, characters that don't need movie-magic makeup, and sets or settings that don't require elaborate changes or construction. Make your movie about normal, modern people who live close to where you live and have similar problems, hopes, or dreams—and you'll be on the right track.

Wheeling and Dealing

A producer has to be good at negotiating. How do you get what you need for what you can afford? Can you compensate someone with something other than money? You might get free or cheap help by giving someone their "big break" to work on a part of filmmaking they haven't done in the past, such as moving a production assistant to a camera operator or assistant director job. To get a key location, you could put a location owner's family in a scene to lower the location fee; or you might offer to place a product in a movie in return for free use of that product (for example, showing and/or saying Rocco's Pizza in a movie in exchange for pizzas to feed the crew every day for a week). Let your creativity run wild—as long as you're not breaking the law.

One interesting example comes to mind. A producer we know needed to entice thousands of people to sit in a football stadium for 10 hours—and not get paid for it. Here's his solution: he found sponsors—big companies to donate their products, such as a TV or computer or stereo, to be given away hourly to the lucky folks sitting in the stands. He allowed the companies, in return, to place their banners around the stadium, which would be shown in the final movie; they considered it free advertising. Everyone benefited: the producer filled the stadium, the people in the stadium had incentive to stick around, and the sponsors providing the incentive got free advertising. You don't want to go overboard with the advertising thing, obviously, but you'll find such creative tactics can sometimes help make things happen in a crunch.

Directing

For your digital feature, you're probably working as both the director and the producer. This means that not only do you need to plan the scenes and make sure the locations and actors are ready when they need to be—producer stuff—but you also need to motivate the actors, choose the camcorder placement and angles (in conjunction with your director of photography, if you're that lucky), and make sure you get the sound and pictures that you'll later need in editing—director stuff.

Directing a feature demands much more than sitting in a special chair behind the camera, sipping a cappuccino, and bossing everyone around. As a director, you must know *why* you are bossing everyone around. You are the one person who has a creative vision for the entire project. You are the last word on the locations, actors, wardrobe, and every other element chosen for the project. You decide how to shoot a scene—the number of shots necessary to create the scene, what should be seen in the frame, how long each scene should last. And you are the primary communicator with the talent, relaying to them how a character needs to be portrayed, directing them on how to say their lines or how to express themselves.

Having said that, you should know that it's generally a huge mistake for a neophyte director to go into a new project with a huge ego. It's important here that we differentiate between confidence and determination, and just plain bluster. A director needs to be a good manager—ideally a "people person," although not all directors are. The director gives everyone involved in the project motivation and direction for their jobs. The best directors communicate his ideas clearly and in turn trust his crew to pull it off without him meddling too much.

Making a feature is a group effort, so appreciating your cohorts goes a long way. (And if you don't have much money, it's also a *volunteer* effort, and volunteers can be difficult to motivate when the going gets tough.) As the director, you must recognize that you are the coach for your team, and whatever you do will affect your teammates and their work, which in turn affects you and your vision. Recognition and gratitude go a long way, especially if no one is getting paid in cash.

Get the Shots

No matter how big or professional your production, the director's bottom line responsibility is to *get the shots needed for editing*. When you think of directing this way, managing all the other tasks—lighting, camcorder operation, location management, directing actors—falls into place. For each scene, you should know what shots you need, including what shots you can "get away with." One thing to realize is that you'll likely shoot the same scene at least three times, not accounting for times that you need to stop because of a mistake or flubbed line.

Here are some of the shot possibilities:

- **Wide or establishing shots**   Depending on the location, you may want to get a shot that sets up the scene, whether it's a wide angle shot of the park in which the next scene will take place or a closer establishing shot in the hallway as the policeman rounds that corner and knocks on the door.

- **Master shot**   The first time you tape a scene, you'll want to shoot a *master* shot—keep the camcorder out of the face of your actors while you get a shot of the entire scene (including the atmosphere and scenery) as it unfolds. This gives you a baseline for your film. When you edit, this will be your main shot, and then you'll layer the other shots over it to create more drama and tension.

- **Two-shot**   In this shot, you are closer to your actors than in the master, and you move with them (when necessary) through their actions. You'll see less background and scenery than in a master shot, but you'll see most of your actors, at least from waist up (depending on how you compose the shot).

- **Medium shot**   With this shot, you're using the camera to get footage from each actor's perspective, which you can later cut into your master to give that back-and-forth conversational look. (One type of medium shot is the "over-the-shoulder shot," where you look over one of your actor's shoulders at another actor.) Most likely, your medium shots are done in separate takes of the same scene— otherwise, the camera operators would be visible in the medium shot. If you've got two camcorders and you want to cheat this a little, you can have them operating at the same time, as shown in Figure 8.4.

On the CD-ROM   With over-the-shoulder shots and close-ups, you need to remember the "180-degree rule." As Figure 8.4 shows, you'll want to shoot from one side of the action only—if you later cut between two over-the-shoulder shots taken from different sides of the action, it will look odd to the audience. (See the Chapter 8 clips on the included CD for good and bad examples of this principle.)

FIGURE 8.4

Here's one way to get your medium (over-the-shoulder) shots more quickly.

- **Close-ups**   If you need to capture particularly emotional moments, you can use the same over-the-shoulder *placement* but go in closer (move the camcorder closer and/or zoom-in a bit) on your subject. Again, you will want to do this in another shot of the same scene— shooting all the action one more time—because changing the focal length of a camcorder in the middle of a scene is not recommended in fiction. You have the luxury of getting all your shots at one focal length and in rich focus, so if you want to do a close-up, it should be a different shot from your medium shot.

 *zoom-in* ──────────────────────────────

Feature films use less zooming than even TV fiction. On a movie screen, zooming in doesn't look the same as it does on TV—when projected, a shot that zooms in on a person tends to look more like a person's head is mysteriously growing bigger rather than fixing on their features in a dramatic way. To create drama, tension, or interest during a shot, film directors will more often dolly the camera (roll it using a special stabilization device and, often, tracks laid on the ground) closer or further away from the actor instead of using zoom.

- **Cutaways**   As with other types of productions, you'll want to get shots of the items that are being discussed—the plane, the bag of money, the diamond ring—if it's relevant to the scene. You'll likely shoot cutaways after the scene is acted, so that you can get close to the items with the camcorder and then edit in the footage later.

- **"Cat in the window" shot**   At every location, you should get a shot that indicates that something *else* could be happening at the location at the same time. A lot of people use animals for these shots—a reaction shot from a cat or dog, for instance. These shots are a last resort when you end up with *nothing* from the other shots that you can use or when there's a mistake in the camera operation or on the tape. The audience will forgive (and sometimes not even notice) if you cut away from your actors while they're discussing something and show a cat sitting in a window or other stationary objects in that room that are reasonably unique—even if you're doing it to cover up a problem.

Using some mix of the different shots outlined above is called getting "coverage" for your feature. You'll almost always want a master shot; you may also want a *reverse* master, which simply films the same scene from a different angle. (From the "downstage left" side of the shot instead of the "downstage right," for instance.) You'll also usually want at least two medium shots—or more if you have more than two actors in the scene. Beyond that, you can get as many shots as you have time and can afford—in budget filming, sometimes it's common to get just a master shot and some medium shots and then move on to the next scene.

This is the magic of feature film—using these different scenes you now have the building blocks for a true movie-style scene. With a feature film, you can *do a scene over* again and get different *takes* of the action. You can cut and splice from two different versions of the same scene. You can cut liberally between different types of shots—master, medium, close-up—if it helps tell your story. Indeed, you *will* need to make these cuts frequently, depending on the style you're trying to use.

If you watch even a few minutes of fiction on television or a movie, you'll see what we mean; nearly all fiction projects will use a variety of shots within the same scene and—if they're any good at all—you don't see any camera equipment in the shot. That means those scenes needed to be shot a number of times—with actors repeating the same lines and gestures—to get all those angles. If you don't take a number of shots of the same scene, you won't be able to use them when you're editing later.

Get Good Sound

As a director, you're also responsible for getting good—even *great*—sound. Without that, you don't have a feature. You need to use good microphones and skilled boom operators, and you need to test constantly on the set to make sure you're getting the sound you need. See Chapter 10 for more on sound-gathering techniques and equipment for your production.

Direct on the Set

You know all the clichés about directors yelling all the time? They're true; as a director, you'll find yourself shouting out directions to your actors and crew. Along with yelling, you need to meet with your actors and crew to discuss what you mean when you yell at them. In particular, get everyone to think about taking it slowly, take their time to begin after hearing "Action!," and remember to hold their places until they hear "Cut!" Taking a few extra seconds throughout the entire process can be helpful to everyone.

It's not always the director who yells on the set—often it's an assistant director—but on your set, you'll find use for the following:

- *Okay... can I have quiet on the set, please!* Not only do you need quiet when you're getting ready to shoot, but shouting this signals to the whole crew and acting team that you're getting ready to roll tape.

- *Roll camera!* You can call out "lights!" and "speed!," but you tend to know whether or not those things are working before you've gotten to this point. "Roll camera!" in this context is a command to your camera operator to start recording. You always want to start recording before the action takes place so that you can confirm that the camcorder is working and so that you can get an *edit handle*—some tape rolling before the action begins that gives you some working room in the editing phase.

 *zoom-in* ————————————————————

On a film set there's another step you usually won't have in digital filming. "Speed!" is called by the sound recordist when the tape (or other recording device) has gotten up to recording speed. That indicates to the assistant director that they can call "Roll Camera!" (then the camera operator responds with "Rolling!") followed by "Mark!" or "Slate!" and then "Action!" If you're not recording audio to your camcorder, you may want to have your sound recordist call "Speed!" as well.

- *Slate!* Put up something in front of the camcorder that indicates what scene and take this is—you'll need to know this later when you're reviewing the tape to find and note the best scenes.

- *Action!* It's probably best on a DV-based production to use your finger to point to your actors when you're ready for them to begin, instead of shouting it out, just in case they start the scene quickly after the command. "Action!" means "start the acting" and, if appropriate, "start the camera motion."

- *Cut!* You know why you yell this, but you may not know when to yell. You should always wait a few seconds after the action in a scene is over—and allow your actors to continue with their action for at least a second or two—before calling "Cut!" Otherwise, you'll be tempted sometimes, in your excitement, to cut a good scene short. If you don't end up with enough of an *out handle* on that scene, it'll be more difficult to edit.

focus

Another issue that professional directors deal with is whether or not to rehearse scenes before filming—some directors and actors believe their performances are more spontaneous and realistic without rehearsal. At the level we're talking about, though, we recommend rehearsing with both the actors and the crew. The shoot will go much more smoothly if you walk through a scene a few times before putting it on tape, so that everyone knows where to stand and move. That said, tape is relatively cheap, so don't be afraid to record a few takes—or even rehearsals—to see which ends up the best or to test different ideas.

Working with Actors

Finding the best actor for a role is essential and challenging. Unless you're doing slapstick comedy, if your characters are not believable, you don't have a movie.

As an amateur, it might be easy to delegate acting roles to your friends and family, and that might work if you've written roles specifically for their personalities so that they can basically play themselves. If that's not the case, though, start rethinking your situation. Just because your friends are outgoing doesn't mean that they will be able to act. In fact, sometimes people who are easy-going in real life are stiff on camera.

Community theaters, colleges, and drama programs in high schools are great places to search for actors. People who desire to act are hungry for opportunity and will jump at the chance to practice their craft and show off their skills.

Hopefully, once you've put the word out that you're looking for actors, you will attract several people to audition for each role. Assessing their abilities is more complicated than having them read a few lines. You want to make sure they look right for the part, but also that they sound appropriate, understand the character, take direction, and that you feel comfortable working with them.

Following are some tips on auditioning.

- Note your first impression. Does the actor fit your vision of the character in your feature? Your first impression is important to, at least, jot down.

- Give each actor a portion of the script to read out loud. Then ask her to modify the way she delivers the lines, even if you think what she did was great. This will allow you to see her willingness to take direction.

- Always give actors positive reinforcement. For example, "That was great—I think you nailed it. Can we try it again, but this time…" There is no point in deflating an actor's ego when he's acting, because you need him to be able to keep control of his emotions.

- Have the actors audition individually and with others to assess their ability to work on the spot as well as with other actors.

- Many actors will come to an audition prepared with a piece to recite or perform. Keep in mind that it may have taken the actor years to perfect that performance, and you may need her to perform your material within a week of first reading it. If you get someone who has a good prepared piece, ask her to read a scene from your movie as well. Cut her some slack and help her get a sense of the character and motivations, but also note how she copes with unfamiliar material.

- Consider asking your auditioning actors to improvise a performance based on a given situation to see how well they can adapt to new situations and what their *range* is. (Consider that an actor like the late John Wayne is effective in certain roles but has less range than Dustin Hoffman, who can fall into nearly any role. Having a Wayne-like actor isn't bad—just make sure he's playing a Wayne-type part.) Throw out a scenario and have the actor act the part. For example, you might have him pretend to be at a dinner party. The host brings out a dish he's been slaving over all day, but it tastes like a dirty sock. How will the actor handle the situation without upsetting the host?

- Can you afford the actor? Does her schedule work? Is she willing to sign a release so that you can use her in your movie without getting sued for profits down the road?

Oops—here's another reason to call an attorney. If you're signing up actors to act in your movie, you need something official for them to sign, even if you're paying them only in copies of the final video. It would be crazy to spend months or years putting together a movie that gets blocked by an actor down the road because you didn't have a contract with him that gives you the rights to use his work in your project. If you have a budget, consider hiring a professional casting director (or get help from someone who has done it in the past) who can provide the appropriate talent releases for legal work, assist with scheduling, as well as manage actors.

After you've hired actors—even if they aren't paid—it is your responsibility, as the director, to help them understand their respective characters and what *motivates* those characters. Yes, it sounds like a tired old cliché that actors need to know their characters' "motivation"—but it's a necessity. In the real world, people have motivation for nearly everything they do. You, for example, might be reading this book because you're motivated to improve your knowledge of video production. We might be writing this at 2 A.M. because we need to get it done before another deadline slips by and our publisher gets upset with us. Those are both real motivations—the type that would inform our characters.

Consider the actor's point of view—you're the actor, and you've just read the script for a scene that comes toward the end of the movie, but the scene needs to be shot *first* because a location is available. The scene: you've just shot and killed your best friend. How do you feel about that? It depends on your motivation. If you're playing a psychopath, you might feel pleased with yourself; if you're an angry person and your friend was cheating with your spouse, you might feel vindicated; if he was coming at you with the gun and you turned it on him, you might feel shocked and confused or triumphant but exhausted. It all depends on motivation.

As a director, it's helpful for the entire cast if you arrange a reading of the script as soon as possible and then discuss the characters and how they relate to one another within the story. This will help you and the actors see where the script might need to be changed or if an actor is not right for a role. Changes will certainly be made as the process continues, but it is best to recognize big changes before everyone is immersed in rehearsals.

Rehearsals should begin as soon as the script is finalized. If possible, conduct rehearsals at the actual shooting locations (or similar locations), because location will affect the actors' performances. For example, if your actors are practicing for weeks in a small room for a scene that will be shot in a huge warehouse, it might be disconcerting for them if their first encounter with the vast location—not to mention the echo—occurs on the day of shooting.

Furthermore, if a scene calls for a couch, make something in your rehearsal room represent the couch. The actors will need to be able to decide how they will move according to where the furniture and other props will be placed—a process called *blocking*, which means mapping out the movements of each actor in a scene. When shooting, it may be essential for the actors to start and stop at specific points—so that they stay inside the lit area or stay within the camera view. Those locations can be marked with tape or chalk on the ground (avoid shooting those markers with your camcorders, though!), but they should also be second nature to the actor.

focus

Learning movie dialogue is different from learning dialogue for a stage play, so don't expect your actors to memorize every line; knowing a scene's worth of lines at a time is enough, as long as they understand their characters. Also, be sure that you give your actors the freedom to interpret their roles before you offer suggestions. Sometimes actors are best able to express emotions through how they move. For example, they may roll their eyes, smack their gum, play with their hair, or breathe more deeply, to emphasize an emotion or feeling. If you are not satisfied with the performance, try not to be too critical, as that can be discouraging. Try describing the character or emotion in a different manner using analogies ("like he's a stockbroker who just lost a million bucks" or "like he's lost in the big city his first time visiting") and ask the actor to try variations. The director should be encouraging to everyone on the set while offering constructive criticism to maintain the vision of the project.

Techniques for Digital Features

Movies shot on digital video will not look like the 35mm movies you see at your local Cineplex. However, DV technology is getting better every day, and how we manipulate it is improving. Professionals and amateurs alike are utilizing DV for their projects because of its cost effectiveness and flexibility in use. The folks with a film background are applying their technical voodoo and know-how to their filmmaking on DV, creating a much more professional product. In this section, we'll share some of their simple secrets.

The major differences between film and video are:

- Film has more visible grain that randomly arranges itself, creating a softness to the image.
- Film has a higher resolution but shallower depth of field.

- Film plays back at 24 frames per second (fps) while NTSC video (National Television Standards Committee—the North American standard) plays back at 30 fps.

In overly simplistic terms, film sees the world a little more like your eyes see the world. People perceive film differently than video—it's slower, bigger, even more *significant*—when they're watching it unfold. Some people call film "romantic" or compare it to fine art. Making video look more like film takes some tricks, including adjustments to lighting, depth of field, shutter speed, color balance, and sharpness. And you can also add to the look by using film-like camera styles, as we'll discuss in the following section.

Lighting

Proper lighting can make your video look more like film. If you've been on a movie set, you already know that one of the most boring times during a shoot is in between shots when the crew resets lights. Film crews spend an enormous amount of time on lighting. Too often, video crews don't do this, but they should. Most people who shoot video either never set up a light or they set up every light they have and over-illuminate the subject.

Read over the discussion of three-point lighting in Chapter 5. For a feature, you'll need to consider the way your lights play on more than one person at a time (at least in some scenes) as well as how lights affect and define the entire set. You'll likely need to pull back your lights to the edge of the set and, at times, compromise on the three-point system (using just a key light and fill light, for instance), particularly for master shots. Then, when you go in for a medium or close-up shot, you'll want to change the lighting again and then get the shot—if you have time and your actors and crew have the patience.

focus ───

Think in particular about backlighting in your feature project—a backlight can help to define your actors against the background, add some subtle definition to their hair and shoulders, and make the video more pleasant to look at. See Chapter 5 for more on backlighting.

You may not have considered that light sources can have different *colors*—at least, maybe you haven't thought about it since high school science class. But your camcorder will definitely pick up the various light colors. For example, typical office fluorescent lights have a green tint.

Lights in your house have a warm color in the orange range, and outdoor light is slightly blue. Film cameras use particular types of film stock to compensate for the color differences. While our eyes and brain can compensate for some odd color casts to white light, camcorders are a bit stupid when it comes to color balance.

That's what *white balance* is for—you tell the camcorder what color, given the current lighting conditions, it should consider as white. (Even if the light is tinted a particular color, when you hold up a piece of paper in that light and white balance to that, the camcorder can correct for the color cast by the lighting.) You should white balance every time you change the lighting or location. If you're not paying attention to lighting while you shoot, your video could look blue, red, or green tinted, unless the white balance is set often or set automatically. (And note that automatic white balance can have its own problems, particularly if a dramatic or sudden change in light occurs, such as a door to the outside opening into the room in which you're filming.)

 *zoom-in* _____

You can also change the color of your shots when editing special effects, so while it's important that you white balance often, if you forget once or twice you may still be able to save the shot using your editing software.

The white balance feature on your camcorder also has the makings of a cool trick—you can use it to fool your camcorder into seeing colors in a slightly different way. For example, without any fancy filters or post-production tricks, you can "warm up" your shot with a rosy quality by white balancing on something that is slightly blue. When you white balance to light blue, it throws the entire spectrum that the camcorder sees closer to the color red to "balance" out the colors. That can warm up skin tones and light, turning a pale shot into something that looks a little more robust.

You can also go in the opposite direction. Instead of white balancing on a white object, you can white balance on a surface that is slightly pink (card stock, a bed sheet, a piece of paper). Your camcorder will see pink and dutifully register it as "white" so it will move its color balance closer to blue, which leaves you with a "cooler" image. (Your camcorder may also have an internal white balance that can be altered as well, creating a further shift in color.) Adjusting the color saturation will also have a dramatic effect on the image, and it's worth experimenting with—you'll find that it's a nice trick to enhance the shots that you're getting.

Depth of Field

Video has a tremendous depth of field—everything stays in focus, causing a flat image. This is particularly true if you are shooting with a wide angle. Film, by contrast, has a shallow depth of field, which means that items at various distances from the camcorder will appear in various levels of focus. The fact is, your eyes work a bit more like that, so video can sometimes look unnaturally "flat" on the television screen or when projected. With that in mind, the following approaches can help you change the depth of field:

- To narrow the depth of field (which is what many videographers try to do to make their video look more filmic), start working with your camcorder's manual settings. For instance, a larger aperture (which translates to smaller f-stop numbers, such as f/2.8) will narrow the depth of field, causing the background to blur. However, by using a larger aperture setting, you're adding to the amount of light that's entering the lens. If your shutter speed is set manually, you'll need to increase its speed to compensate, noting that a faster shutter can make for slightly more stuttered action.

- The less light you use, the more narrow the depth of field. (Of course, with less light, the shot is…uh…less lit!) One trick is to light the set as you normally would and then use a neutral density (ND) filter on your lens (some camcorders have an ND filter built in) to diminish the amount of light entering the lens, which will in turn reduce your depth of field. At the same time, the shot will still have some contrast that it might not have if you simply under-light the scene.

- An extremely simple solution to minimize the depth of field is to shoot with a longer focal length—that is, shoot with the camcorder zoomed in somewhat. The easiest way to accomplish that is to move your camcorder farther away from your subject and then zoom-in to your desired shot size—medium or close-up.

Shutter and Frame Rate

A major difference between the way film and video looks is due to shutter speed and frame rate. Film has a natural "blur," as it is normally shot at 24 fps, whereas video has smooth movement, being captured at 30 fps. You can set your camcorder on *frame* or *film* mode, which simulates 24 fps. However, you'll want to know your camcorder well before you invest in such shots, as some models will toss too much digital information in a frame mode because it no longer shoots every *field* of video. (While video is 30 fps, it's also 60 *fields* per second, or two fields per frame.) When you lose every other field, you lose image quality.

focus _____

A typical NTSC television image is interlaced, which means that it's actually updated in two different steps, called fields, with alternating lines of video being updated separately. Each field of video, then, actually represents half of the lines of an entire frame of that video, but each field is updated before you move to the next frame. The fields update 60 times per second—which corresponds to 60 hertz.

A better solution would be to use a camcorder that has as a true *progressive scan* frame mode, which means the camcorder can capture an entire frame of data—two fields—at a decreased frame rate, with the resulting image looking a little more like film.

A third option is to shoot in the European standard, called PAL (Phase Alternating Line), which has 100 more lines of resolution than the NTSC standard, shoots at 25 fps, and has a normal shutter speed of 1/50 of a second. You should consider several negative factors when shooting PAL in North America, however, such as acquiring a PAL camcorder, using it with software, and then being able to output that footage to NTSC equipment if necessary; this would take a conversion from PAL to NTSC, which could prove to be something you need to outsource at a high price.

A similar issue is shutter speed. If the shutter speed on your camcorder is set to automatic, it will compensate for slow or fast movements, decreasing the amount of blur in your image. By contrast, film tends to blur when you move the camera or move quickly past the camera lens—viewers are used to seeing and relating to that blur, as our eyes blur a bit when we spin around, too. One solution for that is to "go manual" and choose as low a shutter speed as your camcorder will allow—recognizing that it may then allow in a lot of light, which will need to be compensated for using a narrower aperture and/or an ND filter. It is all something of a balancing act!

Sharpness

Video looks sharp. The outline of objects and visible lines appear to have hard, straight edges on video because the pixels on the charged coupled device (CCD) and monitor are aligned in a grid. On film, by contrast, the grains are randomly arranged on the emulsion, which creates a softer, more natural look. As discussed earlier, manipulating lighting, the depth of field, and shutter speed can be used to reduce sharpness, but you should also check your camcorder for a sharpness setting. Turn down the sharpness value if you have that option.

If you'd rather have more control of what your camcorder sees, consider using *diffusion* filters of some sort on the lens of your camcorder. These filters can be used to make things look blurry—and it has been common practice in the past to use slightly softer diffusion filters on leading ladies than on their male counterparts, to make lines on their faces look as smooth as possible. (Check out films with Audrey Hepburn—she was often shot with a "soft" lens.) You can emulate that same thing with a diffusion filter or get a slightly different filmic look with a center-spot diffusion filter, which makes your shot sharp in the middle but blurrier toward the edges.

Of course, you can always decide to add some film-like grain and softness using your computer and effects software. A number of tools and settings in editing and post-production software can manipulate color and sharpness, saturation and grain, as well as make your video footage look more like film. We'll look at some of those options in Chapter 11.

One good thing about shooting without using filters or Frame mode is that you end up with a clean, unmanipulated image that serves as your baseline—and, if you need to, you can go back to your tape and pull that image again for editing. If you have changed camcorder settings and put filters on the lens, you've got a little more to think about, and if the shot doesn't work out, you may have to go back through the entire process again. In other words, there's some risk to being a little too worried about "filmic" results—particularly if it somehow takes focus away from getting good lighting, good sound, and good work from your actors.

Style

One last thing to consider when trying to make your video feature look like film is to add a little camerawork and to develop a shooting style. Many times, videographers—particularly those accustomed to shooting weddings and organization videos—bypass style and shoot in an extremely utilitarian manner. That's a serviceable way to do it, but it's important to recognize that on a professional feature film set, a lot of movement is done with the camcorder to make the shots look more interesting. Those movements are often smooth, well planned, and well timed. If you have a jib available for smooth movement, work with it to its best advantage. If you've got a steadying monopod, try adding some movement to your shots to see how they're able to build drama or heighten tension.

Our best advice for developing a style is to watch movies and television to see what stylistic cues you can grab from the pros. Then, play with those options a little bit, including using odd camera tilts (shoot up to make someone seem bigger and powerful or down to make him look smaller and weak), camera angles or shaking (for earthquakes and crashing space ships), and interesting camera placement. Watch movies and notice how often a foreground object interrupts a camera movement.

For example, the camcorder moves down the sidewalk following little Timmy on his skateboard until suddenly the view is obscured by a mailbox; when you come around the mailbox, you see Timmy running into his house for dinner with the skateboard on the sidewalk. You move in on the skateboard and see a special drawing he made on the bottom of it. These movements and choices may go a long way toward helping your feature look and feel more like a film, even if you don't worry over the other technical tips.

Finally, watch films that appeal to you and pay close attention to how many shots are used in a single scene—over-the-shoulder shots, master shots, close-ups, and cutaway shots. You'll see all of them used in the space of a few seconds. When you have time to shoot them during your own filming, you can play with them in the editing phase. (When you don't have time and you're running over budget, follow the filmmaker's three-take mantra: *Get a master shot, two medium shots, and then get out.*)

Post-Production and Editing

For most character-driven films, you likely won't need to do an extreme amount of special effects work. In fact, we recommend that you remove all car chases, burning buildings, gun fights, and flying scenes from your first film; save them for your second or third film, when a major studio decides to let you spread your budgetary wings and branch out into action. In your first feature, you need to focus on people talking to one another, yelling, screaming, laughing, kissing, and, occasionally, throwing stuff.

You probably won't spend too much time with your special effects software—at least, not until you're ready to use some of those enhancement filters to make your video look more like film. You will, however, spend a good deal of time in your editing software, putting together each scene from the variety of angles that you shot during the production cycle. In fact, if any one word can be used for a feature editor, it's *patience.* You're going to need patience as you sit through a lot of footage.

Watch and Log

Before you do anything else, watch the footage and log the tapes—you need to locate the takes that have the fewest mistakes and make a note of them. Look for the following:

- Which was the best master shot?
- Which are the best medium shots?
- What close-ups, if any, should we use?
- Which shot had the best sound associated with it?

This can take days, depending on the length of your project, but it's absolutely a necessary step—you simply won't have a computer with enough storage space to pull in anything but the best takes and the best angles for use in your editing. You should also compare what you've got against the scene list and make sure that everything that needed to be covered actually got shot. Otherwise, you may need to rewrite or head out and try to get those scenes filmed somehow.

Create the First Cut

The next step is to put together something you can watch. That's called the *first cut*, and it's a collection of your master scenes in the order in which they're scripted. All of these will be relatively uninteresting to watch, because they'll all be taken from one camera angle and probably won't have the best sound. Still, it should take you only a few days to put that cut together, and it will allow you to evaluate the story. You'll know if the film is working, if the writing translated well to the screen, and whether the production was, overall, a success. After seeing the first cut, you may decide to move scenes around, add or delete scenes, cut an actor altogether, or ask someone for more money to continue shooting. It's a turning point for your feature, because it's a moment when you need to decide how to go forward.

Create a Rough Cut

After that, assuming you haven't given up, you'll put together a *rough cut*. Go for good sound, and do your best to use your other angles (medium and close-up shots) to add some variety and interest to the scenes. This can also take a while, but it's useful in letting you know which scenes have enough material to stay in the movie, which might need some help with audio post-production, and which you might need to let go completely.

Work with Sound

From the rough cut (or after multiple rough cuts, depending on how much your story has to change), you'll generally move to a *sound edit*. You need to go through the film and make sure all of the sound synchronizes to what the actors are saying and that the sound is good and even throughout. Using your software, you can change sound levels and perform various sound-effects tasks, as necessary.

At this stage, you can also do some *foley* work (recording footsteps, leaves rustling, and other such sound effects) that you can drop in to make each scene a bit more realistic and vivid. Also, if you must, you can get your actors back in to do some additional recording—speaking the lines while they watch themselves in the final scene so that you can get the best dialogue sound.

For a small production, it's ideal to get your sound "in the field," but if the dialogue can't be heard or understood, you should supplement it by recording your actors reading through their lines again and then *dubbing* it in. You'll have your actors re-record their dialogue so that you can get it recorded crisply and richly in a studio setting. You can then fill in those recordings as needed. (Ain't fiction cool?)

focus

Recording dialogue in a studio can require using an engineer who knows audio, particularly if the sound of the voices is meant to match the environment in which the original scene was filmed. In other words, it's a good idea to avoid doing overdubs in a low-budget production. Still, for some indoor scenes or for minimal problem solving, re-recording dialogue can be a helpful fix.

Create the Final Cut

Finally, months and months later, you'll be building toward your *final cut*. It will include master shots, over-the-shoulder shots, close-ups, cutaways, and, perhaps, some cats in windows. It'll also have sound edits, foley work, and dubbed dialogue (in some cases). Now you're ready to add transitions and effects. You can read more about them in Chapters 9 and 11, but let us state here, for the record—your film probably doesn't need many transitions at all and few effects other than fixing color problems, a few fades and dissolves, and perhaps running it through some of the filters that make video look a little more like film.

For your transitions, realize that audiences are accustomed to seeing straight cuts between scenes in movies. In fact, a jarring example of the overuse of wipes is the movie *Star Wars*, although that technique was used for a reason (to tie *Star Wars* visually to the older, cheesier science fiction to which it paid homage, particularly serials earlier in the century).

You can open segments of your film with a fade-in, particularly if it's meant to suggest that time has passed since the previous segment. You can use a fade-out to suggest that a segment is coming to an end, while allowing the audience to savor their last emotion for the scene. And you can use a dissolve transition to suggest the passage of time within a sequence, usually when you need to montage various shots to give some *exposition* (background information) for a character. Other than that, you'll find that the transitions aren't nearly as important in features as they are in video for television or projects such as music videos.

And...Cut!

In this chapter, we took a whirlwind tour of the world of feature filmmaking, DV-style. DV technology makes it possible to create movies on video that can be easily edited and spruced up; and, with some luck, talent, and planning, perhaps one day they can see the light of a theatrical release, a film festival opening, or distribution over cable TV or DVD technologies. If you've got an idea, months of free time, and the need to follow through on a dream, it can be done!

Basic Editing Techniques

IN previous chapters, you've seen some of the planning, forethought, and execution—the *production*—required to create video projects. In this chapter, we focus on some of the basic editing techniques you can use in nonlinear editing systems such as iMovie, Adobe Premiere, and Final Cut. We also take a look at some of the basics of editing and why technique is important.

Editing is based on one general theory—simplicity almost always wins the day. As you approach video editing, particularly if you're editing seriously for the first time, consider that most of the television programs and movies that you watch may involve complicated camera work, but they often have fairly straightforward editing techniques—cuts, fades, and transitions—applied to them. That said, the editing process is an integral part of creating a coherent video—the decisions you make in your editing sessions are of fundamental importance, even more so than the whiz-bang tools you may have at your disposal.

Knowing something about editing is an important foundation for producing your projects, because you'll need to get the important material recorded successfully before you can edit it. If you don't get the footage you need for your wedding, event, training, or feature video, it won't be available to edit. In this chapter, we include some discussion on the theory behind planning, shooting, and editing footage for the various projects described in this book.

After you have shot footage with your camcorder, you'll need to turn to your software for the next stage of production. Most digital video (DV) editing software works in four stages—capturing footage, editing that footage, adding effects, and outputting the edited movie. We discuss the first two stages in some detail and touch on the third, although both special effects and outputting video are featured in their own chapters (Chapters 11 and 12, respectively).

focus ———————————————————————————————————————

We feature several software applications in this chapter to demonstrate the basics of nonlinear editing. If you need more experience with your particular application, you'll find that nearly all editing packages include online help and tutorials that help get you started, and we recommend that you read the software manual to see how its features correspond to the basics discussed here. (And feel free to ask questions on our web site if you run into a particular problem you can't solve—www.digitalvideoideas.com.)

Capturing Footage

Capturing refers to the transfer of image data from your camcorder or storage disk into your computer's image-editing software. Most nonlinear editing (NLE) applications offer both manually controlled and automatic methods for capturing images. With the manual method, you move to the beginning of a clip that you want to capture, initiate the Capture (or Record) command, and then allow that clip to be captured until you turn off the command. You could capture an entire project this way, and, while it might be time-consuming, it would be effective.

Using automatic methods can be either simpler or more complicated. The simpler automatic method is used by Apple's iMovie—it imports up to an entire tape of video footage and will attempt to break up that footage into clips based on your scene changes. (It does that, for the most part, by creating a new clip every time the camcorder was put on Pause while recording or at every point at which the camcorder was turned off.)

More complicated automatic modes are designed to accommodate a more professional editing approach—that is, you first catalog the video, either in the software or by creating a special file called an Edit Decision List (EDL). After creating an EDL, you can feed it to the software, which, if it's sophisticated enough (as is Adobe Premiere or Final Cut Pro), can use that EDL to run through the tape and import only the relevant clips into the software.

Manual Capture

Manually capturing video is a straightforward process—most software packages offer a Capture command that brings up a set of controls that are meant to mimic the controls on a typical VCR. You use those controls to play the recording and capture footage directly from the camcorder to the computer.

iMovie

With iMovie, the manual method is a standard way of getting video into your computer, as iMovie doesn't work with EDLs or other cataloging approaches. Instead, using the "automatic" mode for iMovie means that scenes are automatically cut into clips as the video is captured.

Here's how to capture video in iMovie:

1. Ensure that your camcorder is connected to your computer, and then click to move the small Camera Mode slider to point to the camera icon instead of the scissors icon, as shown here:

2. Use the controls to move to the portion of your video that you want to capture—you'll notice that the controls are VCR-like. Use the Fast Forward and Rewind buttons to move to a particular portion of the video, and click the Play button to play back the video.

3. When you're ready to import a clip, click the Import button. iMovie will capture the video into a clip. When you click the Import button again, the capture process will end and the clip will be placed on the Clips pane along with any other clips you've captured. (Note that if your video reaches a scene break—where the camcorder was turned off and on or put on Pause—a new clip may be created automatically.)

4. Continue this process for as many clips as you want to capture from your recorded footage.

Final Cut

To capture footage in Final Cut, first choose File | Capture to open the Capture window (Figure 9.1), which you can use to capture clips manually or to log your clips and bring them in automatically.

FIGURE 9.1

The Final Cut Capture window is used for both manual and automatic capturing.

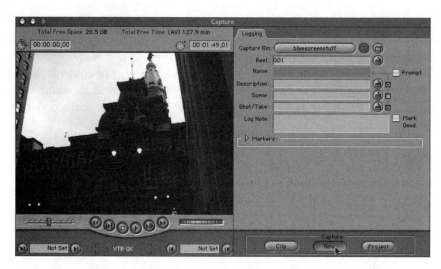

Here's how to capture manually:

1. In the Capture window, use the VCR-like controls to move to the portion of the clip that you want to capture.

2. Click Play to play the clip.

3. Click the Now button in the Capture section of the window (in the lower-right corner) when you arrive at the part of the clip that you want to capture. This will start the capture process.

4. A large window appears. Watch as the clip is captured. When you reach the end of the clip you're capturing, press the ESC key on your keyboard.

5. Back in the Capture window, you can begin the process again for the next clip.

Each clip that you capture in this way will appear in the current project's tabbed window in the Browser window interface, where it is named Untitled and numbered, as in *Untitled 0003, Untitled 0004,* and so on. You can change the name of the capture in the Browser window by clicking the name to select it and then clicking again (after a pause) to activate it for editing. Then simply type in the new name.

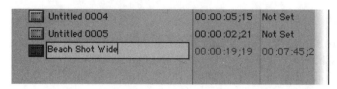

You can also choose to capture your clips to a *bin*, which is a folder to hold clips for your project. To create a bin:

1. Select your project in the Browser window.

2. Choose File | New | Bin.

3. Type in a name for the bin.

4. To set that bin as the capture bin, CONTROL-click or right-click the bin's name, and then choose Set Capture Bin from the menu. A new icon appears, showing that the bin has been selected for capture. As shown in the following illustration, bins are indicated in the Browser window by small folder icons.

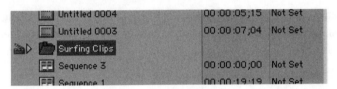

Adobe Premiere

Here's how to capture footage in Premiere:

1. Open your project (if appropriate), and choose File | Capture | Movie Capture.

2. In the Movie Capture window, use the VCR-like controls to move to the beginning of a clip that you want to capture.

3. Click the Play button. With the clip playing, click the small Record button (it's the red circle below the other VCR-like symbols.) The capture continues until you press the ESC key.

Automatic Capture

Manual capture is a hit-or-miss approach, a fact you'll definitely notice if you try it a few times. As you attempt to click or press the capture key at the correct second, you'll invariably overshoot and miss the first part of the clip, or you'll let the clip run a little longer than you wanted before toggling it off (which, of course, is less of a problem). Even if you don't keep the video running and, instead, fast forward to a clip, capture it, and then move to the next one, you'll find that manual capturing is a tedious process that can take a great deal of time to complete.

One solution is to use the professional approach: before capturing, *log* the tape—a manual process of viewing it on a monitor and jotting down the timecodes of your clips. You can then use those times to generate an EDL that your software can use to perform a *batch capture*—capturing only those clips that you've specified. *Batch capturing* uses an automated series of commands that are processed in sequence to capture several clips at once.

 zoom-in ─────────────────────────────

The process of creating a log is called cataloging your tapes, which means watching them to note their contents and taking note of the in times and out times of the best clips. It's a step most professionals take regardless of the type of project, from event video to feature production.

focus ──────────────────────────────────────

iMovie doesn't offer a batch capture feature; instead, it creates individual clips whenever it detects a new scene. After you rewind your tape to the point at which you'd like to start capturing, you begin the capture process and let iMovie continue until you've captured all the footage you want. iMovie will create multiple clips from the various scenes that it detects as it captures. (If it doesn't do that, you'll need to turn on the Automatically Start New Clip At Scene Break preference setting in iMovie's Preferences window. Choose iMovie | Preferences and look under the Import options.) Note that Final Cut Express's Capture Now feature also works in this way, splitting clips automatically at scene changes.

Another professional approach is to watch the footage in your video editing software window and set *in* and *out* points for each individual clip of footage you want to capture. How you do this depends on the software you're using. It's a good way to set your software to capture clips at the same time that you're cataloging your video footage. Doing these tasks simultaneously might require that you spend a great deal of time at your computer, but it's ultimately more efficient than cataloging and then creating your EDL in two steps.

You can then rewind to the beginning and have the software automatically run through the footage and batch capture the clips that you've defined in the logging process by reading the *in* and *out* points you set.

Final Cut

In Final Cut Pro, you set up your batch captures in the Capture window by specifying the *in* and *out* points that you want to capture. (In Final Cut Express, you can't set up batch captures, but you can log a tape by importing individual clips.) Here's how it works:

1. Open the Capture window by choosing File | Capture or File | Log And Capture.

2. You'll be using the logging tools this time. Type in a number for the Reel that will correspond to this tape. (If it's the first tape you're working with, making it **reel 001** is fine; subsequent tapes should have higher numbers, of course.) Also, give the clip a name and a description, if desired.

3. Click the disclosure triangle to reveal the Markers.

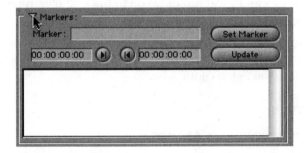

4. Start the video by clicking the Play button.

5. As you reach the beginning of a clip, click the button next to the In marker (the one with the right-facing arrow head, as shown next).

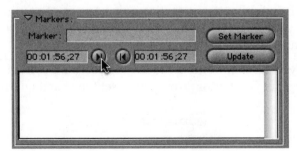

6. Continue clicking that button if you're not yet at the clip—remember that it's a good idea to include a little extra footage before the good stuff starts.

7. Watch the video until you reach the end of the clip, and then click the Out marker button (the left-facing arrow head).

8. If you're happy with the In and Out times, click the Log Clip button in Final Cut Pro or click the Set Marker button in Final Cut Express. Now things diverge somewhat, depending on the version you're using:

- In Final Cut Pro, you'll see a dialog box that enables you to name the clip and mark it as Good. Do so, and then you'll be returned to the Capture window to repeat the steps and add more clips. When you're done logging all your clips, click the Batch button to bring them all in at once.

- In Final Cut Express, click the Clip button in the Capture portion of the window and you'll see a dialog box asking for the name of the clip and enabling you to mark it as Good. Do so, and then the application will immediately begin capturing the clip. After that clip is captured, you can move on to the next clip, repeating the earlier steps.

The Pro edition of Final Cut offers the batch capability, which is one reason Apple uses to justify its higher cost. With the cheaper Express version, you lose the batch capture feature.

Adobe Premiere

Using Premiere, the process is similar:

1. In the Movie Capture window, click the Logging tab on the right side of the window. Name the "reel" (the tape) that you're currently logging.

2. View the movie using the VCR-like controls. When you reach the beginning of a clip you want to log, click Set In. (Note that as you watch, you can click Set In again if you need to start closer to the beginning of the clip.)

3. When you get to the end of the footage you want to use for this clip, click the Set Out button. Now you've set the in and out timecodes.

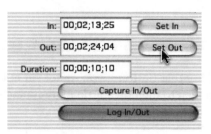

4. Click the Log In/Out button. You'll be asked to name the clip. That clip is then logged and added to the Batch Capture window, where it's ready to be captured at a future time.

How do you later capture that video? In the Batch Capture window, you'll find a list of the clips that you have logged. Make sure your camcorder is connected, and that the appropriate tape is in it, and then click the Record button in the Batch Capture window. That should start your camcorder rolling (rewinding or fast forwarding if necessary) so that it can move through the tape and capture the clips that you've specified.

Timelines

After you have captured the footage from your camcorder to your computer, you're ready to begin editing. (You may need to save the project,

---

Timecode Heads Up

One of the key issues when it comes to dealing with EDLs or even simpler batch captures is timecode, which is generally used with video tape (or other media) to differentiate one frame from another. Timecode uses the format 00:00:00:00, which corresponds to hours: minutes:seconds:frames. Note that the last entry, frames, will be based on the number of frames per second (fps) that were recorded for your video—by default with NTSC video, that's 30 fps; with PAL, it's 25 fps; and with many DV camcorders you can select from other rates.

Timecode can sometimes be broken, and that can spell trouble for any sort of automated batch capture. This often happens when you're shooting several scenes on a single tape. As long as you're recording completely in sequence, using no fast forwards over unrecorded tape, you probably won't break timecode, even if you turn the camcorder on and off between takes. If, however, for some reason you fast forward into portions of a brand new tape and then start recording again, you'll break the timecode. As the camcorder begins recording over that new tape snow, it'll assume that it's at the beginning of the tape and start the count over again. The result is a tape with two or more instances of 00:00:00:00, each followed by a sequential numbering sequence based on elapsed time. That makes it difficult to catalog the tape's contents and impossible to effectively use an NLE's batch capture mode.

To avoid broken timecode, either don't fast forward while you're getting your footage, or blackstripe your tape. Blackstriping is easy and a more foolproof method:

Place the tape in your camcorder, and, with the lens cap on your camcorder and the audio inputs disabled, record nothing onto the tape for its entire duration. Then rewind the camcorder all the way to the beginning, and you're ready to start taping. If you later search around on the tape using fast forward or rewind, you'll still get unbroken timecode, because the timecode has already been written once in a perfect sequence for the duration of that tape.

name it, or work a little other organizational magic before you move on to editing. You may also need to switch out of the capture mode and move into an editing or timeline mode, depending on the software you're using.) You're ready to begin placing the clips of footage in the rough sequence (the *rough cut*) that you'd like to use. Using the editing packages discussed in this chapter, you'll do that by dragging your clips from a bin or other designated storage location onto a *timeline* (see Figure 9-2).

A timeline is an interface element that shows the progress of your video over time, with the audio and video of your presentation divided into different *tracks*. Each track can represent a portion of the project—two audio tracks are often used to represent the left and right of stereo audio, for instance, and multiple video tracks are used in Final Cut and Premiere to help you visualize your transitions and "layers" of video.

In Final Cut and Premiere (among other products not mentioned here), the timeline enables you to *scrub* over that clip, usually by pointing to the *playhead indicator*—a line on the timeline that is used to choose a particular frame on the timeline within your project—and dragging the playhead back and forth.

Playhead (called the Edit Line in Premiere)

Clips

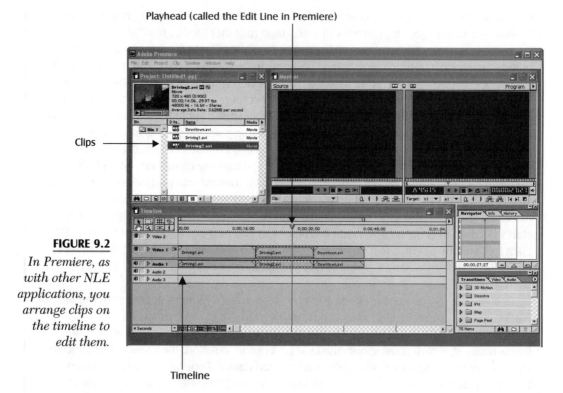

Timeline

FIGURE 9.2

In Premiere, as with other NLE applications, you arrange clips on the timeline to edit them.

zoom-in

Scrubbing lets you quickly glance at different frames in the clip and simultaneously hear the audio associated with that point in the clip. It's a quick way to locate a part of a longer clip of video.

Previewing Clips and Projects

Two typical approaches can be used to preview clips and projects. In simple applications such as iMovie, one window is used to show a preview of the project. When you want to view a clip, you'll see it in the viewer pane; when you want to view your entire project on the timeline, the main viewer pane will be used for that as well.

With other products, such as Final Cut and Adobe Premiere, the NLE software's interface shows you more than one window. Generally, one window is used for viewing clips that you're working on—often that's the *preview* or *source* window and it's used, for instance, to set the In and Out markers for a clip. The other window (often in the middle or on the right, as shown in Figure 9.3) is the *canvas* or *program* window, where you'll see your video as it is currently coming together in the timeline.

Viewer window   Canvas

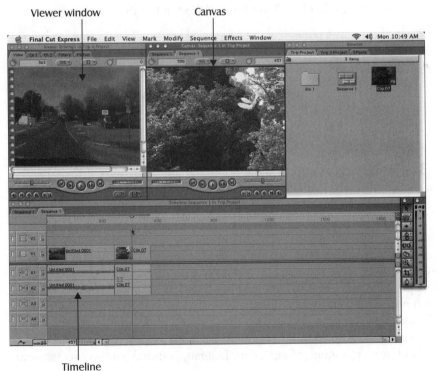

Timeline

FIGURE 9.3

In Final Cut Express, the window on the left (the Viewer window) enables you to edit the individual clip, while in the window on the right (the Canvas window), you'll see the project played back when you use the timeline to preview the project.

As you add edits, overlay clips, titles and special effects you'll make choices about them in the source window and you'll see the results in the canvas or program window.

Trimming and Cropping Clips

In less complicated video editing software, you generally spend a lot of time *trimming* or *cropping* your video clips before you place them in the timeline. (This means you're specifying the portions of the clip you want to keep and discarding the rest of the clip.) Apple's iMovie, for instance, encourages you to do trim and crop—you can split clips, crop them (by selecting only portions that are supposed to survive in the final clip), and then arrange them into a *rough cut* in the timeline interface.

focus ──

A rough cut is editing terminology for the video after you've placed the basic scenes in their final—or at least likely final—sequence, but without titles, effects, or sometimes fine-tuning of each clip.

Here's how to crop in iMovie:

1. Select a clip that hasn't yet been placed in the timeline.

2. In the Viewer pane, use the crop markers (the small triangles below the scrubber bar in the preview area) to select the portion of the clip that you want to keep.

3. Choose Edit | Crop, and the nonhighlighted portions of the clip are moved to iMovie's Trash. You can restore the clip by choosing Advanced | Restore Clip, but only if you haven't yet emptied the project's trash.

In more complex NLE software—both Final Cut and Adobe Premiere work this way—the approach is generally a bit more subtle. Instead of cropping the clips, you're expected to set different *in* and *out* points for each clip. The high-end NLE software assumes you've already done some of your gross "cropping" when you made your edit decisions while capturing the footage—at this point, you should have less reason to go in and crop and cut away too much of each clip. Instead, you make more precise (and less destructive) decisions by changing the *in* and *out* points on a video clip. Now, only the portion of the clip between the two *in* and *out* points will play in the project, even though the entire clip media is still there if you need to change the *in* or *out* points later. The following example illustrates moving the *out* point on a clip in Final Cut Express:

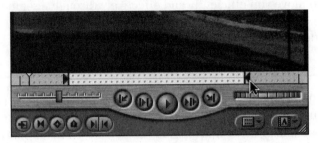

The timeline interfaces often include another important tool for dealing with clips that have already been placed in the timeline. A cutting tool, sometimes shaped like a knife or razor blade, is meant to suggest the tool you would use to cut a clip into two. That can be an important tool to use for adding a transition between clips or to split a clip so that you can place it in another part of the timeline.

The Rough Cut

After you've cropped clips to their *in* and *out* points and split and rearranged clips, you're ready to create a rough cut—a sequence of clips that you can play back in the project's canvas window. To create the rough cut, drag your clips to the timeline in the order in which you want them to appear. This forms the foundation of your video—from here, you'll be able to add transitions, effects, B-roll, overlays, and all sorts of other fun stuff.

With the rough cut accomplished, it's a good idea to make a copy of it as a backup. Many professionals will opt to save the actual data of their project file to computer tape backup, using DAT (Digital Audio Tape) or similar technology. If you don't have DAT available, you can export your project back to DV tape, so that at least you have saved the rough cut so you could re-import it into your NLE software if necessary. (You'll need to go through and split your clips, but that shouldn't be too tough.) From your rough cut, you're ready to dig in and fine tune the way your clips transition from one to the next.

Editing It Together

Spend a little time watching TV shows, movies, or documentaries, and you'll quickly come to realize that most produced segments of film and video are not just rough cuts. Often there's quite a bit of subtle editing going on between the frames that can make the difference between a production that seems cobbled together versus a production that seems polished and fluid. While it can also be the case that TV shows can go overboard with editing, for the most part you'll find that the edits are designed to move you efficiently and effectively through a segment of video. This designed movement helps communicate the message, or story, that the video or film is trying to get across.

focus ——————————————————————————

Of course, the power of the edit can bring about some ethical conundrums, particularly in news, nonfiction, and documentary. If you're shooting home movies or a digital feature, you can edit pretty much anything, transforming it into whatever you want it to be. If you're trying to present a true story, however, you'll need to take care, to the extent that you can, that your edits don't change the meaning of what someone is saying or what actually occurred when you rolled the tape.

Making Straight Cuts

Watch TV closely, and you will see that few special effects *transitions* (wipes, fades, and other effects) are used, contrary to what you might expect, particularly if you've been playing with your editing software a bit. What you tend to see in most TV shows that are aimed at adults are *straight cuts*—transitions from one clip to the next that require no special effects and no overlapping sounds or images; they just move from one shot to the next in an instant. Sure, you'll see fades, wipes, and other effects used in some films—music videos, live sports coverage, and between segments on the 24-hour news—but you'll also find that television shows almost always use many, many straight cuts, once you start watching for them.

We point this out because your initial instinct might be to use your NLE application to load up your video with transitions between the clips, because (1) you can, and (2) that might seem to make it more professional. The truth is, however, a professional video uses relatively few special-effect transitions, unless it's a live-action sporting event or a "Real Cops Gone Bad!" type of adrenaline-driven show. Instead, you'll see that slower paced shows tend to use a lot of straight cuts as well as some special edits that take both sound and video into consideration.

To create a successful straight cut, you need to shoot different angled shots—that is, you'll need the shots we've discussed elsewhere in the chapters of this book, such as establishing shots, medium shots, close-ups, and so forth.

Consider these examples, where straight cuts make sense:

- To suggest continuity between sequential shots of the same scene—an establishing angle, medium, and close-up shot that are moving into your scene. For instance, picture a news feature that starts by showing the outside of a restaurant, then it shows the door of the restaurant, and then it shows the inside—all while the reporter describes how the restaurant was robbed the night before. That's a common place to use straight cuts.

- To show two different people in the same scene. If you watch a TV drama or a movie for craft, you'll see tons of straight cuts between close-ups and medium shots of people as they talk to one another.

We mentioned that your shots should use different angles, which often means that each angle looks totally different—in our restaurant example, the outside will look pretty different from the inside, clearly. If you have a sequence of shots of the same subject, you should make sure you follow the "30-degree rule," which states that your angles (the radial movement of the camera view from the last shot) should vary by at least 30 degrees to ensure that a straight cut doesn't look like a *jump cut*. (In a jump cut, the angle of the camera doesn't change significantly—only the focal length, the zoom level, changes, as shown in Figure 9.4. It often looks like a mistake, particularly when it doesn't happen in a music video. A jump cut might work if you want to simulate someone looking through binoculars or—more dramatically—a rifle sight.)

Because we can define a straight cut as the absence of a special-effects transition—it's just two clips side by side in your timeline—that means you don't need to do anything in particular to make a straight cut in your editing software. As long as you choose the appropriate time to make them, straight cuts are easy—with the rough cut you've created of your clips on your timeline, you already have used straight cuts between them.

FIGURE 9.4

These panels represent a jump cut, which can often look like a mistake in video editing.

However, some clips don't work with straight cuts. In general, you'll want to add special-effects transitions (which we'll talk about more in a moment) in the following (broadly defined) situations:

- **Motion**   If two clips show dramatic or opposing motion (one clip is panning to the left and the other is panning to the right, for example), a straight cut often won't work.

- **Change of location**   A dramatic change of location—not just a change of the angles or positioning of the camera in the same location—will often require a transition. This is a rule that can be broken—a straight cut between locations can be useful to shock your audience with its abruptness. (For instance, a funny shot might be the close-up of someone holding a winning lotto ticket that uses a straight cut to that person driving a Ferrari—the abruptness might add to the humor.)

- **Change of time**   If you're moving from one scene to another and there's a gap in time between the two—the second scene is a week, a month, or a year later (or earlier)—a special-effect transition between the clips (often a fade-out on the first clip) is generally necessary.

Splitting Clips and Inserting Edits

Say you've got one long clip, and you'd like to straight cut to another clip somewhere in the middle of the original. Suppose the long clip shows a train arriving at a destination. You want to show the train approaching the station, then switch to a clip of the person standing up and grabbing his bags inside that train, and then switch back to a clip of the train slowing to a stop.

If the train clip is actually one, long continuous clip, you can perform an *insert edit* to sandwich that second clip in there. With real film, you would literally cut and paste to connect the clip that you're inserting. In a NLE application, you can use a special insert command.

In iMovie, splitting and inserting is a two-step process. First, you place your playhead on the timeline and choose Edit | Split Video at Playhead. What was once one video clip is now two clips, and a new line shows up under the playhead to show two clips. Now, you drag another clip between the two newly split clips.

In Adobe Premiere and Final Cut, you'll use a razor tool for splitting clips. Select that tool, and in the clip's timeline, click where you'd like the split to occur. The following illustration shows the razor tool being used in Premiere.

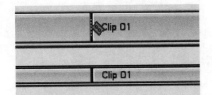

If you'd like to make a more exact cut in Adobe Premiere, place the playhead on the timeline at the frame where you want the cut to occur, and then choose Timeline | Razor At Edit Line. (This step isn't necessary in Final Cut, because the razor tool uses a line to show you the exact frame where the split will take place.)

focus ——————————————————————————————

We'll touch on this later in the chapter in the section "Adding Titles," but splitting clips is handy for more than just editing—you can also use splits to add titles and transitions that occur while a clip is playing.

Unlike iMovie, a more advanced NLE application such as Final Cut won't necessarily open a gap between the two split clips when you want to add another clip between them. In fact, you don't even need to split the clip first in either Premiere or Final Cut to create an insert edit.

In Final Cut, place the playhead at the point on the timeline where you want the insert edit to occur. Then, instead of dragging the clip to the timeline, drag it to the Canvas window. When you do, a number of commands will appear in colorful boxes—drag the clip to the Insert box and drop the clip to insert it on the timeline.

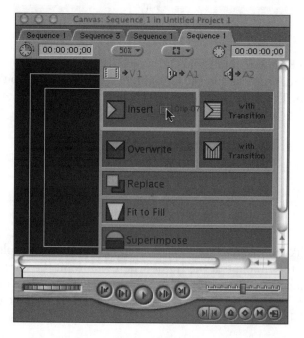

In Premiere, you should first place the playhead (edit line) where you want the new clip to be inserted. Then select the clip in the Project window and choose Clip | Insert And Edit Line. The clip is placed in the timeline, opening a gap into which that clip will fit, as shown next.

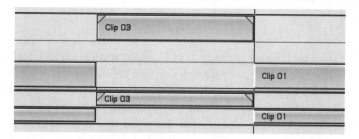

Inserting B-Roll Intercuts

One variation on the straight cut is a straight cut that doesn't take its sound along with it—that's called an *intercut*. With an intercut, you overlay the video *without* adding the audio to the timeline. This is something you might want to do, for example, if a professor is speaking about an important new project downtown, and then you cut to video of that project while the professor's comments continue to be heard. In this case, you're overlaying an original video clip (the professor) with some B-roll video (video of the project) while listening to the audio associated with the original clip.

Most software features an *overlay* or *overwrite* command that turns *off* the audio portion of the insert, usually by turning off or locking the audio tracks in the timeline. How this is done depends on your software. Most products offer a way in which video can be *pasted over* the sound.

In iMovie, for instance, an intercut is done like this:

1. In the timeline, decide which clip is going to include the intercut footage. Select that clip and choose Advanced | Extract Audio Clip. This is an important first step. If you don't do this, the intercut video clip will also include its audio, which is not what you want.

2. Select the clip that you're going to add as an intercut, and, in the Viewer window, choose the portions that you want to use. Choose Edit | Copy to copy that footage.

3. Place the playhead on the timeline where you want the footage to be added, and then choose Advanced | Paste Over At Playhead. That replaces the previous footage with the footage you just copied, as shown in the following illustration. Now the intercut video will be shown, but with audio from the original clip.

In more advanced NLE applications, an overlay edit is accomplished in a different manner, because the timeline has more video tracks to work with; so instead of simply pasting the video over the timeline, you'll continue to work with two separate clips—let's call them the *base clip* and the *B-roll clip*. In Premiere, for instance, you can drag your intercut clip to the moment on the timeline at which you'd like it to appear. Ideally, you should have your base clip on the Video 1B track and your B-roll clip on the Video 1A track. When you drag the B-roll clip to the Video 1B track, that clip's video will automatically appear instead of the base clip video. Shown in this example is a B-roll clip on the track above a base clip:

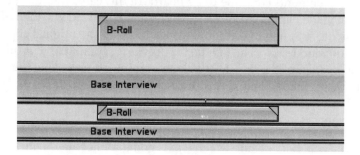

Picture the base clip playing until the playhead reaches the B-roll clip—then the B-roll clip plays until the playhead reaches its end, and then the base clip picks up again.

The problem with this process, however, is that the audio for the overlay clip is still active in the timeline, and it will play along with the base clip's audio. To keep that from happening, simply delete the audio portion of the interclip. Here's how:

1. Select the interclip in the timeline. Both the audio and video portions will become outlined or highlighted.

2. Choose Clip | Unlink Audio And Video.

3. Click the audio clip. It should be highlighted separately now, as shown in the following illustration:

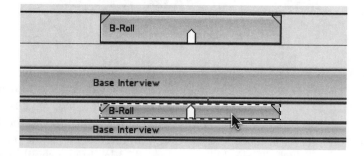

4. Press the DELETE key on your keyboard. That should delete the audio portion.

That's it—now you've got your B-roll clip overlaying the base clip while allowing the base clip's audio to play continuously.

Adding Transitions: Fades, Dissolves, and Wipes

When a straight cut doesn't make sense, a transition might work instead. Generally, you'll use a transition when you need to make sense of an abrupt change in your video—whether you're moving on to a new topic, showing video from a different person's point of view or you're moving on to a different time—a few days or weeks or months have elapsed. All of those types of changes in your storyline can be shown visually to the audience using special-effect transitions.

The following types of basic transitions are commonly used:

- **Fade**   The clips in a video sequence slowly move from black to the full color of the clips—or vice versa. This can be used to start or end a segment or suggest that you're moving on to a new idea, a new sequence, or some other change. Fades aren't to be used lightly, as they tend to relax the audience out of (or into) a scene, telling them "this is over" (fade out) or "this is about to begin" (fade in).

- **Cross-dissolve**   Two clips seem to melt together, as the video of the first clip slowly breaks up and the video of the second clip emerges. When a change in camera angle or location seems too jarring or abrupt to work in a straight cut, you might consider using a cross-dissolve, which can be used to suggest a change in perspective. A cross-dissolve can take a little while to complete, so you don't want to use them too often in a given project. Still, they're an effective way to smooth a cut between angles or to suggest the passage of time.

- **Wipe**   An abrupt way to get out of a scene and move on to the next one—visually, it looks as if the image is pushed or cleared off the screen and replaced by a color, usually black. The type of wipe (left-to-right, top-to-bottom, expanding circles, or one frame of video appears to be pushed off screen by another) can be used to suggest different perspectives. They're a great transition to use for moving on to the next scene while suggesting that the new scene is taking place in a different location—perhaps far away from the first scene.

Most "serious" television shows and feature films—dramatic fiction or nonfiction—use few, if any wipes. They're more common in comedy, music videos, children's programming and in cases where an editor wants to make a show or film look more like an older serial adventure movie. For instance, George Lucas uses wipes frequently in the Star Wars movies, but they're done purposefully to conjure the comic book feel of old science-fiction serials.

Most transitions are easily added using software by selecting the type of transition, setting any *options* (the amount of time that the transition takes, for instance, or the visual characteristic of the effects), and then dragging the transition to the timeline between the clips where the transition should take place (see Figure 9.5). Most transitions need to appear between two clips, but clearly a fade-in or fade-out can go at the beginning or end of a segment on the timeline.

In Premiere and Final Cut, you add transitions by dragging the transition from the Effects window (Premiere) or the Effects tab of the Browser (Final Cut) to a split between two clips in the timeline. Of course, those applications also offer a great deal of customization for transitions, which is beyond the scope of this book. By double-clicking the name of a transition you can see its properties and settings.

focus

One special case is a fade-in or fade-out transition—in iMovie, you drag these transitions to the beginning or end of a clip just as you do other transitions. In the more advanced NLE applications, you can perform fade-in and fade-out transitions in various ways using the timeline—see Chapter 11 for details.

With most software, your video will then need to be *rendered* with a special command before you can see that transition in action, although you may find that you can preview the transition without rendering, depending on the software.

zoom-in

Rendering is a process that the software must go through to "paint" every frame of the video to combine the visual effects of the transition with the original footage.

Adding Titles

Adding titles in most NLE applications is easy—your biggest problem will probably be choosing from the many different types of titles you can use.

FIGURE 9.5

The image is dark because it's fading in from black to full color.

Fade-in transition

The key to titling is to keep it as simple as possible and choose the correct type of title for the moment.

Here are a few popular choices:

- **Over black**   With this option, instead of appearing superimposed over your video clips, the titles appear on a black or solid-color background. You'll choose an over black–style title for a dramatic impact, to make the title easier to read, or to create rolling credits that appear at the end of a movie. You'll likely find that many of the titles your software enables you to choose will have an over black option and an overlay option that enables you to put the title over the video images (see Figure 9.6).

- **Centered**   Centered titles are generally used for opening credits and title sequences—in some cases you'll use them for closing credits as well, particularly if you have only a few people to credit.

- **Lower-third**   Lower-third titles are usually used to identify the people who appear on the screen, particularly in nonfiction such as news segments and documentaries (see Figure 9.7). You'll also find

lower-third titles used for subtitles and for stylized titles such as those used in music videos.

- **Scrolling**   As you might expect, scrolling titles are generally used for credits at the end of a production, particularly one that has a lot of credits to display.

Adding titles in iMovie versus adding them in the more advanced NLE applications can involve quite different processes, so let's take a quick look at the iMovie approach here and save the advanced discussion for Chapter 11.

In iMovie, adding a title is as easy as switching to the Titles effects in the Effects pane (click the button marked Titles, as shown at the lower right of Figure 9.7) and then choosing a title. Click one of the names in the Effects pane and a small sample will appear at the top of the pane. Below

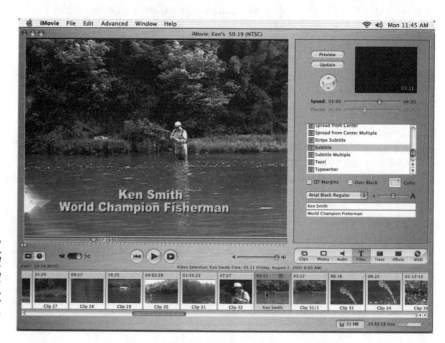

FIGURE 9.7

Lower-third titles are useful for identifying people in documentaries.

the names of the different title types are some controls for those titles—type in your title and choose the fonts and font sizes.

Probably the most important choice you need to make is whether or not to turn on the over black option. If it's turned on, the title will be added as its own clip. When you drag the title to the beginning of a video clip in your presentation, it will be added before that clip. If the over black option is turned off, the title will be added *to* the clip where you drag the title effect, as it will be a transparent overlay. Notice in this clip that the rendering indicator shows up on the video clip itself after a title has been applied to it—that means the title is going to show up as an overlay.

And...Cut!

In this chapter, we took a brief look at some of the techniques used in video editing and in DV editing software to capture the video from your camcorder, to create a rough cut, and then to create transitions. You'll need to dig in and get to know your particular editing software on your own; once you become familiar with the editing options, you'll find that it informs the type of shooting you do and the footage you get. In the next chapter, we take a look at sound and music in your production.

Audio and Music for Your Video

WE'VE all heard the adage: seeing is believing. In video work, however, we can twist that a little—*hearing* is sometimes more important than seeing. Whether you're shooting a home movie, wedding video, documentary, or a feature, your audience has to be able to hear the action (and the actors) as well as see it. If the sound is inferior in a wedding video during the vows, for example, your video loses quite a bit. Your audience wants to hear the declaration of love and commitment, the cracking in the voices, and the softness in tone. In general, sound quality is always more important than you think. As we've said elsewhere in this book, it's often more important to get good sound than it is to get good video.

Once upon a time, in the world before video, sound was not married to film and they functioned in a double-system world where one was recorded separately from the other—one on film and one on tape—which had to later be synchronized together so that the image of a man talking could also be heard at the same time he appeared to talk. In the modern world of video and digital recording, sound can be recorded directly on the tape with the video, where the two live happily ever after. Of course, "living together" has its own set of problems. In this chapter we will briefly discuss some of the issues you will face in recording sound directly to videotape and how that sound can be manipulated during the post-production process in your software.

Getting Good Sound

With today's camcorders, it's possible to point your camcorder and shoot without much thought and get a tolerable image, including sound. Microphones mounted on contemporary camcorders are far superior to what you might have found on the VHS camcorders existing fifteen to twenty years ago. But a professional would never depend on such an on-camera microphone on its own if the idea was to record the best quality sound. We'll cover a few of the rules for getting good sound on your video shoots in this chapter. But realize that there's one golden rule: To get the best sound, you need to get your microphone off your camcorder and as close as you can to your subject. Usually, that means you'll have to deal with the placement of the microphone logistically. If it's not connected to the camcorder and you're busy holding the camcorder, then you may need a helper, or a special type of microphone, or both.

Of course, rules are made to be broken—or, at least, they have exceptions. You'll find that you sometimes have to shoot with a microphone on your camcorder because you're the only person there, or it's the only microphone you have, or it's the best solution for situations where you need to be very mobile. In that case, you should find the microphone on your camcorder is adequate, although you'll need to take some extra care. More than likely, the microphone on a consumer-level camcorder will be an omnidirectional microphone, which means that it will capture sound equally from all directions surrounding the mic, not just from the subject the camera is pointing toward. On higher end cameras, the microphones will often be more of a professional grade. That means, among other things, they tend to have a cardioid pickup pattern. That's a good thing, as you'll tend to get more of the sound that you're pointing at with the mic and less of the sound that you don't want to pick up. (We'll discuss pickup patterns later in this chapter.)

Be aware that other sounds will be picked up by the mic, such as nearby conversations, traffic, a noisy fan, and so on. Unfortunately, this allows you very little control over your sound. And what's sometimes worse is that we get used to ambient sound when we're walking around in our daily lives— our minds filter out some of it to allow us to focus on particular sounds, so we often forget that the mic can hear those sounds. That means, with your camcorder and microphones, you'll probably need to practice a bit in order to get a sense of how sound gathering works and how much extraneous sound you will sometimes pick up when recording. Do some test recording, particularly outside or in areas similar to where you plan to shoot, then return to your editing software and see what the clips' audio sounds like.

If you have no other choice than to shoot with only the camera-mounted microphone, don't shoot where you will obviously have loud background noise and constant interference such as roads with heavy traffic, windy areas, a flight path, busy schoolyard, and so on. If a background sound is preventing you from hearing well with your ears, the microphone will not be able to hear the subject much better.

On the CD-ROM   Check the Chapter 10 section of the CD-ROM for samples of sound gathered using an on-camera microphone versus sound gathered using off-camera mics. The difference can be dramatic.

Using External Microphones

If you want to get serious about location sound recording, use external microphones whenever possible. Most camcorders have at least one mini-plug style microphone port (see Figure 10.1) that will allow you to connect an external microphone—in most cases, these plugs are designed for add-on directional microphones that you attach to the camcorder. That's because the thin wire associated with a microphone that will fit that little jack doesn't really offer high-end quality for long microphone connections. You can use a long cable with such a small connector if it's your only choice, but it'll be a compromised choice.

A better solution for an off-camera microphone is a thick cable that's associated with a *balanced XLR three-prong* connector. Camcorders such as the Sony PD150 and Cannon XL-1s have professional XLR inputs built in, which enable you to connect high-quality microphones directly to the camcorder itself. For camcorders that don't feature XLR inputs, companies

FIGURE 10.1

The mini-plug on many camcorders is good for microphones that are mounted to the camcorder, but not for long stretches of cable.

FIGURE 10.2

A Beachtek box (shown beneath the camcorder) is used to connect XLR inputs to your camcorder.

such as Beachtek (www.beachtek.com) sell small boxes that mount to the underside of a camera, connecting to the camcorder's mini-plug microphone port via a short cable and offering two or four XLR inputs on the box itself.

Having this type of input for external microphones is handy, because it enables you to plug in more than one microphone at a time directly into the camera, control each microphone's volume, and move the microphones independently from the camera in order to get closer to the subjects.

focus

Not to be discounted is the fact that using off-camera microphones makes you appear more professional to your subjects and others—with independent microphones and perhaps a sound person assisting you, you look less like a person with a camcorder and more like a video crew.

Once you have something to plug your microphone(s) into, you'll need to get at least one microphone to plug in. There are two types of microphones that you'll probably consider—one that can be used on a *boom pole* to hold over the subject and one that can be attached directly to the subject. (A *boom* is a telescoping pole that's designed to hold a microphone as shown in Figure 10.3. The word "boom" is used for other types of telescoping poles, too, such as a camera boom.)

Here's a quick look at the types:

- **Boom mic**   A microphone that can be mounted in a boom will generally have a *cardioid* or *hypercardioid* pickup pattern. Cardioid means the mic is designed to pick up sound directly in front of it in a pattern that resembles a heart shape. (The *hyper*cardioid is even

FIGURE 10.3

Here's a boom operator holding a microphone over our talent.

more narrowly focused.) This allows the boom operator and sound mixer tremendous control over what is heard and recorded. If you watch a feature or documentary production in action, you are likely to see a guy with strong arms holding the boom a few inches over an actor's head. The key is to get the microphone as close to the subject while making sure the boom stays out of frame. It takes a great amount of focus and stability to be a boom operator, but all of that hard work pays off in the end when everything you need to hear is clearly audible.

focus ──────────────────────────────────────

As Figure 10.4 shows, a hypercardioid microphone actually picks up sounds immediately behind it as well as immediately in front of it. That means you need to be very careful to be quiet when you're standing behind such a microphone and recording.

- **Lavalier** The second type of microphone to consider is the lavalier (often said "lav," rhyming with "suave") microphone. This is a tiny, generally omnidirectional microphone that can be clipped directly to the person who's on camera. For interviews, you'll often clip the lavalier to a jacket lapel, on a tie, or to a shirt collar. For fiction or for shots where you don't want the microphone to be seen, you'll come up with other options, such as inside a shirt button, attached to a bra strap, or even directly taped to the actor's—or groom's—chest (come

FIGURE 10.4

Here are the basic pickup patterns for the three types of microphones we've discussed.

Omnidirectional   Cardioid   Hypercardioid

prepared with a razor because you'll have to shave a patch of hair to get it to stick). This is a great choice for someone who doesn't have other crew members or an assistant with them because the microphone can be attached to the subject, you can test the sound and choose the volume levels on the camera, and then the microphone can be left to do its job. There is one general problem with lavalier microphones. Because they are usually omnidirectional, they will pick up every sound around them—the rustling of clothing, other people speaking nearby, or any noise within the radius of the microphone. Lavaliers are best for shoots with a small crew or no crew, wide shots where a boom cannot be used because it will be seen, or for interview subjects where it's okay to see the microphone and when a boom microphone might be intimidating.

You'll see other types of microphones, including the handheld variety that we discussed in Chapter 5—usually an omnidirectional microphone that can be used for stand-up reporting or "man in the street" type interviews. You'll see on-camera solutions marketed, from zoom or shotgun microphones (cardioid or hypercardioid) to mini-boom microphones that are mounted on your camcorder but further away from the camera body so that the microphone doesn't pick up camera operation sound. These can record at slightly further distance and, of course, a camera- mounted boom microphone can look professional.

Many companies produce great microphones in a range of prices for the professional and those not-so-professional. Some brands that the professionals use are Shure (www.shure.com), Sennheiser (www.sennheiser.com), Telex (www.telex.com), Sony (www.sony.com), Samson (www.samsontech.com), and Lectrosonics (www.lectrosonics.com). You'll have to consider your needs to make the right decision. For example, if you are shooting a documentary about the music scene in your state, it would be in your interest to pay extra close attention to the sound and how you will record it.

Certain microphones are better for vocals than others, while other microphones are better for recording instruments, conversation, and so forth. Do your research. It will make a tremendous difference when the final product is finished. If you're unable to afford top-of-the-line microphones, consider buying used professional equipment from companies such as Trew Audio (www.trewaudio.com) and www.locationsound.com. Both companies have good reputations in selling used gear at affordable prices.

focus _____

Here's some basic buying advice we've gotten from the sound experts we know. Most audio experts recommend having at least one high-quality microphone in every category—a lavalier, handheld, and boom microphone. Second, it's often recommended that you only buy a wireless microphone if you can afford a top-quality model—a good wireless lavalier microphone is in the $750–1000 range, with the professional-level models costing $1500 or more. Less expensive wireless microphones can sometimes cause more problems than they're worth, as they're prone to interference and the signal can drop out. (If you need a wireless lav for occasional shots, however, a less expensive model will do.) If perfect sound on a tight budget is your goal, you're often better off with lower-priced wired microphones, which can be found at decent quality for less than $100 for a handheld and $150 or so for a lavalier.

Recording Sound

Recording sound has many variables, just like shooting video. If you want the highest quality product, consider hiring someone to deal with all of the sound issues for you. Not only can having the extra hands and ears available make your life a little easier, but you can probably find someone with some experience and equipment who is able to help you either inexpensively or for a share of your expected fees or profits. (Or for the glory of a job well done—don't underestimate other people's love of what they do well and their need for demo reel pieces to show their work to others.) Your audio engineer will be able to keep tabs on how the audio sounds, watch for battery or cable problems and, in general, save you from an editing nightmare— problems with misdirected microphones, background noise, clothes rustling, and other things that may not be apparent while the interview or shoot is taking place.

Whether you're working solo or have an assistant who can watch sound levels for you, here are a few controls found on higher-end camcorders and separate recording decks that can be manipulated for even better audio quality:

- **Mic/Line inputs** You'll likely find a few different audio input ports on your camcorder, particularly if it's a prosumer or professional model. The "Mic" port is what you use for a microphone that doesn't have any sort of amplification built in (which is most of the microphones we're talking about), while "Line" is used when an instrument or a device such as a CD player is plugged in to the camera. In general, it is best not to run a microphone directly into the "Line" port because the sound will be very low or inaudible. Microphones need to be amplified because they don't put out much voltage (the microphone input automatically amplifies), whereas devices such as CD players have a stronger signal and are already amplified before plugging them in to your inputs. Conversely, if you send a line signal through a microphone input it will probably distort because it will be overamplified.

focus ———————————————————————————————————

An amplifier will simply make the signal louder, which is sometimes necessary for unpowered microphones or for mixing audio from two different sources (such as two different microphones or a microphone and a musical instrument). If your microphones are being run through an amplifier—for instance, if you're connected directly to an event venue's sound system in order to record your sound—then you will want to use your camcorder's line-in port instead of a microphone port, if possible.

- **Levels**   These are the main controls monitored by a recordist because they control the *range of volume* of the sound being recorded. (Lowering the levels makes it less likely that the sound will distort, but can make the sound too hushed.) If your camcorder supports multiple microphone inputs, then each microphone input will have its own graphical level control (see Figure 10.5), which you can control from the camcorder. (This is true only of serious prosumer and professional camcorders; on other camcorders you probably won't see graphical sound levels. If you're working with a Beachtek or similar adapter for your microphones, they will likely have manual levels.) The key, when working with a graphical level indicator, is to set a level for each microphone so that the needle or bar on the camcorder does not jump all the way to the top (*over modulation*) and, of course, you don't want it too close to the bottom. Most recordists will "ride the sound" (pay constant attention to it and change it as necessary), compensating for loud or soft noises as they are recorded. A loud noise will shoot the needle to the top so the sound recordist has to be prepared to turn the level up and down when necessary.

- **Mono/Stereo**   Mono will place all of the audio, no matter how many inputs are used, on one *track*, whereas stereo will use two tracks for the left and right channels that two microphones pick up.

FIGURE 10.5

High-end camcorders offer an audio level indicator.

If you record in mono, you will never be able to adjust the level of one microphone against another within a scene, since they are already mixed on the same track, but if you record in stereo, the two tracks—each corresponding to a different microphone or input—can be manipulated in your computer software. Stereo, as you're well aware, can offer a richer sound—however, you'll need to record with two microphones to get a stereo effect. Stereo can have its advantages even for filming in the same scene—you can use a stereo mode to get the same basic sound from two different microphones—from an overhead boom microphone and a lavalier microphone, for instance, which gives you the option (in your software) of making one level of the other louder, depending on which sounds better.

focus —————————————————————————————————————

Another good reason to record in stereo is because you're premixing your sound—if you have a sound mixing board on the set with you, you can run everyone's microphones (and any other audio equipment) into the sound board, then run that board's outputs to your camcorder for recording. With an XLR adapter on your camcorder, you'll be able to get a stereo feed from the mixing board, which would result in stereo sound.

- **Attenuation** An attenuation control—which lessens the sensitivity of the microphone—is a great control to have in rather uncontrollable settings. This setting allows you to record extremely loud sounds that the camcorder is not normally able to handle by turning down the sensitivity of the microphone. For example, you might want to attenuate your microphone levels during a rock concert so that the sound is not distorted. Don't expect miracles, but it will help a little when nothing else can be done.

- **Headphone volume**   It controls the volume of the sound coming into the headphones you or your sound engineer will be wearing. Just because you are riding the recording levels and other controls have been set, it doesn't mean that you are necessarily getting good sound. It's best to listen to what is being recorded. By putting headphones on, you will be able to hear things that everyone else will not be paying attention to, such as the whirring of a fan or the hum of a refrigerator or even the sound of an air conditioner. Headphones isolate you so that you are able to focus on what is being recorded. Set the volume at a comfortable level and listen closely.

 *zoom-in*

Closed-ear or noise-canceling headphones are vastly superior to the typical Walkman-style headphones, although wearing anything to listen to the sound is probably a good idea.

Recording Alternatives

Most of us, particularly at the prosumer level, will record sound to our camcorders. Higher-end camcorders are designed to do a pretty good job and, with an XLR breakout box (such as the Beachtek described and shown earlier) or a very good on-camera microphone, you'll get good enough sound as long as you monitor the levels and take precautions against wind and background noise. That said, recording to your camcorder isn't the only choice. Many professionals will actually plan to get their primary audio from a different recording, with the microphones on their camcorders (or even their boom microphones) working as backups. This is a great approach to take, particularly if you're covering an event or recording an interview that you know you need to get right the first time.

The current professional standard for audio recording is Digital Audio Tape (DAT), with portable recorders available that can be slung over a shoulder and carried around by your sound engineer as he carries a boom pole or constantly checks the levels on the equipment. DAT is expensive, however, with portable DAT recorders starting around $1000 and 120-minute tapes at about $8 a piece. It's even pricier to get a DAT recorder that includes XLR inputs for professional quality connections. Popular portable DAT players are made by Sony (which has some ultra-portable Walkman-style models) and Tascam (www.tascam.com).

So, if you're ultra-serious about your audio—in other words, you've got investors or grants—then DAT might be the best path. For less expensive solutions, however, two other options are intriguing—minidisc and MP3. Sony makes a number of miniDisc recorders that can be used to record CD-quality digital sound to small discs that record 74–80 minutes of audio each, usually for about $2 a disc. MiniDisc recorders are popular for professional radio production, for instance, because they can be coupled with a good microphone and record crisp, clear sound. Consumer-level miniDisc recorders can be had for a few hundred dollars, with the caveat that they have only miniplug connectors for microphones, not XLR. If there's a drawback—and it's a minor one—it's that you'll need to get the audio into your computer via a sound card or sound-in port that may cause you to lose a little audio quality.

A growing category is the digital MP3 player that can also record audio. The advantage of such devices is that they tend to be incredibly lightweight. Some also have extremely high capacity (particularly models built around a portable hard disk), reaching ten hours or more of recording at once. Plus, some of them integrate well with computers, enabling you to use a USB or FireWire (IEEE 1394) connection to copy the audio from the recorder instead of requiring you to record it via a line-in or microphone port on the computer to record the sound. Panasonic (www.Panasonic.com), Tascam, and Archos Technology (www.archos.com), are among others.

Adding Music and Soundtracks

Whether you're creating a home video, a feature, or a business sales video, don't underestimate the importance of music to your final project. Think of some of the all-time most powerful and popular movies, then stop to think about how important the music is in nearly every example, such as "Star Wars," "The Godfather," "Titanic," and so on. Music can create or augment the atmosphere and emotion behind a scene or character. It can express triumph or sadness, elation, anger, or fear. In fact, different music can easily be used to change the meaning of a scene—music can change the same dialogue and actors and direction into a scene that seems ironic or serious or silly. And it's not just big movies that benefit from a soundtrack. Nearly any type of production can use some sort of soundtrack to make it more watchable. (The exception might be legal depositions—they'd be more entertaining with music, but you might not get asked back to edit them.)

Choose Your Music

The first thing to consider in choosing your music is what you are trying to convey to your audience. In a video promoting the efforts of your nonprofit neighborhood improvement service, your audience needs to feel like they are part of a successful effort and that people are overcoming obstacles on both sides. Your audience should feel the sense of accomplishment by the volunteers who build the houses as well as the happiness and gratitude shared by those given homes. Triumphant music with an orchestra might be used as the framework for the house that is going up, and down-home roots or country music or even a soft violin might complement the shot of the homeowner walking in the finished house for the first time. (Where Todd and Nina live, you'd use some blues music in there somewhere, just on principle.)

Picking music is probably more art than science. Just as picking up a camcorder and reading this book has probably made you more aware of how camera angles and editing are used in productions you see in a movie theater or on TV, thinking about the music when you're watching those same productions can be extremely educational. You'll find, first of all, that there's *a lot* of music in TV shows and movies—even newscasts and documentaries—and in the past you may not have even noticed it. The best advice we can give you is to start listening for the emotions in music— not just the words, but the ways that harmonies and melodies and rhythms can be evocative of times or places or feelings. If you spend part of your day semi-consciously cataloguing ideas of how music affects people emotionally, you'll probably become more effective at picking music when you're editing your project.

Another thing to pay attention to when you're watching a TV show or movie is *when* music is used. Video and film editing has a little secret— picking the moments when you're going to use music may be one of the most difficult tasks facing an editor or director. After all, you can follow some rules and guidelines that help you get good pictures and sound, and you can follow some basic techniques to get good cuts and transitions between your clips. But putting the wrong music behind a portion of video—or putting music in when it shouldn't be there—takes a bit more artistry.

You'll find that professional productions use music more than you might imagine, but not at every moment. One of the harder things to do is transition from one scene that includes music to another one. For the most part, scenes with heavy dialogue or story exposition can often do without music. For a wedding video, you might have music in an opening montage and during the wedding reception, but, in many cases, you'll want to leave the music off during the ceremony itself. (Some people prefer music video–style montages for their wedding projects, so you might end up with a song behind the ceremony.)

In a documentary, you probably don't want music behind your interviews, but you might want to choose a soundtrack song to go along with your historical storytelling or reenactments. In a feature film, you may have an intense discussion between two people in a restaurant happen without music or only with background music that suggests there's a band playing. For an argument, you might not have music, but for a love sequence that has a montage feel, you would have music. The bottom line is to get a feel for when music isn't necessary—otherwise, if you have music through your entire production, it starts to feel like a music video.

One trick is to just play with music the same way you might play with transitions or titles—experiment. You can try playing different songs while scenes in your movie are playing to see if the songs work or if the scene even needs background music. Realize, too, that not all of your soundtrack choices need to be your favorite songs, nor must they necessarily be professionally recorded—you may find that very annoying songs, loud songs, flute jazz, traditional melodies, or children playing badly on a wind instrument are ideal for the scene you're editing. Just get in there and experiment until you find what works.

Gaining Music Rights

Once you have some music selected, you run into one of the biggest problems that prosumer and newly professional editors and producers run into. You have to gain permission to use recorded, copyrighted music—which is usually not free. Of course, if you want to use the new U2 song in your home video that your family will see at your summer reunion, no big deal, just plug it in. But if the video you are producing is for public display (even at film festivals), is used to sell a product, or has a profit, organizational, or fundraising component, you're going to need to get permission, and that may prove difficult and costly.

In order to use existing music from the likes of such musicians as Barry Manilow, Nelly, Tori Amos, Tim McGraw, or even Robert Johnson, you would have to get *clearance* (expressed, written permission) through the record company or publishing company representing their work by obtaining what's called a *synchronization license*. In most cases, a large fee would have to be paid to them depending on who the audience is for your project—television, theatrical, people in a business setting watching a training video, and so on. If you personally know the artist, you may get a break on those fees.

In some cases, if you need music for a nonprofit organization or charity, the artist may donate the music. You'll just have to write a convincing letter and get it into the right hands. It's also possible to obtain a *mechanical license* in order to re-record someone's song. (A mechanical license is a license to "cover" a copyrighted piece of music—record your own arrangement of a song.) The Harry Fox Agency (www.harryfox.com)

manages clearances for a number of publishing houses and offers licenses. They contact the appropriate entities to get a mechanical or synchronization license for your production. Special licenses for limited reproductions are also attainable that might be ideal for nonprofits, religious groups, and others that need to create fewer than 2,500 recordings of a particular piece of music.

focus

So what are the consequences of using commercial music? First, if you give a public presentation of your movie and it uses music for which you don't have permissions, you may open yourself up to fines or legal action. Second, if you choose commercial music and you don't have the rights to it, it limits your legitimate venues for distribution—your project may end up not being acceptable to a film festival or to a cable network, public television, or even theatrical release because you've used commercial songs for which the clearances would be too expensive. Likewise, commercial music in company videos, product information videos, or even charitable videos is to be avoided, as it could lead to legal problems as well.

Using Music Libraries

The truth is that, a lot of the time, professionals who are not making video productions for national television or for theatrical release will use *music libraries* for the songs that they include in their videos. These music libraries are generally large collections of CDs of music clips that have been specifically created for film and video work to be used and heard by the masses. Michael Jackson and Britney Spears would not be found in a music library, but tunes reminiscent of their songs in 10-second, 30-second, or even 60-second versions might be found in those libraries.

You can acquire music from libraries by paying either a flat fee for a collection of royalty-free music on CDs or a monthly fee for a certain number of CDs of your choice (symphony, salsa, country, rock, trance, whatever) to be used in projects you create while your subscription is active. In other cases, you can browse royalty-based music online and pay only for a particular song that you want. There are several companies online that can accommodate your needs, such as Digital Juice (www.digitaljuice.com, royalty-free music and graphics library) and Killer Tracks (www.killertracks.com, a royalty-based music library). Sound Dogs (www.sounddogs.com) is also commonly used for music and effects.

Making Your Own Music

Original music that you compose yourself (or pay somebody else to write and perform) is the ideal choice for any video project if you have the time and money to spend creating the perfect accompaniment. If you have musical talent, employ yourself immediately. Your friends and family members who make music should also be strongly considered. It is a great luxury to have complete control of the emotion and tone being set by the music you write or have written. If you use preexisting music, it is likely that you will just settle on something that's pretty close to what you had in mind. And why settle? (Okay—there's the time, effort, money, heartache, and suffering that it takes to create original music. But we mean *aside* from that.)

Acquiring original music doesn't have to be an outrageous expense if you are willing to do a little research. Depending on what type of music you need, it's possible that a little-known local rock band or jazz musician might be interested in promoting themselves in a broader fashion. You could swap services, perhaps. They could create an original piece for you based on your specifications, and in return you could shoot one of their live performances and help them edit together a video or a demo. In the end, you have both broadened your audience, gotten some music video editing (or live concert shooting) practice, and fulfilled each other's needs. You might consider a high school band, church choir, or local symphony as well. Exposure is good incentive for those seeking to be more successful at their passion. It never hurts to ask.

If you don't feel confident asking others to trade services, or more honestly, don't have the energy to commit to returning the favor, you might want to consider creating your own music. Those of us who have no idea how one note fits together with another to make a sound that makes sense have been given a miracle. There are companies such as SmartSound (www.smartsound.com) that have created computer software that enables you to compose your own royalty-free soundtracks. (Some versions of Adobe Premiere come with SmartSound QuickTracks, for instance, shown in Figure 10.6.)

Apple offers a product called SoundTrack that does much the same thing; it's also designed to work directly with Final Cut Pro 4. Their applications enable you to take some royalty-free tracks and then set the parameters for variables such as tempo, key, time signature, note selection or exclusion, timbre, and so on. The computer generates the music accordingly, turning a typical royalty-free track into something that fits the pacing and rhythm of your video more exactly. It may require some trial and error before you create the perfect piece, but at least you don't have to do it from scratch.

Foley Work and Sound Effects

Footsteps, doors slamming, water dripping, a whirring fan, chalk on a chalkboard are all sounds that a *Foley artist* might re-create. A sound can

FIGURE 10.6

SmartSound QuickTracks is a plug-in for Premiere that you can use to create custom, royalty-free soundtracks.

be created in post-production by a professional Foley artist if the original recorded sound was unsatisfactory or, perhaps, not pronounced enough to convey the action or emphasize a point. (Or maybe you didn't record the sound at all when you were shooting the scene.) It may seem superfluous, but again we encourage you to watch some TV shows and movies to illustrate our point. Do you hear car doors slam? Footsteps on gravel? Grandfather clocks or church bells?

As you've seen earlier in this chapter, a lot of video and film work is done with directional or lavalier microphones, so how did they get that perfect sounding car door? Did they really get a church to play those bells over and over again on cue? Probably not. In a lot of those cases, the footsteps and bells were added in much later, during post-production. You may want to do this, too, to add dimension and detail—using sound—to your productions.

If you've seen any of those specials on TV about how movies are made, you have probably seen the elaborate rooms of materials and devices used to make sounds. For example, a Foley room might be outfitted with different types of flooring so that the Foley artist can record herself walking on hardwood floors or linoleum or through sand, carpet, leaves, or any number of surfaces. The artist has the ability to create a wealth of sounds, including punching sounds, car screeches, or whatever else you can imagine. With a decent microphone and a bit of creativity you can do the same. You can even use your camera while on location and record sound effects while other scenes are being prepped. There are no true rules in this business, so make it happen in whichever way works for your particular situation. The key is to keep in mind that, at some point, you may want to add these sound effects, so think about how you can get them ahead of time or most efficiently.

You can also take the easy way out—*effects libraries*. Programs such as iMovie have a few effects built in—dogs barking and so on—but the professional solution is an effects library that can be rented or purchased in much the same way that a music library can. An effects library will have hundreds of sounds from chirping birds to crashing waves to jackhammers and wind chimes. The libraries usually have variations of each sound as well, but you can always manipulate the sound once you have it within your editing software. Once the sound has been imported into your editing program, you can place it on an active audio track (see Figure 10.7) and then, in the more advanced NLE applications, you can apply special effects to it, as well.

Along with some of the music library companies already mentioned—particularly Digital Juice and Sound Dogs—many professionals use a company called Sound Ideas (www.sound-ideas.com). Their 6000 series is the most widely used effects library for production work. But it's not the only one—online companies such as SoundFX.com (www.soundfx.com) and SoundEffects.com (www.soundeffects.com) have listings of several effects libraries.

FIGURE 10.7

Adding a sound effect to an existing video project

Adding Narration

Narration is widely used in every style of filmmaking from corporate videos to feature films and television documentaries and even in home video. A narrator helps the audience have a greater understanding of what is shown on screen. Narration is sometimes referred to as *voice-over* or *V.O.* A voice-over is voice *only*—you don't see the speaker—placed over existing video. For example, in a nature video you may see ants in their happy little ant home and hear a voice telling you that the queen ant is cozy in her nest while her soldier ants have been building new tunnels for her move to a brand new queen's boudoir that they have been busily constructing. You hear a voice, but you don't see the speaker—that's voice-over.

Generally, a V.O. will give you information that is not readily apparent in the existing video. There's no need for narration if what was shot tells the story or illustrates the idea clearly. Narration would be redundant. In feature films in particular, V.O. should be used sparingly, only when necessary or for stylistic reasons like in "American Beauty" in which the main character played by Kevin Spacey provides the voice-over to make it *his* story. Some other feature films that have utilized narration for stylistic reasons are "It's a Wonderful Life," "Soul Food," "Casino," "Goodfellas," "A Clockwork Orange," and "Forrest Gump." As a very general rule, V.O. is seen as something of a cop-out for screenwriters, who are expected to be able to tell their story without resorting to narration. That said, some of the best movies made have had voice-over, so it's one of those rules that are made to be broken.

With the microphone on your camera or with an external microphone plugged in to the camcorder, you can record voice-over in almost any quiet setting. The key is to minimize background noise to virtually nothing. Book a sound or recording studio if you have access to one in your town—if not, a quiet room in your house or office should work. Many times, local bands will improvise a recording studio or practice room, which would work perfectly for recording your narration. (It never hurts to ask, and they probably wouldn't mind giving you studio time if you offer to use some of their music in your work.)

 *zoom-in*

If you need to record voice-over while you are on location (and your location budget doesn't include high-end trailers), a great impromptu studio is inside your car. After all, it's closed off from the rest of the world and is well padded with plastic and fabric, so sound will not bounce all over the place.

Timing is the most important factor to consider when recording voice-over. The scripted copy has to fit the length of the video. Monitoring the timing can be accomplished in a variety of ways. The most accurate technique would be to run the video (with the sound muted, of course) while recording the narration. This will help the voice-over *talent* (the individual you've hired or cajoled into reading the narration) not only with timing, but also with the motivation for their readings, giving them a sense of the emphasis and emotion behind the words by looking at the scene simultaneously. If you are unable to run the video during recording, make sure you use a watch or stopwatch (or your editing software) and get an exact length for the video clip that you're narrating. You will have a little flexibility when editing the voice-over in your software, but it's best to make your voice-over fit the video as well as possible when recording.

With or without the video, it is wise to record the V.O. at different tempos and rhythms, various inflections and emphasis, with varying degrees of emotion, volume, and maybe even accents. It's hard to be objective when recording, so give yourself options for editing. But as mentioned before, make sure you are timing each recording and keeping it under the length of the video clip in question. If one take is too long, you may not be able to cut it down to fit the video, even if it was the best take.

focus ───────────────────────────────────────

If you end up recording the V.O. in multiple sessions, it becomes important to record in the same place or at least under the same conditions (with the same microphones and equipment and at the same levels and ambient noise) each time so that it sounds consistent throughout the story.

Who will be delivering the voice-over? Your best friend, though he or she may be readily available and free, may not be the right person for the job. Does your project need a voice with a heavy English accent, Southern U.S. accent, Midwestern U.S. accent, or the precise diction of a news anchor? It's important to choose the appropriate voice for the job. It's helpful to work with someone who is familiar with what they're doing, as amateurs tend to speak too quickly, breathe too loudly, and inflect very unnaturally when reading. (Some pros are the same way or, worse, they have too affected of a "radio voice" to make good voice-over speakers.)

Are you planning to do the voice-over yourself? That's fine—don't immediately think that voice-over requires a deep baritone. Most people have interesting voices and, particularly if the piece is about you, using your voice may be the best solution. (It's definitely the cheapest.) Here are some hints:

- **Know the material**   Write your voice-over script out and read through it a number of times. If you know what you're going to say, you'll sound more natural.

- **Relax and read slowly**   The biggest mistake that people make—even those used to speaking into a microphone—is speaking too quickly. You get nervous when the Record button is pressed and it's only worse if the material is actually a bit too long for the amount of time you have. Relax, take a big breath before pressing the Record button and then read as slowly as you comfortably feel that you can. Realize that a video voice-over isn't radio—most of the time you want it to sound like you're comfortably chatting and recounting a story.

- **Break it up and give yourself some practice tries**   Don't go into the recording session assuming you can record three minutes of perfect speaking straight without a break. Instead, break the narration into smaller chunks and be ready to do it in a number of different takes. You'll improve as you go on, but it's always going to be much easier to do 30-second chunks.

Editing Tips for Sound

Should you mess around with the volume and other settings on your clips' sound first? Or lay down all of your video clips and then try to match sound and soundtrack to them? Like everything else in this book, there is no one way to do anything. Some folks prefer to edit sound before picture, while others wait until the very end. Many times your project dictates what comes first. Commercials and music videos are generally projects in which sound might be edited before the picture since both are limited either by time or content such as music. In those two cases, the editor would simply lay down the song or the voice-over and then pop in the images in the desired manner. With music videos, the timing of the music usually dictates when to cut the video clips, whether you're editing to the beat or against it.

For documentaries, event video, and organizational projects that are driven by the pictures and the story, the typical approach is to lay down a rough cut of your clips, then do a sound edit so that the sound flows nicely while you add in overlays and intercuts. Once you've got a video that tells the story and is visually interesting, you can find places to drop in some soundtrack music or, if necessary, sound effects. Many other projects can "cut picture before sound"—you can edit your pictures first, then make the sound match. Big Hollywood movies are generally edited according to a script, plugging in scenes in the order in which they should appear and working with the sound once the picture is locked in place.

It may seem like sound is a minor element, but as we mentioned at the beginning of this chapter (and it can't be said enough), bad sound will make a potentially great project awful. When Nina and the screening committee for the film festival she works with have looked at all of the submissions that come in from around the world, they've found that bad sound can eliminate a film from being selected even if the film is well shot and the story is compelling. If the sound is poor, it makes the entire project unprofessional for screening and unwatchable for large audiences. No one wants to ride the volume button on the remote control throughout a TV show or movie, and no one will sit in a theater for long and listen to muffled voices or poorly matched volumes. Conversations should flow smoothly with people's voices at virtually the same level and quality, music shouldn't overpower dialogue, transitions from one scene to the next should be smooth and seamless, and sound effects should be believable.

Sound also is the most important element in creating the mood for a scene or project. Pop in a DVD of your favorite movie with a Special Features section and look for scenes that were not used in the film and compare them to the scenes that were used in the film. The unused scenes will seem bland and lifeless in comparison to the perfectly *mixed* scene in the film with music and sound effects. (For Hollywood productions, audio often goes through the same kind of *mixing* process that pop music does to give it a rich tonality and to meet various Dolby and surround sound standards.) Imagine "Apocalypse Now" without sounds of war and destruction and music and voice-over. It wouldn't be nearly as rich an experience. Watch and listen closely next time you see a movie or check out the Academy Award winners and nominees for Sound Design and Editing—and then watch those movies—to get a sense of why they're considered the best.

So, how do you create the perfect mix for your project? For simple sound editing, most editing software such as iMovie, Adobe Premiere, and Final Cut Express will have the capabilities to do a basic sound edit. If you'd like to be more precise with your sound edit, you can download a free version of ProTools, the premier sound editing software used by professionals, from www.digidesign.com.

Here are a few tips from some of the sound experts we interviewed:

- Match your volume levels of original recorded sound from scene to scene, person to person. Put simply, you'll do this by listening to your video as it passes from clip to clip and making sure that each clip has about the same level. You can change levels in your software by selecting a clip and then either dragging a volume slider or moving a level indicator up and down (shown is Final Cut):

focus

With higher-end editing software, you can get a little more exact with your sound while at the same time making sure the levels are correct for conversion to analog and playback on a television. The standard normal level at which you should set in your editing software is –12dB (though to be safe, one sound recordist we know works around –20dB) while for analog it is 0dB. At 0dB, digital audio will distort and be virtually unusable, whereas analog sound is more giving and handles distortion more gracefully. If your original recording levels are above or below –12dB, you may need to use your software to change those levels. In Premiere and Final Cut you'll make those changes using the level line, which you can drag up and down in the timeline.

- You will have several tracks of sound to accommodate dialogue, voice-over, music, and effects. Familiarize yourself with recognizing what tracks of sound take priority in various situations. For example, if you have voice-over, you will want to bring down the sound that was recorded during the shoot in order to clearly hear the voice-over. Also, in general, your background music track will be at a lower volume than your tracks with dialogue. There are always exceptions, but you will be safe following these simple rules.

- Just like editing images, you will have to build in transitions between shots such as fades and dissolves in order to move from one scene to the next smoothly. Some cuts will be fine as they are, but many times an effect will need to be rendered such as a cross-fade, fade-out, or fade-in to match the effect put on the video or to emphasize the scene. For example, at the end of a video, most sound and picture do not abruptly end, but rather they fade out slowly. These tiny details will make a huge difference. Most editing software is capable of rendering simple effects, and in Final Cut or Premiere you can easily create small keyframes to fade out audio—in this example, we're using Final Cut to fade an audio clip:

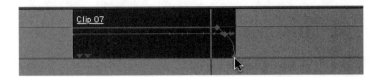

- Editing sound stylistically can help build your characters and the action in your video. Imagine a horror flick—many times you know that something terrible is going to happen because the audio will lead you. The music will build up in the previous scene before you see the killer at large, for example. You can also lead the viewer toward an emotion with narration, dialogue, or even sound effects. (Consider the difference that a distant siren can make in a scene where someone is committing a crime or is trying to get away from the police.) You can also punch up the sound of something to make it more dramatic.

Our best advice is to remember that sound is vitally important to your production and, as such, it's important that you prioritize getting good sound when you're planning and executing your production shoots. Get good sound with good microphones and half the battle is won. The other half takes place in your editing software, where attention to detail, creative Foley work, a good soundtrack, and clever audio editing can really help make the difference between a mediocre, well-shot video and an outstanding, well-shot video. When people see what you can do, they'll ask for more.

And...Cut!

In this chapter, you learned about microphones and recording technology, you read some tips for being a better sound engineer, and you got a quick overview of how camcorder inputs work and what controls you'll find on prosumer or better camcorders. You also learned about soundtracks and soundtrack software, sound effects, Foley work, and narration. The chapter finished up with some bullet point suggestions on how best to edit sound in your video editing software. In the next chapter, we'll build on your newfound knowledge of audio editing by looking at the visual special effects and clever editing tricks that today's NLE applications allow you to accomplish.

Special Effects

IF you enjoy the "magic" that computers can muster, you'll enjoy playing around with special effects. What we call special effects can range from active and animated transitions (twists and turns on the fades and wipes we talked about in Chapter 9) to commands that change the brightness, color saturation, and general appearance of your video. You can use special effects to slightly enhance or dramatically change the look of your video. You can use effects for fun or to improve the telling of a story. You can use them to fix mistakes or to better communicate ideas.

Of course, special effects aren't actually magic. Each frame in digital video is an individual picture made up of thousands of tiny dots, called *pixels*. Each pixel has a certain color or intensity, which can be changed using computer software and sophisticated commands. By applying a particular special effect command to a series of frames—whether the frames comprise a second, two seconds, or ten minutes of video—you can rework the pixels. The result can be anything from a subtle shift in colors to special transitions, to the layering of images so that a person can appear to be standing in front of a weather map, a beautiful sunset, or a space station.

In this chapter we'll look at three different levels of special effects. We'll start with some of the basics that you'll find in all sorts of nonlinear editing (NLE) applications, from iMovie to Adobe Premiere: brightness, contrast, color, and tonal quality of the image. We'll include fun effects such as soft focus and fog filters. Then, we'll look at some higher-end effects, which you're more likely to find in Final Cut or Adobe Premiere. These effects require additional settings and expertise. Finally, we'll look at some of the techniques that go along with these effects to add motion, animation, compositing, and other tricks.

Special Effects Basics

For starters, let's focus on some of the basic special effects that you'll find in nearly any NLE application. In the broadest sense, a special effect in computer-based editing is simply a command that enables you to "paint" individual frames of video. Because video is composed of individual frames—about 30 per second in North American standard (NTSC) video—each frame can be accessed as if it were a still image, such as a JPEG or TIFF that you might manipulate in Adobe PhotoShop or a similar application. This allows you to make a number of adjustments that are similar to those you might make to still images, such as adjusting color, brightness, and contrast. In the higher-end applications these adjustments are called *filters;* in applications such as iMovie, color adjustments are bundled along with the other effects.

Filtering Colors and Appearance

Don't like the color in your video, or a portion of it? Change it. We'll look at how to change color in a number of different NLE applications, starting with the simplest.

iMovie 3 Color Effects

To change color in iMovie 3, select a video clip (or multiple clips) on the Timeline, and then click the Effects button on the right-hand side of the interface. Now, click the Adjust Colors effect; it should be at the top of the list. When you select this effect, the controls change slightly, displaying three sliders at the bottom of the effects panel: Hue Shift, Color, and Lightness. Move these sliders to change the color settings for the selected clip. You'll see a preview of the color change in the small window at the top of the effects panel (see Figure 11.1). When you have finished making choices, click Apply to apply the effect to the selected clip(s).

FIGURE 11.1

Here's an effect being previewed in the effects pane in iMovie.

focus

As you may have noticed, iMovie renders all effects, transitions, and titles immediately after you apply them to a clip. With special effects, this can mean waiting a long time after clicking the Apply button while the red line that denotes rendering time creeps along in the clip's box on your Timeline. You may be able to work with iMovie while it is applying the effect, but you won't be back to full speed until the effect is finished rendering. For this reason, it's ideal to get most of your editing and transitions done, saving all your effects for later in your project.

iMovie has a number of other effects that are designed to alter the overall color of each selected frame. The Black & White effect changes all selected frames to a grayscale. Sepia Tone turns the image a reddish brown, which is meant to suggest an aged black-and-white photo or film. Sepia Tone is also commonly used to give images an American Old West appearance.

Final Cut Effects

In Final Cut, more effects are at your disposal than with iMovie. They are more powerful than iMovie and relatively easy to add, but they can be more complicated to work with. As with Final Cut's titles and transitions, you access the effects by clicking the Effects tab in the Browser window and then opening one of the effects folders (which Final Cut calls *bins*). For basic effects, open the Video Filters bin, where you'll find a number of subfolders that hold some of the filter effects we want to look at.

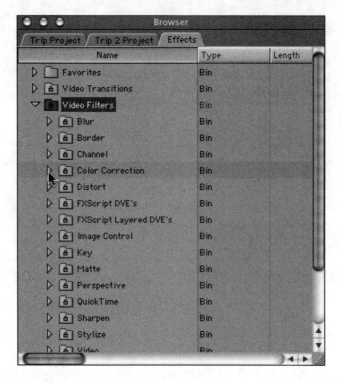

For starters, open the Image Control bin and note the Color Balance filter. Drag the filter to a clip in the Timeline and drop it on the clip. Now, double-click the clip to select it in the Viewer window (by default, it's the window farthest to the left at the top of the screen). It is in the Viewer window that you can make changes to a clip's settings once a filter has been applied to it.

 zoom-*in*

You can also select a clip in the Timeline and then choose Effects | Video Filters. Then choose the type of filter and the filter's name to add it to the Filters tab in the Viewer window.

When you double-click the clip, it appears in the Viewer window. Click the Filters tab; you should see the controls for the filter that you dragged from the browser. (In fact, you'll see controls for *all* of the filters that have been added to this clip.) The following illustration shows the Color Balance filter.

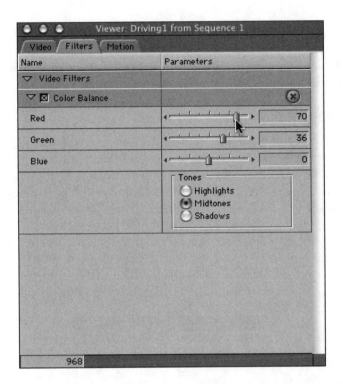

Select one of the sliders and move it around to see what it can do. The image in the Canvas window should change to reflect the changes you're making in the filter's controls. (If you don't see the image changing, check the playhead on the Timeline to be sure it's over the clip that you're currently editing.) Note that the changes have been previewed but they haven't been applied; they still need to be rendered. Until they're rendered, you won't be able to see many of the effects in motion—you may only be able to look at them a frame at a time. When you've changed settings to your liking, select Sequence | Render Selection. (You can also choose Sequence | Render All to render other effects or transitions you might have in your project.) When the rendering is done you'll be able to watch the clip with the newly applied filter.

 *zoom-in*

It's a good idea to move through your clip frame-by-frame before rendering in order to see whether the effect looks good on every frame that you've selected. If not, you can make changes to the settings for individual frames in order to improve them. This attention to detail may take a little longer, but it will help your final project look as good as it can.

Final Cut offers plenty of filters to keep you busy for a while; in the Image Control bin alone you'll find simple effects such as Brightness & Contrast, Tint, and Sepia. Venture outside the Image Control bin and you'll find a wealth of others—we'll look at a few more later in this section.

Adobe Premiere

Adobe Premiere's approach to adding effects is similar to Final Cut's. With a clip selected in your Timeline, move to the Effects window and click the Video tab. The Video tab contains a number of folders that house various video filters. For example, open the Image Control folder (you can either double-click it or click the disclosure triangle next to the folder icon) to see filters that are similar to those we've already discussed, such as Color Balance, Black & White, and Tint. (Brightness & Contrast and other similar filters are under the Adjust folder.) Drag one of these filters to your Timeline and drop it on the clip that you want to change. The Effect Controls window appears, where you can choose the settings that the filter provides.

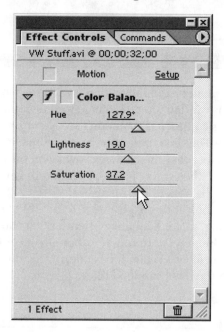

To remove a filter from a clip, select the clip and make sure that the Effect Controls window appears (if not, use the Window | Show Effect Controls command to make it appear). In the Effect Controls window click the small Trash icon to delete the effect from the clip.

The preceding steps are essentially all it takes to add filters in Premiere. Of course, the learning curve comes in figuring out what each effect is for and how best to use it. You can experiment with them to get a sense of when you might use a Gaussian Blur, a distortion filter, or a stylizing filter. Not every project needs all these effects, but they are handy for cleaning up video that doesn't look its best or for adding fun effects to home videos, short films, features, and similar projects. You'll probably find that it's useful to play with the color levels on many of the clips you shoot, if only because the colors we tend to have in our offices and studios can be dull compared to what we're used to seeing in Hollywood movies. By playing with contrast and color settings, you can sometimes make your video clips a little more vivid and pleasant to watch.

Applying Effects Over Time

The second type of effect takes place over time—you literally watch the effect as it occurs in the video. This type of effect can be anything from a picture slowly changing colors or getting brighter to a special effect that is applied more intensely as the clip plays on. For instance, NLE applications offer a "film look" or "film noise" clip, which makes video clips look like the aging film scores of years ago. By applying this effect over time, you can create a clip in which the film noise appears to increase as the clip goes on. You could use this effect to suggest that the clip is getting worse and worse until it breaks or bends, as if it were being eaten up by a projector.

On the CD-ROM We've put an example of this effect on the Chapter 11 section of the included CD-ROM.

You could also apply an effect over time to suggest that the sun is coming up, an earthquake is occurring, or an image is starting to blur (which might be handy if your protagonist has had his drink drugged and is falling asleep). And, as you'll see a little later in this section, you use this motion technique in Final Cut and Premiere to add an effect that is a basic staple for any video editor—a Fade In or Fade Out effect.

iMovie

iMovie 3 allows you to set Effect In and Effect Out times for nearly all the special effects that it offers, enabling you to create some basic effects over time. The effect occurs as you watch the clip. For instance, say you choose to make the clip gradually change from its original color to black and white using iMovie's built-in Black & White effect. If you set an Effect In time of three seconds (3:00), the clip will start out at its normal level and then will gradually fade to black and white until it reaches the full setting at the three-second mark. The rest of the clip will play in black and white until it ends.

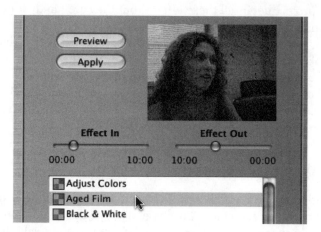

The Effect Out slider can be used to achieve the reverse effect. Set it at two seconds (2:00), for instance, and the clip will revert from black and white (or whatever effect settings you've made) to the original color level, so that it's back to normal just as the clip ends.

Adobe Premiere

Adobe Premiere's ability to work with effects over time is impressive. Premiere employs a concept called *keyframing*, in which you designate a particular frame in the video as special—a *keyframe*—and then set an effect or filter for that frame. Then, you designate another keyframe and choose *different* settings for that keyframe. Premiere automatically fills in the frames between the two, gradually progressing from the first keyframe's settings to the second's. If, for instance, the first keyframe's settings are for full color and the second keyframe's settings are for black and white, the frames in between the two would start out at nearly full color and progress slowly toward the final frame of black and white. When you playback the rendered video, the effect would appear to take place over time.

focus

You often don't have to set an initial keyframe because most NLE software assumes that the first frame of a clip is a keyframe, as is the last frame of the clip. So, to gradually change a clip to black and white as it is played, you would simply set a keyframe half way into the clip and change its color settings to black and white. The clip would begin in color (assuming that it was shot in color) and then gradually change to black and white as it approached the defined keyframe.

Here's how it works:

1. Make sure that the clip you want to use for keyframing an effect is on track Video 2 or higher and click the disclosure triangle next to the track's name (such as Video 2 or Video 3). Doing so reveals the Keyframe Line.

2. Click the Display Keyframes button under the name of the track (e.g. Video 2)—it's the diamond-shaped button.

3. Drag an effect filter to the clip in the Timeline (this example uses Color Balance).

4. Place the playhead at the point on the Timeline where you would like the first keyframe to appear.

5. In the Effect Controls window (shown are the controls for Color Balance), click the small Enable Keyframing box (when you do, a tiny stopwatch-like icon appears; that means this effect will now change over time between keyframes).

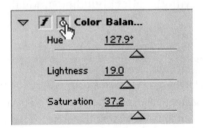

6. Set the effect's sliders and options so that they reflect the settings you want for the first keyframe in this clip.

7. Drag the playhead to the location where you want the next keyframe; you'll see a small diamond representing the first keyframe you set.

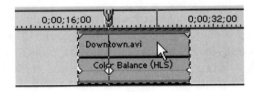

Every time you place the playhead and change the settings for the effect, you create another keyframe. After setting a few keyframes, your clip will show the keyframes in the Timeline.

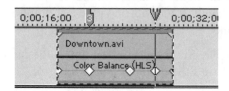

 focus

If you end up with a keyframe you don't want, select it in the Timeline. A small checkbox appears over on the left side of the Timeline under the track name where you're adding keyframes (Track 2, Track 3, etc.). Click the checkbox and the keyframe will disappear.

That's it. Now, when you render this effect, the levels of the effect will take place over time, with the effect building gradually from one keyframe setting to the next.

zoom-in

You can use keyframing to both increase and decrease an effect. For instance, you can have a clip that goes very red, using a Color Balance filter, and then have it go back to normal settings. To do this, you use two different keyframes: an initial keyframe that is set to red and placed midway in the clip so that the clip builds toward that keyframe, and a second keyframe that is set at the original color settings toward the end of the clip. After going to red, the clip will slowly change the effect to normal as it works toward the second keyframe.

Fades in Adobe Premiere and Final Cut Express

Unlike Adobe Premiere, Final Cut Express doesn't allow you to change a filter's settings over time using keyframes. And unlike iMovie, it doesn't offer simple Effect In and Effect Out settings. (Final Cut Pro is capable of doing this.) With Final Cut Express, however, you can use keyframes to set in and out points for audio and video *fades*, which, as discussed in Chapter 9, are a common type of transition.

On the CD-ROM   The fade is a classic (and classy) transition that is used to begin and end "sequences" in your video. You can also use fades to suggest the passage of time or to cleverly cut together interview footage. See the Chapter 11 section of the CD-ROM for examples of the fade effect.

The process for creating fade effects is similar for Premiere, so we'll cover both applications in this section. (Fades in iMovie are discussed in Chapter 9; they are added in the same way as other transitions are added: by dragging them from iMovie's list of transitions and placing them on the Timeline right before or after the clip to which the fade will be applied.)

Final Cut

In Final Cut, you create fades using *overlay lines*. You display these lines in clips by clicking the Clip Overlays button at the bottom left of the Timeline.

These lines are used to set *levels*. In an audio clip, the lines can set the volume level; in a video clip, the line is used to set the *opacity* of the clip. You can drag one of these lines to change a video clip's opacity from 100, the default, to something lower. The lower the line, the darker the clip.

Because the line is lowered or raised uniformly across the clip when you drag, you'll need to add keyframes if you want the video to fade up from black or fade down to black. To add a keyframe, click the Pen tool in the toolbar or press P. Now when you point at the line, you'll see the Pen tool icon. Click the overlay line to create a keyframe.

Add a second keyframe to drag one or both of the keyframes up and down. That will enable you to have the levels move gradually up or down with the video clip, the audio clip, or both.

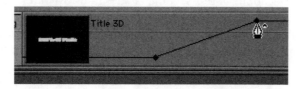

To cause a fade in to occur quickly, place the keyframes closer together; if you want the effect to occur more gradually, place them farther apart.

focus

To remove keyframes, right-click them or click and hold the mouse on the Pen tool in the toolbar to choose the pen with a minus sign, which can be used to remove keyframes.

Adobe Premiere

In Premiere, your video must be on track Video 2 or higher in order for you to create a fade effect. To create fade effects, you'll work with Premiere's *opacity rubberbands* feature, which looks almost exactly like the keyframes in Final Cut Pro. Here's how it works:

1. Enable the rubberbands line for the video clip by clicking the disclosure triangle next to the track's name (as in "Video 1" or "Video 2"). This is the same step you'd take for working with keyframes.

2. With the line revealed, make sure the small Display Opacity Rubberbands button is clicked (it has a red box with a line through it). Note that this is different from the Display Keyframes button discussed earlier.

3. Click on the line to create drag points (which are just like keyframes) and drag the little boxes to create the fade effect.

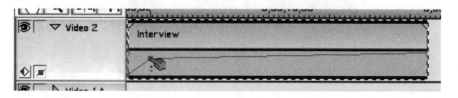

Adding Motion Effects

The pro-level NLE applications that we're focusing on offer numerous effects with all sorts of settings that are outside the scope of this book. Some of the effects are obvious and some of them will become obvious when you work with them a little and test different settings to see how they work. Others have documentation to clarify their function; in fact, some effects have buttons in their control panels that enable you to view help or link to the effect's web site (particularly for third-party effects).

One type of effect that is common to both Adobe Premiere and Final Cut is the capability to use keyframing to add motion effects to video—for example, moving the picture around on the screen, changing its size, and so on. And, by combining motion and layering, you can place "picture-in-picture" style graphics and images or create your own titles and transitions.

Basic Motion

The basic idea with a motion effect is simple. You begin by creating keyframes in a clip, and then you change the position of the clip in the Viewer window from one keyframe to the next. For instance, with both Adobe Premiere and Final Cut you can set a clip so that it scrolls from one side of the visible display to the other, or from top to bottom. You can also resize a video image in either application; so, using keyframes, you could cause the image to grow or shrink on the screen. This capability can be handy for creating transitions or for building evening news-style graphics and overlays.

Final Cut

We'll start with Final Cut's capability to add motion to a clip. First, some motion effects can be added and adjusted without adding keyframes—they are built in. Double-click a clip in your Timeline and, in the Viewer window you'll see a tab called Motion. Click the tab to see a number of basic effects that you can apply to any clip in Final Cut. Each effect has a disclosure triangle next to it that can be used to reveal the effect's settings. Figure 11.2, for instance, shows the Basic Motion controls.

The Basic Motion controls enable you to change the scale or rotation of the image, or move it around on the screen by entering a different center point. (The center point, by default, is called 0,0, representing the x and y coordinates of the center of the screen. So, to move the image to the left, you would enter something like –30,0; to move the image up, you might try 0,–40, and so on.) If you change any of these numbers or settings, the

FIGURE 11.2

Every video clip in Final Cut can be altered using these basic effects.

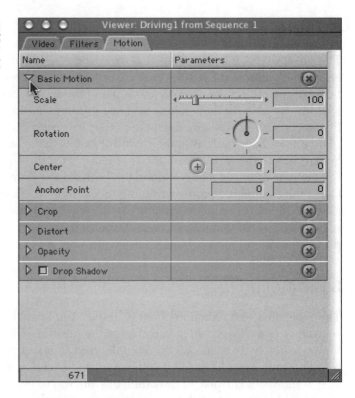

video will continue to play as normal after rendering, even if it's positioned halfway off the screen or at a funny angle.

In fact, all of these options are essentially another way to access motion effects that you can accomplish with your mouse in the Canvas window. If you'd like to use a more hands-on approach with these effects, you can drag the image around in the Canvas window to change it. First, at the top of the Canvas window, click the small menu to select it. In the menu, choose Image+Wireframe; doing so enables you to see the wireframe controls that allow you to change the video by clicking and dragging.

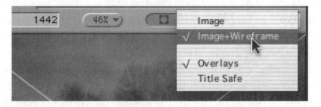

Now, using your mouse, you can click and drag different parts of the image in the Canvas window to change the Basic Motion settings for the selected clip. Click in the middle and drag, for instance, to move the image around on the canvas. Get to one of the corners of the image to resize it. Or, if you mouse around a bit, you'll see the circular cursor that enables you to rotate the image; click and drag to rotate the image. When you have finished, you might end up with something that looks a little like the following illustration.

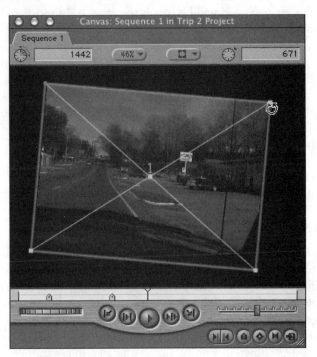

So far, these "motion" effects are actually static—you can move things around, but they don't move during playback. Of course, this is where keyframing comes in. With Final Cut, you add keyframes to the clip in the Canvas, which will enable you to set one motion preference, and then move to the next keyframe and set another motion preference. Final Cut obligingly adds the motion between the two keyframes. For this keyframing, use the keyframe button in the Canvas window—it looks like a small diamond. In the Canvas, locate the first frame that you'd like as a keyframe and click the keyframe button or press CONTROL-K.

In the Canvas window, you'll see the wireframe turn green, indicating an active keyframe. Change the settings on the Motion tab. Next, move to another part of the clip and set another keyframe; then, make additional changes to the video—you can rotate, resize, or move the image around on the canvas. (If you drag the image to the edge of the Canvas, try not to push it all the way off, as it will be tough to retrieve. In most cases, taking the video image too close to the edge, even if you can see a little bit of it, will mean it won't be visible when viewed with a TV. You can use the Wireframe menu in the Canvas window to turn on the Title Safe indicators, which can help you see where the edge of a typical TV screen would be.)

When you have finished rotating and moving, you should be able to move the playhead back and forth on the clip to get a basic sense of how the final effect will look. Render the image (Sequence | Render Selection or Sequence | Render All) to see the final motion effects.

On the CD-ROM   Check the Chapter 11 section of the included CD-ROM examples of these motion effects.

Adobe Premiere

Premiere also offers keyframing options and techniques, including the capability to control the motion of the video image. With a clip selected in the Timeline, choose Clip | Video Options | Motion. Doing so brings up a special Motion window, which you can use to change the motion of the video image across the display. To change the motion of the image, drag the beginning and end points on the line in the motion pane, which is on the right side. As shown in Figure 11.3, you can add keyframes on that line simply by clicking it and dragging the new keyframe box that appears. These keyframes enable you to add to the motion that is occurring. When you manipulate these lines and keyframes, you create a path for the video image as it crosses the visible area.

At the bottom of the Motion window are a few other motion options. You can use the Fill Color option to place a different color in the background, so that when part of the visible area is not covered by the image, it's covered by this fill color. In the center of the window are settings you can use to change the angle of the image (Rotation), the size of the image (Zoom), and the amount of time to wait before this clip's motion begins (Delay). Note that you can use these settings without a motion path, if desired, to simply make the image bigger or smaller over time (using Zoom) or to rotate the clip while it's playing back.

For example, here's how to make a clip disappear, which might be handy for a transition effect:

1. Select the clip in the Timeline and choose Clip | Video Options | Motion.

2. In the Motion window, place the Start image in the center of the Visible Area. You can use the Center button to help you place it perfectly.

3. With the Finish image selected, change the Zoom setting to 0%.

4. Move the Finish image to the portion of the Visible Area to which you'd like it to disappear. You can even choose a location outside of the Visible Area.

5. Click OK.

Now, at your discretion, you can render the effect using the Timeline | Render Work Area command. (You can also use the Timeline | Preview function if you'd like to see the effect more quickly without rendering.) Once rendered, the image will appear to shrink to a dot and then disappear when the clip ends. In the Timeline, you should have a video clip that this image overlaps, which will make the transition appear to be more seamless.

Graphic Overlays

The motion and resizing capabilities of advanced NLE applications also provide the capability to *overlay* graphics on top of a moving video image.

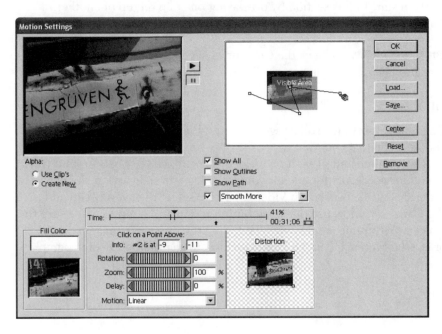

FIGURE 11.3

Here's an example of creating a motion path in Premiere.

As an example, think of the local news. The floating box above the anchor's head that illustrates the story that she's covering can be created using the motion tools. To do so, shrink a still frame image that is above the motion video of the anchorwoman. You'll need to create the overlay graphic in a program such as Adobe PhotoShop or a similar application. Create an image that is 720 × 480 pixels; if your application has the option, use a "TV-safe" color palette. Most NLE software can deal with TIFF, high-quality JPEG images, or other common image formats.

Alternatively, you can use two motion clips to create a picture-in-picture effect. This approach is useful for sporting events—for example, for overlaying interview footage and B-roll (interview the student athlete in an overlay box while the game is played at full size) or showing two views at once (show the archer pulling his bow at full size and show the target in a smaller overlay).

This process of creating graphic overlays is also called *compositing*, as you essentially take two different clips and make a composite of them— bringing them together to create one new image. Overlaying two clips, as we'll discuss in this section, is fairly simple. Creating titles in sophisticated NLE software is a more complex type of overlay compositing. In a later section we'll discuss the type of compositing that mixes two different clips to create the "blue screen" effect, which enables an actor or subject to be placed in front of a graphical background, like on a television weather report or in superhero movies.

We'll start in this section by overlaying one clip on top of another in Final Cut and Premiere.

On the CD-ROM   Check the Chapter 11 section of the included CD-ROM for sample clips of overlay techniques and uses.

Final Cut

Begin by importing a still image using the File | Import | File command or choose a clip that you want to use for the overlay. Next, drag the overlay clip to the Timeline and place it on a video track above your background track. (In other words, if your anchorwoman footage or main action clip is on Video 1, put the overlay on Video 2.) Then, select the overlay clip and in the Canvas window use the small button menu at the top to make sure that Image+Wireframe is selected. Then, drag the onscreen image to resize it or use the Motion tab in the Viewer window to change the size of the graphic.

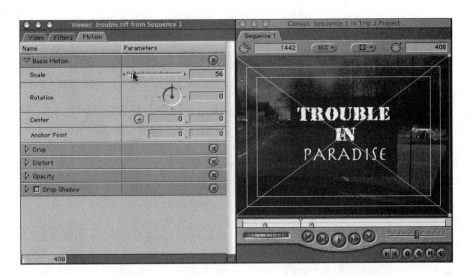

Once the overlay image is the size you want, you can drag it to the portion of the screen where you'd like it to be—assuming you don't want it in the center. Note that you can also use the Motion tab's controls to change the rotation of the image and specify its location more exactly.

For the record, you can combine these movements with the Basic Motion effect discussed in the preceding section so that the overlay starts out full size, shrinks in the middle, rotates, and then moves to the top corner (picture the two preceding illustrations in motion). This capability could be used to create a fun graphic that adds life to your home video or an organizational or training tape.

 *zoom-in* _____

One good use for these overlay techniques is in training videos or any video that uses PowerPoint or similar presentation slides. Instead of taping the speaker standing in front of the slides, you can overlay the slides, and then move them up to the corner of the video, as an overlay, while the trainer is speaking. This technique allows the viewer to see the slides in detail while adding visual interest to what might otherwise be a less-than-thrilling stand-up presentation.

Final Cut has additional filters that might be of interest when you're working with overlay video. On the Motion tab, you'll find two filters in particular that you might want to look at—Opacity and Drop Shadow. The Opacity controls add sophistication to overlay images by enabling you to make them either fully visible or partially transparent. Use the slider to pull the opacity toward zero to see through the overlay graphic. Click the checkbox next to Drop Shadow, and then click the Drop Shadow disclosure triangle to see controls for altering the appearance of a drop shadow that appears beneath the overlay graphic. Again, using this feature makes the overlay look a little more professional.

Adobe Premiere

Begin by importing a still image (use the File | Import | File command) or choose a video clip that you want to use for the overlay. Next, place the overlay clip on the Timeline above the base clip (the one that will be the background video for this overlay). If you've placed a still image clip, you must render the work area (Timeline | Render Work Area) to see the still image clip overlay the clip below it.

To change the size of the image or move it around on the screen, make sure the clip is highlighted in the Timeline, and then choose Clip | Video Options | Motion. You'll see the Motion Settings window. Here you can choose to make the overlay image smaller (choose one of the keyframes and change the Zoom level to something less than 100%), you can use the keyframes to draw a path for the image to move around, and so on. In Figure 11.4, we've set the image to shrink over time to 30% while moving to the top-right corner. The 30% is assigned to a keyframe that is about halfway along the path; the Finish keyframe is also set to 30%. These settings cause the image to shrink and move for about half the time it's on the screen and then to sit in the corner for the remainder of its duration.

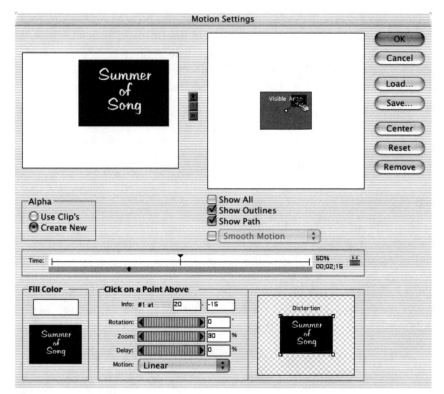

FIGURE 11.4

In this Motion Settings window, we've set the overlay image to shrink (note that the image is much smaller in the motion area to the right) and move toward the top-right corner. The appearance of the final clip is shown in the left-hand preview pane.

 *zoom-in*

You can experiment with the Skew command in the bottom-right corner of the Motion Settings window to see other interesting effects you can create with the overlay clip. The Skew command is designed to stretch and pull the image in different directions so that it's no longer rectangular, but can be all sorts of odd shapes.

Once you've made your choices and closed the Motion Settings window, you must render the workspace again to see it in action.

Titles

Titles are a basic component of most video productions, which is why they were touched on in Chapter 9. They can also be used in conjunction with some of the concepts presented in this chapter, particularly if you're interested in titles that do more than just appear and disappear or creep across the screen. In essence, the titles you'll work with are similar to overlay graphics—you'll create a clip that has either a colored background or a transparent one. Then, you'll either add the title as a base clip (before your first video clip, for instance) or use the title as an overlay clip, using some of the same techniques we discussed in the preceding section. In either case, let's look at Final Cut and Premiere to see what they can do with titles.

Chapter 9 covers creating titles in iMovie.

Final Cut

Creating titles in Final Cut is fairly easy. You start in the Browser window by selecting the Effects tab. Scroll down through the effects to find the Text bin; open it to see some of the *video generators* that can be used to create text—and hence titles and credits—for your editing project. (Video generators are effects that create new video clips instead of altering existing ones.) Additional video generators—for example, Title 3D and Title Crawl—can be found in the Text bin.

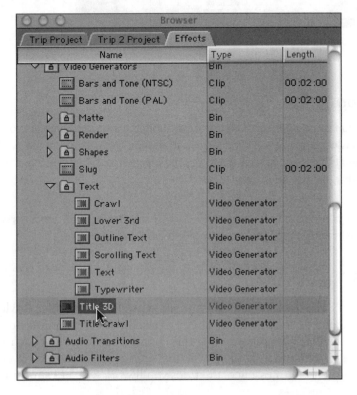

To generate titles for your project, begin by dragging one of the Text generators to your Timeline and placing the clip on a video track. A window pops up enabling you to enter the text for your title, as shown in Figure 11.5. Choose the fonts, font sizes, and other options you want to set regarding the appearance of the font. Then, click Apply.

You can change the length of the title clip by dragging it once it's in the Timeline. To make other changes, start by double-clicking the clip, which places it in the Viewer window. Next, click the Controls tab to see the controls for the titling video generator. Click the Text Entry & Style button to see a text entry window such as the one shown in Figure 11.5. Otherwise, experiment with the other controls to see how they affect the appearance of your title.

To put your titles in motion, use either the Motion tab or the Image+ Wireframe control in the Canvas window. Then you can manipulate your title sequence as you would any graphic images or picture-in-picture images as discussed in the preceding section, "Graphic Overlays." Specifically, you can move the title across the screen following a path over time, you can shrink it or grow it over time, and you can rotate it. In fact you can have quite a bit of fun! (Just remember that your titles must be readable by your audience!)

On the CD-ROM   Check the Chapter 11 section of the CD-ROM for sample clips that show various possibilities for working with titles and motion.

FIGURE 11.5

Here's an example of a text window from the Title 3D video generator.

You may be tempted to create scrolling credits on your own—and you can. Here's how:

1. Create a title clip and drag it to the Timeline.

2. Move the playhead to the beginning of the clip in the Timeline. (Use the ARROW keys so that you get to the very beginning.)

3. In the Canvas, make sure the Image+Wireframe option is turned on.

4. Drag the image in the Canvas down to the bottom of the screen so that it's barely visible. (You can send the text all the way off the screen if desired, as long as you can still see part of its wireframe.)

5. Click the Keyframe button (it looks like a small diamond) in the Canvas window. Doing so sets this first frame as a keyframe.

6. Move the playhead to the end of the clip.

7. Head back to the Canvas and drag the text's wireframe up to the top of the Canvas window; note the line that appears, showing you the path it's going to take.

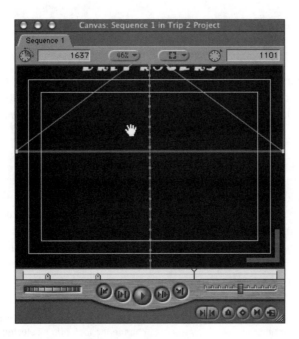

8. Click the Keyframe button again.

9. Render the clip and watch it play back. The text will scroll up the screen for the duration of the clip—the longer the clip is, the slower the scroll will be.

What's interesting about the process is not the scrolling up or down—that can be accomplished using the Title Crawl video generator, which animates the scroll automatically. (In fact, Title Crawl has some useful options, including the capability to fade text at the top and bottom of the scroll using the Mask Start and Mask End features.) Instead, what's fun with this motion is to come up with more creative paths for the titles to travel—or to toss in rotation and other features that can make the titles fun to watch.

Adobe Premiere

Premiere takes a slightly different approach to titles, although it is as flexible as Final Cut in this regard. You won't find titles in the effects folders. Instead, you create a new title by choosing File | New | Title in Premiere. Doing so brings up the Adobe Title Designer, as shown in Figure 11.6. The Title Designer offers too many features to touch on them all in this section, but suffice it to say that if you're familiar with drawing and type tools you should be able to put together basic text and graphical titles for your videos fairly easily.

zoom-in

One item worth noting is the Templates button at the top of the Title Designer window. Click the button to gain access to templates that facilitate the setup of certain themed title screens. Also, notice the motion control in the Title Designer window, which enables you to switch among still, roll, and crawl titles.

When you save the title and close the Title Designer window, the title is added to the Project window in Premiere and you are now free to work with it. To add it to your project, drag it to the Timeline; if you'd like it to overlay existing video, make sure you put it on a track that is above the video you want to overlay. Now, with the title in its track, you can manipulate it as necessary. For instance, you can add a fade to the title, just as you might add a fade to a regular clip using opacity rubberbands, as discussed in the section, "Fades in Adobe Premiere and Final Cut Express."

Use the shapes to drag shapes for your title.

Use the Object Style properties to change the look of the selected object.

FIGURE 11.6

Building a title in Adobe Title Designer has similarities to the basics in drawing programs such as Adobe Illustrator and Corel Draw.

Choose a title style.

Use the Transform properties to quickly change various qualities of the selected object.

You can also add transitions to the title clip and drag some filters onto the clip, allowing you to change its characteristics in the same way that you'd use video filters to change any other type of clip.

Compositing Video

The last concept we'll touch on before leaving you on your own to experiment with your editing program is the effect that we call *compositing*. In this context, the term essentially refers to putting two video clips together so that they become one; you might call it *superimposing* one image on the other or you might call it *masking* one image so that another one shows through. In either case, the idea starts out pretty simply but can become a little complicated once you dig deeper in your editing program. (As was mentioned earlier, creating graphics and title overlays is a form of compositing, and you can generally use the word interchangeably. You're more likely to hear it used in this context, though, when talking about mixing together clips to create a clip with a new look.)

Let's start at the simple level. The use of compositing that may come to mind most immediately is the weather portion of a newscast. If the meteorologist is standing in front of a moving map, you're witnessing video compositing. The reporter is actually standing in front of a screen or a painted wall. The backdrop is a uniform color that offers contrast to the clothes that most of us would wear on camera (certain shades of blue and green work best). Using software, the uniform background color is made transparent, so that another layer of video will show through, causing the person to appear to be standing in front of a large electronic map or something similar. With the two clips of video now viewable together, we consider them to be *composited*.

 zoom-in ————————————————————

Because of the way compositing works, it's important that your foreground image—the meteorologist, for instance—not have any of the background color in his tie or on his suit. If that happens, the background images will show through that color of clothing.

In another example, you might have a still image that you want to use as a frame for your video. The still image might be a title that says Happy Birthday!, or perhaps it's an image of a television set with a portion designed so that the motion image shows on its "screen." In this case, you're creating a portion of the video that is transparent so that the video below it only shows through the cutaway hole, often called a *mask*. (In the case of the "Happy Birthday!" message, you could have the video playing *through* the words, for a stylized title screen; in the case of the television screen, you could make the screen transparent so that it looks like your video clip is playing on the TV screen.) It's the same process, although a mask is sometimes easier to accomplish when, as in our example, you use an image (instead of moving video) and the image can be created with a uniform color that can be turned transparent.

Using Final Cut or Adobe Premiere to turn a portion of a video clip transparent isn't difficult. What's tougher is getting a video image that has a background color that is uniform enough to be easily *knocked out* of the image. Even if you have a wall in your studio painted a specific shade of bright green, you must light it uniformly, so that portions of it aren't darker than others. In addition, you must correctly light the people in front of the background and have them stand far enough forward to avoid shadows on the background. Shadowy backgrounds can be more difficult to turn transparent because the software looks for a light green, not the darker green that the shadow creates. (The software can compensate for some of this; in fact, some video filters allow amazing flexibility for knocking out a background color. As a general rule, however, the better the color is when it comes into the software, the better the final composited video will look.)

Let's look at the basics of transparency. As an example, we'll create a mask that creates a transparent box in a still image through which video can be seen. You can also use this technique for making the background transparent if you want a "Superman flying" or meteorologist look to your video, but you'll need to find an appropriate color background against which to shoot. As you may know, this second technique has taken over Hollywood, particularly in the age of digital effects. If you can perfect it for your editing (or even if you don't *quite* perfect it), you can have a lot of fun with your home movies or in producing low-budget features.

Final Cut

To begin in Final Cut you'll need a graphic image that has an area that can be turned transparent. Ideally the area is a large box or other shape that is a different color from the rest of the image, meaning that you can use the color *only* in the section that will be replaced with video (see Figure 11.7). Note that if you use the color in other places—even text—the color will be replaced with the video behind it. This could be a cool effect, but if you don't want the video image playing through your text, use a different color.

Once you have an image that works, you're ready to bring it into Final Cut and make the color transparent. Here's how:

1. Import the image (remember that a 720×480 pixel image works best) into Final Cut using File | Import | File.

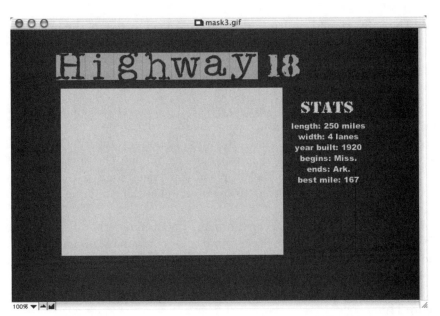

FIGURE 11.7

Here's an example of the image that we're going to use to overlay moving video—the box is in bright green.

2. Drag the image from the Browser to the Timeline on a video track that is above the video that you'd like to see filter through the image.

3. Click the Effects tab in the Browser and open the Key bin.

4. Drag the Chroma Keyer effect to the image's clip in the Timeline.

5. Double-click the image to make sure it's selected in the Viewer, and then click the Chroma Keyer tab in the Viewer.

6. This window looks complicated but it doesn't have to be. Simply click the eyedropper icon, and then click the area of the image, shown in the Canvas window, that you would like to turn transparent.

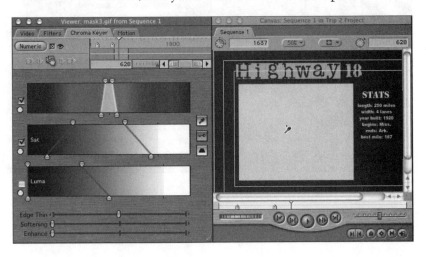

7. The video should appear in the chroma-keyed section of the image in the Canvas. (If not, try turning off the Sat and Luma checkboxes on the Chroma Key tab in the Viewer.) Transparency is keyed to that color and video will show through it (see Figure 11.8).

So, for the Superman/weatherman effect, the trick is to accomplish the exact opposite: Make a background color invisible so that the actor is placed in front of a different background—the tops of buildings zooming by or a radar screen, for example. It's the same basic technique. The difference is that you must shoot against a backdrop and you'll need some patience to knock out a live background color as opposed to knocking out one that you create in a graphics program.

As mentioned, creating the weatherman effect can be very difficult, because the uniformity of the background color is of utmost importance. The key is to follow the advice laid out previously—use uniform lighting on the background and avoid shadows. Fortunately, the software can often compensate for some differences, but not all of them, as shown in Figure 11.9).

We encourage you to shoot some video against a blue screen and experiment with the Chroma Key filter. You'll find that you can play with the filter's ranges and options to get a better result. In our example, after playing with the saturation (Sat) and the colors that the Chroma Key filter was supposed to attempt to knock out, we didn't have much luck. Then, we completely turned off the Luma setting. The result is shown in Figure 11.10.

FIGURE 11.8

With your transparency set up, the video will show through the transparent portion of your image.

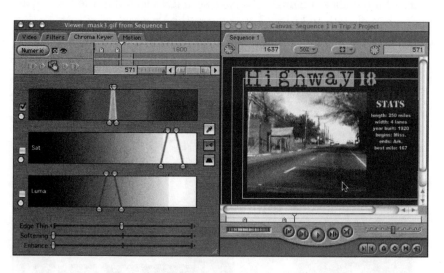

FIGURE 11.9

Here's an example of a green-screen effect that we tried to create. The background, lit only by sunlight, had a wide variety of blue shades in it.

zoom-in

The video that you place a person in front of should move very smoothly and uniformly, if it moves at all. Otherwise you'll end up with an effect that may make your audience seasick or, at the very least, will seem incredibly unrealistic.

FIGURE 11.10

When we turned off the Luma setting, we got a near-perfect result for the "weatherman" effect.

Adobe Premiere

In Premiere, creating an image overlay with some transparency is even easier. First, create an image similar to Figure 11.7, with a portion that has a unique color that you can make transparent. Then, import the image into your project (File | Import | File) and place it on the Timeline on track Video 2 or higher, above the video that is going to show through.

With the clip placed, creating the transparency is simple. Select the clip and choose Clip | Video Options | Transparency. In the Transparency Settings window, choose Chroma from the Key Type. Now, in the Color section of the window, click the color that you'd like to turn transparent. The Sample area should show the color going to gray if it has been successfully turned transparent.

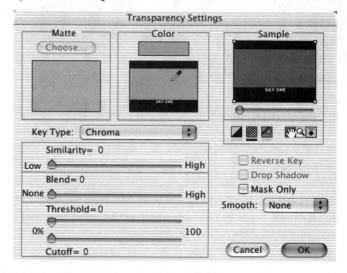

Click OK in the window and you're finished with the clip. Now all you need to do is render the work area (Timeline | Render Work Area) to see the two video clips together on screen.

And...Cut!

In this chapter you got a whirlwind tour of some of the special effects features that are possible in NLE applications, particularly the more advanced Final Cut and Adobe Premiere applications. We began by looking at basic video filters, then we moved on to a discussion of applying effects over time. We then moved on to motion effects, including animation and video overlays. We ended with transparency compositing, which enables video from one track to show through a clip on another track. In Chapter 12 we'll discuss outputting your project to various media.

Output Your Work

YOU'VE shot the raw footage, you've finished the editing and special effects work, and now, more than likely, you're sitting in front of a computer screen staring at an edited piece you know so well you could mouth it backwards in your sleep. You're probably also nine months late and you've at least tripled your budget (or lost that much money in productivity at your paying gigs). Regardless of how you got to this point, it's time to move to the next step: getting your work from the editing software into a format that is useable for playback, exhibition, or distribution. In other words, you're ready to show your work to the world—or, at least, to your friends and family.

Options for Output

People like to call digital video a *killer application*, which can be defined as a reason to use a computer that's so compelling—like editing digital video—that a person will actually buy (or upgrade) a new computer just to be able to perform that new function. One reason that digital video (DV) is considered a "killer app" is that it offers higher quality than typical consumer analog formats, making it useful for higher-end applications. Digital editing suites offer most of the tools of nonlinear editing (NLE) bays costing hundreds of thousands of dollars, squeezed into packages that cost less than $1000—in fact, some editing tools are downright cheap.

Another reason that digital video is an advance in video technology is that it puts a number of output mediums within range of the consumer. Granted, digital video technology is only part of the story; it also helps that powerful computer processors and special optical writers are also available for a reasonable cost. But the confluence of all these technologies means you can get video images out of your camcorder, edit them and return them to tape, and then output them to DVD or CDs or display and transmit them over the Internet relatively easily and without an extraordinary investment.

Here's an overview of some of the output options discussed throughout this chapter:

- **Tape**   This category includes both digital tape and analog tape. The most obvious output option might be to send your edited video back to the camcorder. This enables you not only to archive the video on MiniDV tape (or whatever tape format you're using), but also to copy the video to any other analog technology that can accept your camcorder as an input. This means you can easily create VHS or Betamax tapes or transfer the video to a broadcast-quality format.

- **Optical disc**   With certain software and DVD-Recordable hardware, you can create a DVD using your edited digital video. Depending on the software you use, you can even create DVD menus, video chapters, and many of the items you would expect from a DVD that can be played in consumer electronic equipment. (If you don't have much experience with DVD movies, know that they can be handy, allowing you to instantly move to different *chapters* in the movie in the way you might move to different tracks on an audio CD.) But DVD isn't your only option—another popular approach is to create Video CDs, which can also be used to display video in many consumer DVD players. Although the quality of Video CDs isn't as high as the quality of DVDs, they have the advantage of requiring only a CD-Recordable drive, which many existing PC and Mac systems already have.

- **Computer file**   You may have good reason to simply export your project to a different digital movie format and save it as a QuickTime, Audio Video Interchange (AVI), or other computer file. Using various *codecs* (compressor/decompressor software routines), you can compress the movie, choose a size, and so on. Then you can play the movie back from your hard disk (provided that you have a compatible playback application) or store it (and transfer it to others) via a data CD, DVD, or other removable computer medium.

focus ────────────────────────────────

The difference between creating a DVD movie (or a Video CD) and a data DVD (or a data CD-R) can be a bit confusing at first. With a DVD movie or Video CD, the disc is written in an industry-standard format that is recognized both by computers and by consumer electronic equipment such as DVD players that are hooked up to televisions. By contrast, a data DVD or data CD-R is simply another storage medium for computer files. You can save a QuickTime or AVI computer movie file to a data CD and copy it to hard disk or play it back in a computer application that knows how to display movie files.

- **Internet**   An extension of the computer file approach is creating a digital movie file that is suitable for the Internet. Movies can be shown or distributed over the Internet in a variety of ways: They can be displayed as part of a web page, attached to an e-mail message, or downloaded to your user's computer via the web or file transfer protocol (FTP). The essential requirement is to create a file that can transfer quickly enough. If you're sending an e-mail attachment or a movie that is intended for downloading, it must be a relatively small movie file—which usually requires a small image size as well as lower quality images than the original. You might also look into *streaming* Internet technologies, which enable you to use special Internet servers to play a digital movie to Internet viewers without requiring them to download the whole file first; it works a little like digital cable or satellite TV. This method requires an interest in Internet technologies and may require some software, but some of that software is freely available.

In the following sections, we'll separate the preceding options into the analog approach and the digital approach. In the analog approach you put your video back on DV tape (or other media) and then transfer it to analog tape. In the analog digital approach, you create a digital movie file and then either write it in special formats to an optical disc for playback in consumer DVD and CD players or leave it as a computer file but deliver it on data disks or over the Internet.

Output for Analog Delivery

Creating Internet video is fun, but there's nothing like getting your project back to the small screen (your TV) as soon as possible. So, once your video is essentially the way you want it, you're ready to export it to your camcorder. (Once it's there, you can always return to your project on the computer to make corrections.)

Exporting to a DV camcorder is relatively straightforward. Depending on your software, you may have to first select a command that *renders* all your titles, transitions, and special effects if they haven't been rendered already. (Rendering is the process whereby your editing software "paints" any transitions or titles to each frame of the video that needs to be altered.) Rendering can take time, as the software must step through all the math required to turn your commands for effects into actual frames of video. Of course, the length of this process depends on your computer's speed, the software, and any hardware you have added to improve speed.

With the video effects rendered, you're ready to export. Ideally, you should use a new DV tape for this export, although you could record a short edited piece to the end of one of your raw footage tapes for the same project. Obviously, which option you choose depends on the length of the project. (Before any export procedure, do a little math to make sure you have a tape that is long enough to hold your project.) Using a blank tape is a bit safer because you can keep the Record tab on your raw footage tape in the Off position, meaning you won't inadvertently record over it.

 zoom-in ————————————————————

If you opt to use an existing tape, it's best not to break timecode (as discussed in Chapter 9), which might happen if you fast forward into the unrecorded portions of the tape before outputting your video. You can get around this in one of two ways. First, you can simply record some extra time at the end of the raw footage, keeping the lens cap on and the microphone off so that you continue the timecode into "safe" space on the tape. Second, you may be able to set your software to create a "handle" of blank space before it begins recording as well as after it's completed recording the project to tape.

Getting Your Video on DV Tape

Pop your new or existing tape into the camcorder, cue it to the right spot (if relevant), and make sure your IEEE 1394 (also called FireWire or i.Link) cable is connected. Now, in your editing software, choose the output command and then make choices that enable you to output to the camcorder.

focus ————————————————————

Your camcorder isn't the only option. A number of manufacturers offer DV VTR decks, enabling you to record and play back MiniDVs directly. They tend to be expensive, but they are a good idea if you manipulate MiniDV tapes often and you don't want to wear out your camcorder's mechanism.

Here are some of the export commands for various types of software:

- **Apple iMovie**   In iMovie, choose File | Export to see the Export dialog box. In the dialog box, choose To Camera from the Export menu (it's the default option). Now, enter the amount of time that iMovie should wait before beginning to output the video (so that the camcorder can get up to speed) as well as how much black should run at the beginning and end of the video. (Don't make this too long or you might mistake the tape for a blank one in the future.) Click OK to begin the export. (iMovie renders every effect as you add it, so there's no wait at the time of export, assuming you don't attempt to export while the rendering is ongoing.)

- **Apple Final Cut**   Final Cut's command is File | Print to Video, which brings up the special Print to Video dialog box (see Figure 12.1). In this dialog box you can make a number of choices such as the type of leader that the video will have (color bars, black, a slate, or a countdown) and the audio tone. Then, you choose what to print— either the entire project you've put together or just a portion between In and Out points that you've set previously. Finally, you choose the amount of black to use as a trailer to the video that is output and click OK. Final Cut then writes your video to disk, which includes rendering any transitions or effects that require it. This can take a while, but it ensures a cleaner transfer.

focus ————————————————————————————

How do the In and Out points work? In the Canvas window, while viewing your project, you can set an In point and an Out point for your project. This can be handy if you only need to export a small part of a large project. The In and Out point controls are small buttons on the Canvas window; place the playhead in the Canvas window and then click one of these buttons to set an In or Out point.

- **Adobe Premiere**   Premiere offers a number of commands that you can use to get your project back on tape, depending on what you want to put there and how you want it presented. For final presentations you'll usually use the File | Export Timeline | Print to Video feature, which enables you to add color bars and blank handles to your video. The Export Timeline | Export to Tape feature is a little more straightforward, enabling you to simply put a particular clip or series of clips on tape without the color bars and other features of a final presentation. The Export to Tape command can be used to control your camcorder; with the Print to Video feature, you must press Record on your camcorder manually. Whichever command you choose, Premiere immediately builds a *preview* which includes

FIGURE 12.1

Here's the Final Cut Print to Video dialog box.

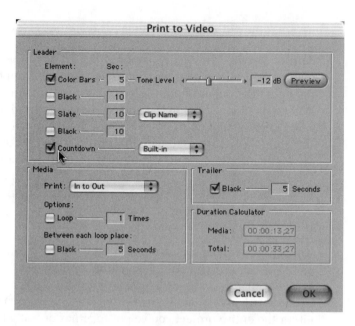

rendering any effects that must be rendered before the video can be output to final. When this is finished, you'll be able to make choices in the Print to Video or the Export to Tape dialog box. Choose Print to begin the playback; choose Export to Tape to begin the export to your camcorder (or other DV deck).

focus ——————————————————————————————————————

The Print to Tape feature can be used to send video directly to a non-DV target device, such as an analog VCR, if the device is connected via video-out ports. These ports are present on some computers or often can be installed via an expansion card.

Once you've put the software's Print or Export command into action, all you have to do is wait (and, perhaps, hope you don't run out of tape). When the export process has finished, the camera usually will stop on its own. If you used a Print to Video command in Final Cut or Premiere that requires manual control of the camcorder, you may have to press Stop on the camera to get it to stop after the video signal has finished.

Getting Your Video on Analog Tape

We've covered outputting to DV tape, but what about analog tape? What do you do if you want to put your video on VHS and distribute it to friends? In most cases, you can simply connect a special analog cable to your camcorder that gives you analog-out cables using composite connectors. Plug these connectors to the analog-in ports on the VCR or TV to use the camcorder as you would any external VCR-like device. The yellow connector is for video; the white (left) and red (right) connectors are for audio.

 *zoom-in* ————————————————————————

Some camcorders have an S-video out option that you should use if your analog device supports S-video in. S-video offers higher quality than the yellow composite cable; you should still use the audio composite cables for the audio connection.

Although the camcorder-to-VCR connection is the easiest, it isn't the only option. Software that supports a Print to Video command (notably Final Cut and Adobe Premiere) can be used on PCs and Macs that have direct analog-out ports either built in or on a PCI expansion card. These ports enable you to connect cabling directly between the computer and the VCR, and then play back the video to the ports so that the picture can be seen (and recorded) on the analog device.

If your computer doesn't offer analog audio/video ports, a breakout box, such as those described in Chapter 2, will. In fact, if you plan to create a lot of analog video tapes, and putting the video on DV tape seems superfluous, a pass-through DV box is an ideal choice. It enables you to use a IEEE 1394 (FireWire, i.Link) connection to the box and then analog cables from the box to your VCR.

Finally, if you're in the market for a high-end duplication solution, you'll find VCRs designed to accommodate both MiniDV (or DVCAM) and VHS (or S-VHS) recording. These VCRs allow you to quickly move video from one format to the other, or you can stack two such decks together to enable you to copy video to and from Betacam SP, and other professional-level formats.

Output for Digital Delivery

The flip side of outputting your project to DV tape is exporting it to a digital movie file. Much like a text file that can be translated into different word processing documents, a DV movie can be translated into various other digital media formats so it can be used and viewed in different ways. With your NLE software, it's possible to take your edited DV movie and export it—in its new sequence and with all its effects and titles intact—to various other digital movie formats. You may want to do this for the following reasons:

- To play back from a hard disk or removable media disk of some sort
- To translate to DVD movie format
- To translate to Video CD format
- To translate to various Internet-friendly formats and codecs
- To translate to movies suitable for Internet streaming

All these are valid reasons for creating digital movie files. Once your edited movie is in a digital movie file format, it can be translated, burned, compressed, packaged, and delivered in many different ways, all of which we'll touch on in this section.

For the most part, you'll use your NLE software to create a digital movie file before you move onto any of the other steps, so we'll cover that first. It isn't always the case, however, that you have to take this step. Certain applications, such as iMovie and iDVD on the Mac side or Pinnacle Edition on the PC, can output directly to DVD without requiring you to first create a digital movie file. (Or, at least, they hold your hand through the process.)

Digital Movie Choices

Before we get into the nitty-gritty of individual applications, it's worth noting that there are a *lot* of choices to be made when it comes to exporting to a digital movie file. You may have to make the following choices:

- **File type**   When you save to a digital movie file, you may have the choice of the file format you'd like to use, depending on the software. Most of the time, the software will use the default for your operating system. On the Mac, the default is QuickTime and in Windows, the standard file format is AVI. However, your software may enable you to save to the MPEG-2 or MPEG-4 formats, which are discussed a little later in this chapter. You'll also likely find options for exporting to various still image formats or even to sequences of still images.

• **Movie size**   While movie size works hand-in-hand with compression schemes (discussed next), you'll often have to make movies smaller in terms of pixels—and hence smaller on the computer screen when played back—if you're trying to reduce the file size. So, for instance, you have the option to export your movies at lower resolutions (such as 320 × 240 or 160 × 120) instead of at the full DV resolution of 720 × 480. Lower resolutions are ideal for movies that will be sent over the Internet, as they require considerably less data to complete the picture.

• **Compression scheme (codec)**   You may be prompted to choose the codec that is used to compress your video, and you may be prompted to compress the audio. We'll look at these schemes a little later in the chapter. At the outset, particularly for creating DVD movies, you will probably opt for uncompressed video instead of codec. Once you move to Internet video, however, choosing the right codec becomes very important.

As mentioned, we'll explore each of these items as we move through the remaining sections of this chapter.

Exporting to a File

Let's look briefly at the same applications we discussed earlier in this chapter to see how they export to digital movie files:

• **Apple iMovie**   Apple iMovie takes a basic approach to exporting movies. You can export them to QuickTime format relatively easily, using predetermined compression and size schemes that Apple has identified for the task at hand. So, if you'd like to export a video that is optimized for sending as an e-mail attachment, or if you'd like to format the exported movie as Full DV quality, these choices are available (see Figure 12.2). You can also choose Expert Settings, where you can explore the controls that the underlying QuickTime technology makes available. In the Save Exported File As dialog box, you can use the Export menu to choose from a number of different formats, including saving the movie as an AVI or MPEG-4 movie (see Figure 12.3). You can also click the Options button to choose codecs and compression settings.

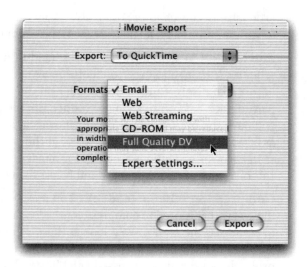

FIGURE 12.2

The basic iMovie controls make exporting as a digital movie file fairly straightforward.

- **Apple Final Cut**   With Final Cut, you choose File | Export | QuickTime to begin the process. Doing so brings up a Save dialog box where you can not only save your file, but also make many of the same choices that iMovie offers. (After all, all Apple tools are built on top of QuickTime, which is the technology that enables digital movie translation on a Mac.) In this dialog box you can click the Options button to see the options that relate to a particular file format. For instance, if you choose QuickTime Movie and click Options, you'll see the codec and quality settings relevant for a QuickTime movie; if you choose AVI and click Options, you'll see different options because the different file formats require different codecs and settings.

- **Adobe Premiere**   Exporting to a file in Premiere varies depending on the platform on which you're using Premiere, which is weighted

FIGURE 12.3

Click the Options button and you'll discover even more options for saving your digital movie file.

toward QuickTime on the Mac and toward Windows Media technologies on a PC. In either case, the command is simple: Choose File | Export Timeline | Movie. In the Export Movie dialog box, you can give your movie a name and choose Save to save it in the default movie format. You can click the Settings button to see the Export Movie Settings dialog box (see Figure 12.4). In this dialog box, you can choose what portions of your project to export (video or audio only, for instance) and you can choose different file types. If you choose a different file type (for instance, by choosing QuickTime in the Windows version of Premiere), you can click the Next button to move through the specifics of the codec, frame size, frame rate, and so on (see Figure 12.5), which we'll cover a bit later. When you've made your choices, click the OK button to export the video.

Getting Your Video on Disc

Writeable CD and DVD technology has become fairly pervasive on home and hobbyist computers—so much so that creating your own movie DVDs is a viable and affordable alternative to recording to VHS tapes—and DVDs have the advantage of being easier to ship through postal mail or delivery services. So if you have a DVD-R drive and software that is capable of creating DVD movies, we encourage you to consider DVD technology for displaying, archiving, and distributing your final projects.

Even if you don't have a DVD-R drive, you have options—particularly if you have a CD-R drive, which is even more common. A CD-R drive (or, more likely, a CD-RW drive) writes to special CD-Recordable and/or CD-Rewriteable discs that can store upwards of 700MB of data. Usually data is stored on a CD-R in the form of computer data, which can be mounted on your computer's desktop and accessed as if it were on any

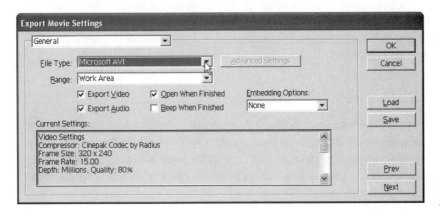

FIGURE 12.4

Premiere offers tools for exporting to a variety of formats.

FIGURE 12.5

*Click Next and
you'll discover
some fairly
advanced
settings.*

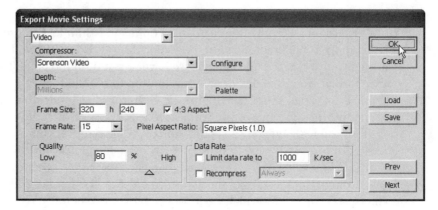

other sort of removable disk. DVD-R and DVD-RW work much the same way, except that their capacities reach to 4.7GB or more.

With certain technologies you can write data to these discs in a different way. With a DVD-R drive and the correct software, you can take a movie that is saved in the MPEG-2 format and write it to a DVD-R disc in the DVD-Video format for playback in a consumer electronic DVD player. With a CD-R drive and the right software you can write an MPEG-1 format movie in the Video CD format, which can then be played back on many consumer DVD players as well as on computers using special VCD playback software. We'll look at each option in turn.

Creating a DVD

Creating a DVD-Video formatted DVD requires three things: a DVD-R player, DVD-R media, and software that can properly encode the disc. Ideally, the software should also be able to help you design the disc. After all, DVD movies tend to have attractive menus, the capability to access different video clips, and a chapter feature that enables you to move directly to different parts of a long movie. Although not all DVD-Video creation software offers all these features, it has become somewhat easier to create DVDs for playback in consumer DVD players.

focus ———————————————————————————————

Adobe announced Adobe Encore DVD for Windows XP at the time of this writing. It is a $549 package for professional-level DVD creation that integrates well with Adobe Premiere as well as other Adobe tools. If you're interested in pro-quality DVDs from the Windows platform, Encore DVD might be the right road to take. On the Mac side, you can export video from Premiere for use with iDVD, Apple DVD Pro, and third-party tools.

Apple iDVD

You start the DVD creation process by properly exporting your movie in a format that the DVD software can handle. In iMovie, this is really simple, as iMovie includes an iDVD panel that makes moving the video to the iDVD software incredibly easy (see Figure 12.6).

You access the panel by first clicking the iDVD button in the effects section of the iMovie window. Then, you can define different chapters for your movie by placing the playhead on the Timeline and clicking Add Chapter to begin a new chapter at the playhead's location. When you have finished creating and editing your chapters, click the Create iDVD Project button to launch iDVD and begin editing the DVD.

focus ———————————————————————————————————————

You aren't required to have chapters in your video, but they're helpful for long videos that are placed on a DVD, as they serve the same function that tracks do on an audio CD—they let you move quickly to a part of the video. iDVD works with the chapters you define in iMovie and turns them into what iDVD calls "scene selections."

In other applications, your goal will be to export your video to files that offer the highest quality possible—that generally means QuickTime or AVI files with no compression (or DV/DVCAM selected at the compressor) at the same 720 × 480 resolution that the original footage was in. This can

FIGURE 12.6
iMovie's integration with iDVD is handy for burning DVD-Video format discs.

take a little longer to export, but once you've done that, the DVD burning software can help you deal with the files. (You should also be aware that the files you create when exporting full-quality DV clips can be enormous—about 3.5MB per second or 210MB per minute of video.)

In iDVD, for instance, you also have the option of importing exported files using the File | Import command, which is handy if you haven't been editing the video in iMovie 3. Once you've added a few clips, you can arrange them on what will be the DVD's menu (see Figure 12.7). In iDVD, you can choose themes for the DVD in the interface "drawer" that is shown on the left side of Figure 12.7.

When you choose a theme, each clip in your project is displayed on the DVD menu according to that theme. (This menu will be viewable whether you're watching the movie on your computer or using a consumer DVD player and a television set.) You have other options for customizing the DVD and various settings that are outside the scope of this book—iDVD has a Help | iDVD Help command and Apple maintains a web site to help you learn more about the program.

Once you have arranged the items the way you want them, you can click the Preview button to see how the disc will work. Then, you can click the

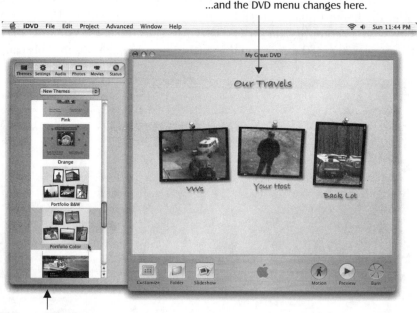

...and the DVD menu changes here.

FIGURE 12.7

iDVD lets you create a DVD-Video disc visually.

Choose a theme here...

Burn button twice to spin up a DVD-R disc and burn the project to the disc using your DVD-R drive. iDVD is responsible for both encoding the video as an MPEG-2 file and then writing that file to the disc in the DVD-Video format.

Final Cut can work with iDVD as well, but it's a bit more manual—instead of gaining direct access from within Final Cut, you export your project as a Final Cut movie using the File | Export | Final Cut Movie. This allows you to maintain chapter markers that you set in your project, which can then be translated by iDVD or Apple DVD Pro. Chapter markers tag a particular frame as the beginning of a new chapter. iDVD uses these markers to create its Scene Selection menu, which enables the viewer to jump to specific chapters.

To create a chapter marker, follow these steps:

1. Place the playhead on your Timeline where you'd like the chapter marker to appear (and, hence, where you want a new chapter to start).

2. Choose Mark | Markers | Add. You should see the frame in the Canvas window with the word "Marker 1" or similar.

3. To edit the marker, choose Mark | Markers | Edit.

 zoom-in ——————————————————————————

You can accomplish both Step 2 and Step 3 by pressing M twice instead of accessing the menu commands.

4. In the Edit Marker window, click the Add Chapter Marker button to add the code that shows this to be a chapter marker. You can also rename the marker.

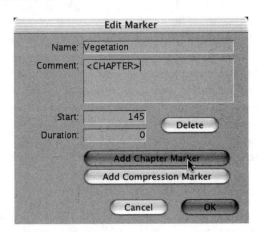

5. Click OK to set the marker.

6. Now that you've created chapters, you must export the video properly. Choose File | Export | Final Cut Movie. In the Save dialog box, give the movie a name, and then choose the portion you want saved in the Include menu.

7. While you're still in the Save dialog box, pull down the Markers menu and choose DVD Studio Pro Markers. Click Save.

focus

DVD Studio Pro is Apple's professional-level DVD mastering software; the chapter markers work just as well in iDVD.

That's it—you've exported successfully. The exported Final Cut Movie can be brought into iDVD, where the chapter markers will be recognized and automatically broken out as a sequence of scenes that can be accessed individually. (This happens by default, but you can change the behavior in iDVD | Preferences, so that the software will ask you before automatically adding individual scene selections that correspond to the chapters.) To import into iDVD, choose File | Import from iDVD's menus. You can also use the Movies button in the iDVD interface to see all the movies that iDVD finds in the Movies folder and any others that have been customized.

When you import a movie with chapter markers, iDVD will either automatically create the Scene Selection button (so that each chapter/scene can be selected individually) or you'll see a dialog box asking you whether you want the scenes created. Clicking OK causes both the movie and the scenes to be added to the iDVD menu (see Figure 12.8).

Pinnacle Expression and Impression DVD Pro

Pinnacle Systems offers two software packages that are similar to Apple's offerings, but they are available only for Windows-based PCs: Pinnacle

FIGURE 12.8
When you import a movie with chapter markers in iDVD, iDVD creates a Scene Selection button automatically.

Expression and Impression DVD Pro. Pinnacle Expression has a "cutesy" interface but it's a powerful package, enabling you to collect video clips, perform rudimentary edits (cuts and deletes, mostly), and then place them in a DVD, Video CD, or Super Video CD (SVCD) interface. Used in conjunction with basic editing software it's a robust home solution.

You begin by either capturing raw clips from your camcorder or by opening edited movie files from your hard disk. From there, you can arrange and design your DVD or Video CD using templates and editing tools (see Figure 12.9). Finally, you burn the disc.

focus ——————————————————————————————————

Super VideoCDs are only supported by a limited number of consumer DVD players. They offer better quality, but less compatibility, than a standard VCD.

Pinnacle Impression DVD Pro is the more advanced package, offering options for creating more sophisticated DVDs. Although the process is similar to Pinnacle Expression—you import video, still images, and other assets into the project—you also have a Timeline. The Timeline enables you to create DVDs with menus, add subtitles, and create a number of effects that the consumer-level software isn't capable of.

FIGURE 12.9

*Pinnacle
Expression
offers a simple
interface that
enables you to
burn home
movies and
video clips
to DVD or
Video CD.*

Creating a Video CD

A Video CD (VCD) is an interesting alternative to creating a DVD for a
number of reasons. First, a VCD is cheaper to create because CD-R
media is cheaper than DVD-R media. (This will probably be true for some
time to come although, presumably, the gap will continue to narrow.)
Second, a video CD requires only that you have a CD-R drive in your
computer, not a DVD-R drive. (Many of today's computers come standard
with a CD-R drive and almost any modern computer has a CD-ROM
drive that can be used for playback of VCDs.) Third, a VCD will play back
in many consumer DVD players, making it almost as useful as a DVD for
distributing to friends or clients. And, finally, a VCD can be played back
on a computer that is equipped with a CD-ROM drive—no DVD drive is
required. (Special playback software is required, but it can generally be
downloaded as shareware.)

The main drawback to a VCD is that it offers lower quality and less
running time than a DVD. About 70 minutes of footage will fit on a VCD
and the quality of the image is similar to an image that has been recorded
on VHS. VCD also has a slight drawback concerning its perception by the
public. People in the United States in particular are more familiar with
DVDs than with VCDs, which have, reportedly, proven more popular in

Asia. If you're willing to brave the drawbacks, however, VCD is an inexpensive way to put video on a disc and distribute it easily.

Creating a VCD is a two-stage process that is similar to the DVD process: First you encode the video file, and then you write it to disc. For a VCD, the encoding is MPEG-1 instead of the MPEG-2 format that is used for DVDs. You'll need software that handles both of these steps.

On a Mac, VCD isn't something that Apple's low-cost software (such as iDVD) currently allows, so you'll need a third-party solution. The most popular is Roxio Toast (www.roxio.com), which can handle both encoding and writing to the disc. Toast has been around for a while (it was Adaptec Toast until Adaptec spun out the Roxio brand for its software) and it's a time-honored solution for burning data CDs and DVDs as well as VCDs, audio CDs, and all sorts of disc-related projects. Other CD burning options are available, but you'll need an application capable of translating your video into MPEG-1 format.

For Windows, Roxio makes the popular Creator software, which can be used both for VCD and for regular DVD creation. The DVD Builder interface in the software enables you to graphically build the menus for your DVD or VCD and then burn the project to CD-R media.

Video for Internet Distribution

There are two basic ways that you can distribute video over the Internet: as a deliverable movie file or as a streaming movie. A deliverable movie is one that you can send via e-mail, post on a web site, or place on an FTP server. The movie must be small enough (in terms of file size) that it can be transported reasonably easily across a typical Internet connection.

A streaming movie works a little differently. It is of relatively low quality, but it is designed to appear in the user's movie player in real-time, so that it can be watched before it has been completely downloaded from the Internet. The process is similar to creating a deliverable movie file, but you generally must set specific options to get a streaming movie to work. You'll also need a special server (or space on an ISP's server) that supports streaming media.

Internet Deliverable

Creating a movie for delivery over the Internet requires two major decisions: how big will the file be and in what format. The file's final size will affect how "deliverable" the movie seems to your target viewer. For entertainment purposes, most users won't want to download a movie that is more than a few megabytes unless they have a broadband connection, in which case they might go for a 10–50MB movie, depending on how interested they are in it. (They may, however, be willing to view that movie using *streaming* technology, which is discussed in the next section.) For internal corporate and organizational use, you might be able to convince your audience to spend a little more time downloading the video. For sales and product demonstrations, you'll want the process to be as painless as possible.

To make video files smaller, you have to decrease the resolution and increase the compression. Doing so results in a lower-quality image— sometimes *much* lower quality than the original DV files. But, a lower quality movie is the trade-off if you want a movie that can be downloaded in a reasonable amount of time.

We also mentioned file format. To be useful over the Internet, the file must be stored in a format that is accessible to a large number of Internet users. If you're creating the file from a Macintosh, you'll likely choose QuickTime as your file format; if you're starting from Windows, you might choose AVI. You should also consider your target audience. QuickTime is useful for nearly all Mac users, but many Windows and UNIX-based users don't have software that supports QuickTime. (QuickTime is popular on Windows PCs, but not pervasive.) Mac users are less likely to be able to view AVI files, although the newer the Mac the more likely it is to support AVI files out of the box. (Most Macs can play back most AVI files, but it can take some downloading and configuring to make it happen.)

focus ————————————————————————————————————

Before you get too deep into creating Internet files: In our experience, NLE applications are decent, but not great, at creating the optimum files. If you need good-looking, but small, highly compressed files, your best bet is to consider a third-party application. Discreet (www.discreet.com) makes the very popular Cleaner application for both Windows and Macintosh. With Cleaner, you begin by exporting uncompressed DV video from your NLE application. Then you load that video into Cleaner and use it for the compression step—videos tend to come out smaller, crisper-looking, and better optimized for the web.

iMovie and Final Cut

Some NLE applications have the capability to save or export directly to a movie format that is appropriate for Internet delivery. iMovie, for instance, includes the option in its Export dialog box. Choose File | Export, and then choose To QuickTime from the Export menu. You'll see options in the Format menu that enable you to choose size and compression settings that

Apple has determined are good for the tasks mentioned, such as e-mail and web playback.

Final Cut is a bit more complicated, but not much more. Choose File | Export. The Save dialog box appears. Give the movie a name, and then choose a file format from the Format menu. In most cases you'll choose QuickTime Movie. You can then open the Use menu to choose a target Internet connection and the quality level. You can also do things a bit more manually, by clicking the Options button and choosing settings for your video and audio tracks (see Figure 12.10).

Experiment with these settings to get the best balance between video quality and file size so that the files perform well on the Internet. As you experiment, you'll see Sorensen codecs, the H.261 and H.263 codes, and the MPEG-4 codec—these are all useful for creating highly compressed files. (We'd suggest using the Sorensen codec for most of your Internet deliverables.) You can also choose fewer frames per second—12 to 15 frames per second still shows full motion, although it won't be as fluid as full motion (about 30 frames per second for NTSC video). You can also compress the audio quite a bit to get a smaller file.

Adobe Premiere

In Premiere, follow these steps to export a movie suitable for Internet delivery:

1. Choose File | Export Timeline | Movie.

2. In the Save dialog box, give the file a name and choose Settings.

3. To choose a format for the movie, select either Microsoft AVI or QuickTime from the File Type menu. Click Next.

4. On the Video screen of the Export Movie Settings window (see Figure 12.11) choose the compressor settings, the size of the movie in pixels, and the frame rate. (You'll likely want to choose Square Pixels from the Pixel Aspect Ratio menu, so that you can translate DV pixels into computer pixels for a truer picture.) Click Next.

5. To set up audio, choose a frequency and quality level. (The lower each is, the less space your movie will take up. Of course, the quality of the audio will degrade as a result. Note that video is much more file space intensive than audio, so you may not need to alter these settings much.) When you've finished, click Done.

6. Check that the file is named correctly, and then click Save. Premiere will begin translating, encoding, and saving the movie file.

FIGURE 12.10

In Final Cut you can access the QuickTime compression settings for your exported movie.

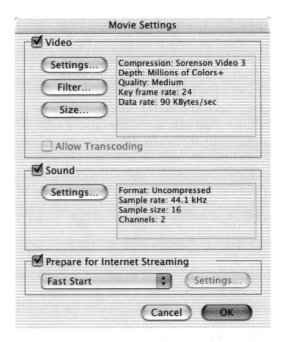

Internet Streaming

Creating the movie file for Internet streaming is very similar to creating one for Internet delivery. Your goal is still to compress the file so that it's easy to send over the Internet, but this compression is a little different. Because the entire file doesn't have to be sent before the movie is played, the key is to make the movie as efficient as possible for transport and playback on a frame-by-frame basis. A larger file size is acceptable for a streaming media file, because the entire file doesn't have to arrive before your recipient can begin viewing it. What's more important is that you choose

FIGURE 12.11

You'll make many of your compression decisions in the Export Movie Settings window.

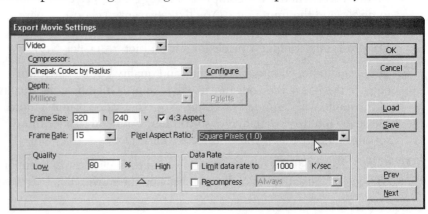

a good format for the streaming video and that you make the correct setting choices. This section will begin with a quick look at all these components that make up Internet streaming.

QuickTime

QuickTime is a jack of all trades—it's commonly used for streaming as well as for regular Internet deliverables. A QuickTime movie must be *hinted* for streaming—hinting simply means the movie file is encoded with special data elements that make Internet streaming of that file work more efficiently. You'll find the hint setting when you choose preferences for a movie that you're exporting. (The following illustration shows iMovie, but any QuickTime-enabled application will allow you to choose similar settings.)

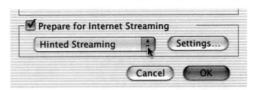

With hinting turned on, the file can be used with QuickTime Streaming Server (http://www.apple.com/quicktime/products/qtss/), a server application that is available for free from Apple. You can also use a hinted QuickTime file on an ISP's account if the ISP supports QuickTime serving, which many Apple-centric ISPs offer. And, of course, Apple's own .Mac service (http://www.mac.com) supports QuickTime streaming.

MPEG-4

The latest MPEG standard (MPEG-4) is optimized for streaming; this compression scheme is based, in part, on the QuickTime file format technology. The goal with MPEG-4 is to be able to deliver something similar to DVD-quality MPEG-2 video, but at a much lower data rate, the idea being that MPEG-4 could do for video what MPEG-3 ("MP3") did for Internet audio.

focus —————————————————————————————

If you aren't familiar with MP3 audio, then that last sentence is probably meaningless. MP3 technology essentially made it possible for CD-quality songs to be recorded into computer files that could be easily transferred over the Internet. That made file swapping, single-song sales and all sorts of new listening and marketing possibilities come about. MPEG-4 could do for video what MP3 did for audio—make it possible to transfer high-quality video in ways that would change the way that video is viewed and marketed.

MPEG-4 is gaining some acceptance in the market, although Mac tools seem to be incorporating MPEG-4 a bit more quickly than Windows applications. (That makes sense because MPEG-4 is based, in part, on QuickTime technology.) MPEG-4 has competition from both Windows Media and Real Media, which are proprietary formats that have a great deal of acceptance in the community. The potential with MPEG-4, however, is that it is a cross-platform solution that does away with some of the headaches of proprietary solutions.

In many applications, MPEG-4 is simply another choice for your streamovie format. Because MPEG-4 incorporates its own compression scheme, you don't have to make as many choices when you select it. You may have to simply choose a quality setting, a size for the video, and whether or not to turn on server hinting.

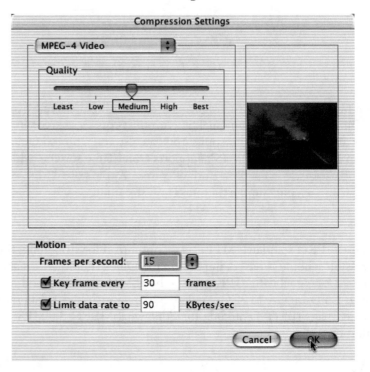

Then, save the movie and make it available on an MPEG-4 compatible streaming server. (MPEG-4 can also be viewed in compatible browsers even if you place the file on a regular web server. It's a file format—just like QuickTime or AVI—that can be downloaded as well as streamed. It just happens to be *optimized* for streaming.)

Real Media

One of the more popular formats for streaming is the Real Media format, owned and managed by Real Networks (www.real.com). Real Media players are very popular downloads, so it's a safe assumption that the majority of Internet users can either view a Real Media file or get a viewer fairly quickly. Real Media's compression schemes are good, and are particularly effective at lower bandwidths, such as over lower-bandwidth analog modem connections. Real Networks was the first company to make streaming work on a large scale, and it has since made a point of adding a number of services and a great deal of content to keep people interested in its player applications.

To make Real Media streaming files available to others, you must encode the file and place it on a Real Media server. The encoding can be done either with a Real Media product or via the Real Media export feature of some Windows-based NLE applications. (For instance, Adobe Premiere can export to Real Media format.) Third-party encoders can be used as well, such as Discreet Cleaner, mentioned earlier, which can create Real Media files as well as QuickTime and Windows Media files. Once the file is encoded, you make the file available via a link from your web page. The link causes the Real Media player to be launched and the media stream to be played back to the user.

Windows Media

Of course, Microsoft's technology for streaming can't be ignored. Windows Media is a very popular approach to creating streaming files, offering wonderful quality, particularly for high-bandwidth connections. Windows Media files can be created by a number of Windows-based NLE applications such as Premiere and Pinnacle Edition, tools made available by Microsoft (http://www.microsoft.com/windows/windowsmedia/WM7/encoder.aspx), and third-party applications such as Discreet Cleaner and others.

The main advantage of using Windows Media is that the required player is already installed on a majority of PCs, thanks to Windows itself. Files are generally saved as AVI movies, encoded, and then placed on a Windows Media-capable server. This server can be bought, configured, and installed on a permanent Internet connection, or you can purchase server space via an Internet provider that makes Windows Media services available to its webmasters.

And...Cut!

This chapter covered getting your movie from the Timeline in your editor to your audience, whether that audience needs a tape, a disc, a computer file, or a movie that is delivered via the Internet. In the next chapter, we'll move on to something a bit less technical but probably more difficult—marketing your film and actually getting it seen by an audience.

Glossary

THE video-editing world may have as many or more insider terms per sentence as the technology world does! We've tried to tone down their use in the pages of this book, but some are bound to slip through. What follows is a list of some of the terms we've used in this book and some quick and easy definitions. Feel free to stick your tongue out at any of these terms if that makes you feel better.

16:9   The traditional ratio of width to height, respectively, for motion pictures and the standard ratio for high-definition television.

30-degree rule   A rule in editing that states that the camera angle for each cut between clips of the same subject should vary by at least 30 degrees, particularly for a wide shot/medium shot/close-up sequence. Otherwise, the edits can look like *jump cuts* or mistakes.

accessory shoe   A connector on the top of many cameras designed for an external flash, light, or microphone.

analog formats   As opposed to digital formats, these are the technologies that record video and/or sound as signals of electricity instead of a series of numbers. Analog formats for video include VHS, Betacam, and Hi8.

aspect ratio   The ratio of width to height in the display of a recorded image.

back light   A light that is shined on the back of your subject in order to put highlights on arms, shoulders, and around the hair or head. The back light is designed to add a three-dimensional element to the shot.

BetaSP   The professional level of Sony's Betacam video tape format.

blackstriping   The process of recording black to a tape so as to mark it with timecode. Subsequently recording over the tape with your important video will overwrite it, but with no risk that timecode will be broken. (Without blackstriping, it's possible that you could break timecode and have the camcorder start counting up from 00:00:00 somewhere in the middle of the tape.)

boom   An extending pole used to hold a microphone or a camcorder. This enables you to put your equipment closer to the action than you might otherwise.

breakout box   A general term that refers to a device that enables you to connect multiple components to a central component or recording device. For example, you might use a breakout box to connect analog sources (VCRs and audio playback devices) to a computer via a FireWire/IEEE 1394 cable in order to digitize those sources.

B-roll   Footage of the surroundings, buildings, or objects that are involved in the action of your production or are discussed in an interview. (In feature films, these may be the exteriors of locations that you're simulating on a sound stage.) This footage can then be used for intercuts in the editing process.

capture and batch capture   Some editing applications call the process of copying a video clip from a digital camcorder to a computer the "capture" process. In addition, with batch capture, you can specify the clips to be captured using their timecode, and then the software will capture them all automatically.

CCD (charged coupled device)   A small chip that registers various levels of light and turns them into digital values that can be recorded. The CCD is found in computer scanners and many different types of cameras, particularly digital cameras that create computer files instead of film images.

chromakey   A type of compositing, or image layering, where one image shows through a certain color of another image. For instance, a meteorologist might stand in front of a green wall and, in compositing, you can replace that green color with the image of a weather map.

cinéma vérité   A "fly-on-the-wall" style of documentary filmmaking that follows the subject and shoots more continuous footage rather than setting up staged interviews and re-creating actions.

close-up   A zoomed image that isolates a subject from the background and surroundings. See *tight shot*.

codec or compressor/decompressor   A software program that uses sophisticated math (algorithms) to compress a video file, so that it takes up less hard disk storage space but is still relatively true to the original. The codec is also responsible for decompressing the file at playback time. Compression is useful because uncompressed footage takes up a great deal of disk space, which makes movies impractical to work with and store. But compression can have an adverse effect on the quality of the image (the more it's compressed, the more it may lose detail) when it's played back, depending on the codec's technology.

cropping   In video editing, see *trimming*. In photo editing, cropping means to cut the portion of an image that falls outside what you want to keep.

DAT   Digital Audio Tape, a common choice for recording high-quality sound in digital format when you're not recording directly to a camcorder.

degrade   An analog video image will begin to lose detail and gain visual "noise" after it's been copied, particularly if it's multiple generations (copies of copies) away from the original. Digital video doesn't lose quality in this fashion.

depth of field   The range of distances at which a camera's lens will show items in focus. A shallow depth of field shows a smaller range of distance in focus, while a large depth of field shows a larger range of images in focus. Video tends to have a large depth of field, but you can take steps to lessen it.

digital camcorder   A motion video camera with built-in recording and playback capabilities that's capable of producing computer-readable files instead of an analog signal recording.

digital formats   As opposed to analog formats, these technologies record video and sound as ones and zeroes—numbers that can be read by a computer and edited using software. Tape formats include MiniDV, MicroMV, and DigiBeta, among others.

digital movie file   A collection of computer data stored in a format that the computer recognizes as motion video and audio. Some of the most common digital movie file formats are QuickTime, MPEG, and AVI formats.

digital still photography   As contrasted with digital video, the process of taking non-motion (single frame) pictures with a digital camera.

digital zoom   The ability of a digital camcorder to make an image appear larger—and, hence, closer—as it's being recorded. Digital zoom does this by interpolating the pixels in an image to approximate a larger image, which sometimes results in blocky or "pixilated" results. This is contrasted with *optical zoom*, which generally offers the appearance of closer images at high quality because no information has to be approximated.

digitizing   The process of turning an analog signal into a digital signal, generally resulting in a computer file that can be manipulated by software. An example would be importing video from a VHS tape to a computer as a digital movie file so that video can be edited.

DVCAM   Similar to MiniDV, this is Sony's professional-level digital video tape format.

DV Stream   The standard format for raw digital video footage that is used by many digital video camcorders.

DVD-R   Digital Versatile Disc-Recordable; a standard that enables a computer to write data to special writable DVD-R media. Using special software, a computer with a DVD-R optical drive can translate a digital movie file into a DVD movie, which can then be played back in standard DVD consumer and "home theater" players.

DVPRO   Similar to MiniDV, this is Panasonic's professional-level digital video tape format.

edit decision list   A list, either on paper or in electronic form, that details the in and out times for each clip that you'd like to import into your editing software. The in and out times are recorded according to the tape's name or number and the timecode as marked on the tape.

exposure   The combination of shutter speed (the length of time the lens stays open) and the aperture size (how large the lens opens) for your camcorder's lens determine how much light the CCDs "see." That exposure determines how bright the image is as well as the *depth of field*.

eyeline   An imaginary line that represents where an interview subject or actor should be looking, whether it's toward the camera, off camera, or at another person or thing. For example, in an interview, you may want the eyeline level with your camcorder and looking just off to the side of the lens, where the interviewer should be seated.

fade   A type of transition effect where each frame becomes either successively lighter (a fade in) or successively darker (fade out).

fill   A light compensates for shadows created by your key light. The fill light or fill reflector is used on the opposite side of the subject from the key light (if the key light is on the left side of the camcorder, the fill should be on the right side) and generally has the same or lower intensity and is typically more diffused.

filmic   A term meant to suggest that a video format, effect, or technique has qualities that make it look more like the images were recorded on motion-picture film. This may be accomplished by the manipulation of color saturation, the addition of grain or imperfections, or the use of focus and depth of field to create a film-like appearance.

filter   In editing software, a visual effect that enables you to change the color or other picture qualities of the video image.

filters   Protective, colored, or textured glass or plastic that fit over a camera's lens to change the properties of light and/or to protect the lens from dust and scratches. Ultraviolet, neutral density, and polarizing filters are common.

FireWire   Apple's name for IEEE 1394 technology, which is an advanced type of high-speed serial communication port found on most DV camcorders.

gain   The level of input signal that is recorded by an electronic device. For instance, you can increase the audio gain on a camcorder, which boosts the audio signal as it is received.

Hi8   Using 8-millimeter tape, this analog standard offers 400 lines of resolution and relatively small footprint tapes that are well suited for camcorders.

IEEE 1394   A common technology used to connect computers and external digital devices, particularly devices that require a high-speed connection. Also called FireWire and i.Link, an IEEE 1394 port is commonly found on digital camcorders so that they can be connected to personal computers. The IEEE 1394 technology can be used to transfer digital image data and to control the camcorder from within your software.

i.Link   Sony's name for IEEE 1394 technology, which is an advanced type of high-speed serial communication port.

intercut   An editing technique where you change the visual portion of an image without changing the audio that's heard beneath it. (For instance, while interviewing a police officer, you intercut to video of the scene of a crime while still hearing the officer talk.)

in the can   A common term for saying that footage has been successfully shot and recorded. (In filmmaking, film would be exposed by the camera and then returns to its can for processing.)

in the field   A common term for shooting on location or away from a studio, which generally suggests you have less video equipment and it needs to be more mobile.

jump cut   An editing technique where you cut to a clip of the same angle of the same subject but at a different focal length. This cut/close-up/cut/ medium shot/cut/closer type of editing can look like a mistake if it's not done very purposefully.

keyframing   Selecting certain frames between which a special effect will occur and/or change over time. For instance, you can use keyframing to set a start frame near the beginning of a clip and an end frame later in the clip and then have a special effect occur between the two—such as the clip becoming gradually black and white.

key light   The name given to the main light source when you're illuminating a shot. The key light can be a special light that you control or the sun and is typically the brightest light source on the subject.

lavalier   A type of microphone that is clipped to the clothing (or taped to the body) of your subject or actor and often associated with wireless transmission devices.

linear-editing systems   A system for editing video productions that requires you to work with the base recording in the sequence that it was recorded, either overlaying or replacing portions of the video or audio with new footage from other tapes and sources. This system is complex and slow and requires multiple recording and playback decks along with control units to accomplish sophisticated editing.

long shot   An image that is composed so that the people or subjects in view are tiny to the point of being almost unrecognizable. Sometimes used with a slow zoom to establish visual interest or perspective. For instance, a long shot might start with a distant shot of Times Square in New York where you see thousands of people and then slowly zoom in on your actors as they walk up Broadway, placing them in an environmental context.

lower-third title   A type of titling that's usually used to identify the on-screen speaker, the time of day, language subtitles, or some similar bit of supplementary information.

mask   A portion of an image that is cut or outlined to be transparent so that another layer of video can show through it.

medium shot   An image that has a single subject as the focal point but still shows that subject in its environment. For instance, you may see the writer typing on her computer, but you can also see that she's sitting in her apartment. (A closer shot may not reveal the environment, as you'll be too close to her.)

megapixel   A camera or camcorder that has a CCD with a resolution over 1 million pixels. A *2-megapixel* camera offers a CCD with over 2 million pixels and so on. Megapixel CCDs are of more use when taking still photos than when recording digital video.

MicroMV   A digital technology created and marketed by Sony that is useful for in-camera digital editing as well as for taking still digital photos.

MiniDV   The most common tape format for consumer digital camcorders, MiniDV tapes can be used to record 30, 60, 90, or more minutes of digital video.

MOS   Recording without sound.

motivation   In acting, the reasoning behind a line, action, or scene; the emotions or logic that prompt or motivate a character to action.

MPEG   Stands for *Motion Picture Experts Group*, and is used in video to indicate a file format created by that group. *MPEG-1* is one type of standard MPEG file format and compression scheme for video stored at compression rates and sizes that are appropriate for computer playback. *MPEG-2* is a file format and compression scheme that is used to create DVD movies and VideoCD-format movies. *MPEG-4* is a file format and compression scheme that is suitable for Internet playback and Internet streaming.

neutral-density filter   A piece of glass or plastic placed in front of a camcorder lens or an electronic setting that cuts down the amount of light that enters the lens.

nonlinear editing (NLE)   A style of editing that enables you to manipulate the base clips in your video presentation in a random access manner, moving and manipulating them at will, because the clips are in digital format. Contrast this with *linear-editing systems*.

NTSC   Stands for *National Television Standards Committee* and refers to the standard for North American television. In order to create NTSC format video (which is necessary for playback on NTSC video players and televisions), you'll need to record (with your camcorder) and play back (with your VCR or similar equipment) in the NTSC standard. NTSC video is recorded at 29.97 frames per second and 525 lines of resolution.

one-chip camera   A digital video camcorder that uses only one CCD to detect and record all light and color information, as opposed to three-chip cameras, which record red, blue, and green separately.

optical disc   A CD or DVD disc that is read with a laser. Includes recordable varieties that can also have data "burned" to them with a laser.

optical zoom   The ability of a lens on a camcorder to change focal length so that images appear to be closer. This can be contrasted with *digital* *zoom,* which uses electronic enlargement routines to make a digitally recorded image look larger (and, hence, appear closer).

optics   The mechanics of a camera or camcorder—the lens, autofocus capabilities, and so on—that are used to resolve an image onto the recording surface, whether that surface is film or a digital sensor. The term is sometimes used to differentiate from the *digital* features or capabilities of a camcorder.

over black titles   A type of titling where the title image or words appear over a solid color background instead of over the video images in an overlay.

overlay   Placing one video clip over another. In some editing, the overlay is an *intercut,* which means the overlay image completely obscures or replaces the original image. In editing, overlays can also be *composited,* meaning the overlay can be combined in various ways with the original to produce a new image or a clip that is a combination of both.

PAL   Stands for *Phase Alternating Lines* and refers to the television standard that's dominant in Europe and Asia. Editing PAL video requires PAL equipment. Some videographers prefer to shoot in PAL format for digital video that they intend to transfer to film, as the PAL format uses 25 frames per second, which is close to film's 24 frames per second.

pan   Moving the camera in the "x plane" (horizontally) to the left and/or right.

pixel   A "picture element." Pixels are a sophisticated way of saying "dot." All things being equal, the more dots that a CCD uses over the same amount of space to record an image, the higher the resolution of that image.

polarizing filter   A piece of glass or plastic that attaches to a camcorder's lens to change the angle at which light enters the lens. Excellent for eliminating many types of glare. Can be useful for seeing through glass or under the surface of clear water.

post-production   The phase of your project that takes place after you've recorded the basic footage. This phase includes cataloging the footage, editing it, adding special effects, making any changes or additions to the sound, and then outputting your project to tape or transferring it to various media.

practicals   Lamps or lights that the camera can see in the studio shot—often these are used to set the atmosphere or finish out the appearance of a set to make it look more realistic.

pre-production   The planning phase—research, scripting, finding actors or subjects, storyboarding, scheduling—of your video project that takes place before you begin shooting footage with your camcorder.

prosumer   A term meant to suggest a non-professional who works with electronic equipment or techniques that approach professional quality.

QuickTime   Apple, Inc.'s layer of multimedia technology that includes the ability to play back digital movies and a file format in which those movies can be stored. QuickTime is also a translation technology, making it possible for any QuickTime-enabled application to translate between file formats if the application's author chooses to add those features.

rack focus   Using the camcorder's manual focus to change the emphasis in a framed shot. For instance, with this technique you can focus on an item in the extreme foreground (such as an alarm clock about to ring), then *refocus* (instead of zooming or moving the camera) on something in the background (such as your actor in bed) to change the focal point of the shot without moving the camera.

render   Whenever you create a transition or special effect in an editing program, you're essentially directing that application to change each frame of the clip that has been selected for the effect. This change, which uses mathematical algorithms to repaint each frame, is called rendering. The more complex the render process, the longer it will take your computer to accomplish.

resolution   The number of dots or pixels (in a given area) used to record or represent image data for a digital video (or digital still image) file. In digital video, the resolution of a CCD can range from 270,000 pixels to 1 million pixels or more. The higher the resolution, the more detail can be resolved. (Resolution isn't the only measure of picture quality, however, as the quality of a lens and the sophistication of a camera's internal optics are very important.) In a final, full-resolution digital video computer file, the resolution is always 720 pixels by 480 pixels.

rough cut   An edit of your project where the foundation clips are loosely placed in the order that follows the basic storyline of your project.

Rule of Thirds   Camera composition technique that suggests that key elements should not appear in the middle of your frame, but rather on grid lines and intersections designated by the lines drawn at one-third points both horizontally and vertically.

scrolling titles   In this type of title effect, text moves from the bottom of the screen to the top of the screen—this is the standard end-of-movie credit sequence.

shoot   As a verb, to record images with your camcorder. As a noun, it's a planned event for the purpose of recording video images, as in a "video shoot" or a "photo shoot."

straight cuts   An editing technique that moves directly from one shot to another (or one distinct camera angle to another) without a special-effects transition such as a wipe or fade.

streaming video   A digital movie that is transmitted over the Internet and begins to play just as the data arrives instead of waiting for all (or most) of the data to be transmitted. Streaming video often requires that the file be saved with special keyframes or "hints" and that it be saved using certain codecs. Streaming video sometimes requires a special player application and may require that the file be stored on a special type of streaming server on the Internet.

SVHS   Super-VHS, offers better resolution than VHS. SVHS-C stands for Super-VHS-Compact, which offers the same resolution as SVHS with a smaller tape that's better suited for camcorders.

take   An attempt to get a scene (or a portion of a scene) recorded. In some types of video, particularly fiction, training, or promotional videos, you'll typically try multiple takes in order to get the scene acted, presented, and recorded well.

tape stock   Blank tapes for recording video images. The terminology is a holdover from the term "filmstock," which is useful to distinguish between film that hasn't yet been exposed and film that has. (Filmstock hasn't yet been used, whereas "film" suggests that it has.) The same is true with video. The main difference is that tape can be rerecorded and film cannot.

three-chip camera   A digital video camcorder that uses separate CCDs to detect and record the red, green, and blue colors in an image. Produces higher quality video than a one-chip camera and is most evident on professional-level cameras.

tight shot   An image that is zoomed in so that the camera appears to be very close to the subject. If you're shooting a person, their face likely fills the entire screen. Same as a close-up, although it's common to say "Get in tight" or "Get in tighter" to instruct a camera operator to frame a close-up.

tilt   Pivoting the camera in the "y plane," up and/or down.

timecode   A digital code that's added to a special track on the tape as video is recorded, noting the minutes, seconds, and frame numbers of each individual frame of video. Using timecode enables you to move directly to (or simply make note of) a particular frame in the video.

trimming   An editing term that means to cut portions from the beginning and/or end of a clip, leaving only the parts that you want to work with.

two-shot   Framing a video image so that you can see two people simultaneously in an interview or newsgathering situation. One example is the standard evening news two-shot that shows both anchors at the news desk.

USB (universal serial bus)   A connection technology for computer peripherals. While the original USB standard is designed for less-intensive applications, USB 2.0 is a high-speed technology that's suitable for transferring large files (such as video and photo files) between computers and external devices.

VHS   A very popular analog video format used a great deal for home recording. VHS offers 250 lines of resolution and uses relatively large footprint tapes for recording.

VHS-C   VHS-Compact, uses smaller tapes than VHS but records at the same resolution.

video generator   A special effect that creates a video clip instead of simply altering an existing clip. (For instance, special effects for titles.)

white balance   A setting that indicates to your camcorder what color should be considered "true" white given the current lighting conditions.

wide shot   A video image that uses the widest angle of the camera's lens (no optical or digital zoom) to maximize the extent of the scene that can be recorded. This is good for shooting crowds or expansive backgrounds.

XLR or balanced cables   A type of connector and cable that's used for high-quality audio connections, offering less noise and better sound fidelity than RCA-style or mini-plug connectors.

Index

A

accessory shoe
    camcorder, camera, 9
    defined, 313

Adobe Premiere
    See also Adobe Systems, Inc.
    introduction to, 23–24
    batch capture in, 212–213
    compositing video in, 286
    digital movies, export techniques for, 296–297, 298
    fades in, 264, 11–12
    graphic overlays in, 274–275
    and Internet movies, 276–277
    keyframing in, 262, 264
    for the MAC, 29, 30
    motion effects in, 270–271
    Print to Video command (analog tape), 293
    special effects, immediate, 260–261
    special effects, time-phased, 262–264
    splitting clips in, 221–222
    tape export commands (DV tape), 291–292
    titles in, 279–281

Adobe Systems, Inc.
    Adobe Encore DVD, 298
    After Effects, 23, 29
    Digital Video Collection, 29
    Photoshop, 24
    Premiere (See Adobe Premiere)
    Title Designer, 23

analog video, adapting/importing
    introduction to, 35
    analog format, defined, 314
    breakout boxes, 36
    camcorder connections for, 36
    Dazzle Hollywood DV Bridge, 36
    digitizing cards (PCI expansion), 36–37

Apple
    See also iDVD; iMovie; Macintosh computers
    DVD Studio Pro, 302
    SoundTrack music software, 245, 246

archiving
    DVD-R, burning, 35
    hard discs, internal/external/RAID, 34–35
    tapes, raw footage/rough cuts, 33–34

aspect ratio
    16:9, camcorder support of, 11, 313
    defined, 314

audio/sound
    See also microphones; music; sound effects
    audio inputs, camcorder, 11
    audio recording, introduction to, 14
    digital audio tape (DAT), 169, 240
    in documentaries, 115–116, 132, 134, 138–139
    extraneous/background noise, 232–233
    feature film audio, sound editing, 169, 202
    Foley work (sound effects), 245–247
    good sound, importance of, 115–116, 158, 231–232
    headphones, volume controls on, 240
    home movies, sound in, 56, 60–61, 62
    interviews, sound recording/editing in, 104–105, 111
    interviews, synchronizing/combining audio tracks in, 109–110
    level control/riding the sound, 238, 239
    mic/line inputs, camcorder, 237–238
    minidisc recorders, use of, 241
    mono vs. stereo recording, 238–239
    MP3 discs, players, 241
    narration, adding, 248–249
    organizational videos, ambient sound in, 159
    sound editing, discussion of, 250–251

sound editing, tips for, 251–253
sound levels, analog vs. digital, 252
sound levels/quality, weddings and events,
    68–69, 73
for vérité videos, 118
voice over, discussion/tips for, 249–250
wedding and event videos, sound in,
    68–69, 73
AVI (digital movie format), 294
Avid Technology, Inc.
Avid Express DV, 24
Avid Free DV, 24
Mac-based editing tools from, 29

B

B-roll
B-roll intercuts, inserting, 222–225
defined, 87, 314
in documentary filming, 127–128
in interview editing, 108, 110
shooting (for organizational videos),
    158–159
back light, defined, 314
Beachtek. See breakout boxes
BetaSP, defined, 314
blackstriping, defined, 314
Bluetooth wireless technology, 13
boom, defined, 314
breakout boxes, XLR (Beachtek)
defined, 314
uses of, 234, 240, 293
breakout boxes (analog), 36
Burns, Ken, 117, 138
business videos. See organizational videos

C

camcorders, analog
See also analog video, adapting/importing
CCD resolutions of, 7
formats for, 4
Sony Betacam SP, 3
camcorders, digital
See also CCDs (charge coupled devices);
    optical discs
defined, 316
digital recording, advantages of, 2–3
formats for, 3–5
manufacturers, choosing, 6

one-chip, defined, 320
three-chip camcorder, defined, 323
three-chip vs. one-chip camcorders, 6–7,
    8–9, 10
camcorders (general)
See also camcorders, analog; camcorders,
    digital; formats, camcorder
introduction to, 1–2
accessory shoes for, 9
aspect ratio (16:9 support), 11
audio inputs, 11
camcorder settings (wedding/event videos),
    77–78
color temperature, importance of, 149
flash capability, 12
inexpensive camcorders, usefulness of, 15
lenses/lens quality (See filters and lenses)
lighting, on-camera, 11
manual overrides, 10–11
multimedia features, 12
multiple, synchronizing settings for, 76–77
overexposure and zebra setting, 55
renting vs. buying, 14–15
S-video output on, 293
steadying devices for, 133–134
used camcorders, buying, 15
variation between, 76
white balancing, 77, 149, 196
Canon Corporation
GL-1 w/ key light, 101
GL-1 w/ screw-on UV filter, 17
XL-1 camcorder, 11, 233
XLR connectors on, 11, 233
Canopus
DVRaptor, 23
ProCorder, 33
capture, image
introduction to, 206
automatic, 206, 209–210
batch capture, defined, 314
batch capture (Adobe Premiere), 212–213
batch capture (Final Cut Pro), 211–212
batch capture (iMovie), 210
manual capture (Adobe premier), 209
manual capture (Final Cut), 207–209
manual capture (iMovie), 207
NLE (nonlinear editing) in, 206
scrubbing, 213–214
Timecode/timelines, 213–214

"cat-in-the-window" shot, 189
CCDs (charge coupled devices)
    introduction to, 2, 6
    defined, 314–315
    image quality of, 6
    one-chip, defined, 320
    one-chip vs. three-chip camcorders, 6–7,
      8–9, 10
    resolution (pixels) of, 7
    still photography, use in, 7
    three-chip camcorder, defined, 323
chapter markers, creating, 301–302
chromakey (blue screen)
    defined, 315
    use of (in organizational videos), 144–145
cinema vérité, defined, 315
close-up, defined, 315
compositing video. See special effects
compression, file
    See also MPEG (Motion Picture Experts Group)
    codec (compressor/decompressor),
      defined, 315
    DT movies, file size vs. resolution, 295
    DV Stream, raw file sizes in, 31
    DV Stream and file compression, 31
    importance of, 31
    Internet movies, file size/compression in,
      306–307
    and Internet videos, 306–307
    MPEG and compressed video, 12–13, 31
    vs. quality (DVD movies), 300
cranes
    CobraCrane, SkyCrane, 168–169
cropping, defined, 315
cross-dissolves, adding, 225

D

Dazzle Hollywood DV Bridge (A/D conversion), 36
degrade, defined, 315
depth of field
    defined, 315
    in feature films, 197
diffusion filters, use of, 199
digital audio tape (DAT)
    DAT recorders (quality/cost), 240
    defined, 315
    in feature filming, 169
digital editing (general)
    See also editing software (general); editing
      software, nonlinear (NLE); See also

    specific tasks (e.g., home movies,
      interviews)
    B-roll intercuts, inserting, 222–225
    camcorder editing effects, 13–14
    capture (See capture, image)
    clips, previewing, 215–216
    clips, trimming and cropping, 216–217
    cross-dissolves, adding, 225
    digital formats, defined, 316
    Edit Decision List, 206, 210, 213
    ethical issues in, 218
    fades, adding, 225
    jump cuts, 219
    linear vs. nonlinear (NLE) editing, 20
    Mac vs. PC, 20
    PC editing, introduction to, 19–20
    projects, previewing, 215–216
    the rough cut, 217
    splitting clips, inserting edits, 220–222
    splitting clips (Adobe Premiere, Final Cut),
      221–222
    straight cuts (no transition effects),
      218–219, 323
    Timecode/timelines in, 213–214
    titles, adding, 226–229
    transition cuts, typical situations
      needing, 220
    transitions, adding, 226
    wipes, adding, 225–226
Digital8 format, 4
digital movies. See movies, digital
digital video, working with
    See also DV Stream
    archiving, 33–35
    capturing (copying to computer), 30–31
    DV vs. film (cost/quality), 113–114
digitizing, defined, 316
Discreet (Cinestream)
    Cleaner series of encoding tools, 33
    and Internet movies, 306
    as lower-cost editing software, 24
documentaries
    introduction to, 113–114
    B-roll, importance of, 126–127
    background, awareness of, 131
    camcorders, selecting, 115
    digital video vs. film (cost/quality), 113–114
    educational, 121
    framing: the rule of thirds, 130–131
    "getting out of the way," 124

historical, 119–120
historical/stock footage, sources of, 136–137
holding your shot/getting handles, 128–129
labeling/protecting your footage, 129–130
logging/organizing your tapes, 135–136
microphones, selecting, 116–117, 126
moments of silence, importance of, 129
nervous interviewees, 126–127
personal, 120
pre-shoot interviews, reasons for, 124–125
pre-shoot interviews, techniques for, 125–126
public domain, fair use, 136
reality (vérité) video, 118–119
saddlebags, 134
safety tabs, MiniDV tapes, 130
scripts, writing/outlining, 121–123
sound edit stage, 137–138
sound mix stage, 139
sound quality, importance of, 115–117
sound quantity, importance of (B-roll), 132, 134
stabilizers, camcorder, 131–132
steadying device, counterweighted, 134
still photographs, use of, 137–138
styles, introduction to, 117
subjects, unpredictability of, 119
telling the story, 114–115
tripods/monopods, 133–134
DV Stream
See also digital video, working with
introduction to, 12–13
alternative file formats, translating to, 31–33
defined, 316
file compression, importance of, 31
file compression vs. quality, 32:15
DVCAM
and Real Media, 32, 311
translating to other file formats, 31–2
defined, 316
format, 4
DVDs. See optical discs
DVPRO
defined, 316
format, 4

E

edit decision list
creating/using, 206, 210, 213

defined, 317
in organizational videos, 161
editing. See digital editing (general); editing software, introduction to; editing software, nonlinear (NLE); See also specific tasks (e.g., home movies, interviews)
editing software, introduction to
See also Adobe Premiere; editing software, nonlinear (NLE); Final Cut; iMovie
Adobe Premiere, 23–24
Avid Express DV, 24
Discreet (Cinestream), 24, 33, 306
DPS/Leitech, 24
Final Cut Express, 28–29
Final Cut Pro, 28
iMovie, 27–28, 29; 207
Media 100, 24
Pinnacle Studio, Pinnacle Edition, 24, 25
Vegas Video, 24
editing software, nonlinear (NLE)
arranging clips on timeline using, 214
defined, 320
and digital movie files, 294
graphic overlays using, 271–272
in image capture, 206
image capture using, 206
inserting B-roll intercuts using, 223–224
in Internet movies, 306
for the Mac, 25
previewing clips and projects with, 215
splitting clips,. inserting edits with, 221–222
vs. linear editing, 20
event videos, filming. See wedding and event videos
exposure
defined, 317
manual exposure (wedding/event videos), 78
overexposure and zebra setting (home movies), 55
eyeline, defined, 317

F

fades
See also special effects
adding, 225
defined, 317
feature films, creating
introduction to, 165–166
actions, describing, 174–175

actors, working with, 191–194
adaptations, permissions for, 171
audio, discussion of, 169
auditioning, tips on, 192
"cat-in-the-window" shot, 189
characters, descriptions/conventions for, 174
close-ups, 188
costume designer, responsibilities of, 180
cranes (CobraCrane, SkyCrane), 168–169
crew needs (food, etc.), 170
cutaways, 188–189
depth of field, importance of, 197
dialogue, memorizing/interpreting, 194
diffusion filters, use of, 199
digital audio tape (DAT), use of, 169
directing, introduction to, 186
directing: getting the shots, 186–189
director, responsibilities of, 180
director commands, on-the-set (Roll, Cut, etc.), 190–191
director of photography, responsibilities of, 179
expenses, 170
in feature films, 189–190
film vs. digital video, 194–195
first cut, creating, 201
final cut, creating, 202–203
good story, importance of, 170
jibs (Micro Jib, full jib, Super jib arm), 169
lighting, types of, 169–170, 195–196
line producer, responsibilities of, 179
locations, contractual agreements regarding, 183
locations, listing/visualizing, 181–183
locations, scouting, 182–183
locations, typographic conventions for, 173–174
master shot, importance of, 187
medium shot, 187
microphones, types of, 169
motivation, actor, 193
multiple/repeated shots, importance of, 189
necessary equipment, 167–170
"180-degree rule," 187
options, securing (contractual), 172
post production and editing, 200–203
producer, responsibilities of, 180
production designer, responsibilities of, 179
progressive scan frame mode, 198

props, typographic conventions for, 175
rehearsals, script readings, 193–194
reverse master shot, 189
reviewing footage, logging tapes, 201
rough cut, creating, 201–202
scenes, structuring, 173
script, basic elements of, 173–175
script, example of (typical), 174
script breakdown/master list, developing, 177–179
sharpness, image, 198–199
shooting schedule, developing, 183–185
shutter speed and frame rate, 197–198
slate, defined, 190
sound editing, 202
story, outlining/developing, 175–177
the (story) treatment, 172
storyboard, creating, 180–181
style, developing, 199–200
two-shot, 187
wheeling and dealing: sponsors and perks, 185
white balance in, 196
wide (establishing) shots, 187
"Ferris effect," 61
file size. See compression, file
fill, defined, 317
film
    cost/quality vs. digital video, 113–114
    filmic, defined, 317
filters and lenses
    See also zoom
    filter, defined, 317
    lens quality, 10
    ND (neutral density) filters, 17, 320
    polarizing filters, 16–17, 321
    UV (ultraviolet) filters, 16, 17
    zoom and wide-angle adapters, 17
Final Cut (-Pro, -Express)
    introduction to, 28–29
    batch capture using, 211–212
    compositing video in, 282–285
    editing individual clips in, 215
    export commands, digital movie, 291
    fades in, 264, 265–266
    graphic overlays in, 272–274
    and Internet movies, 275–276
    manual capture using, 207–209
    motion effects in, 267–270

Print to Video command (analog tape), 292, 293
    tape export commands (DV tape), 291
    titles in, 276–279
    video effects, selecting/applying, 257–260
final formats. See output
FireWire. See IEEE 1394 (FireWire)
flash capability, built-in, 12
Foley work (sound effects), 245–247
formats, camcorder
    analog (VHS, 8mm, Hi8), 4, 5
    choosing, 3–5
    Digital8, 4, 8
    DVCAM, 4, 8
    DVD-CAM, 4
    DVD-RAM, DVD-R, 8
    DVPRO, 4
    MicroMV, 4, 5
    MiniDV, 4, 8
    MPEG4, 8
    resolutions, typical, 4
formats, file. See compression, file; DV Stream;
    formats, camcorder; MPEG (Motion Picture
    Experts Group); output
frame mode, progressive scan, 198
frame rate
    See also shutter speed
    film vs. video, 197–198
    PAL (Phase Alternating Line), 198

G

gain, defined, 318
graphic overlays. See special effects

H

HabbyCam
    Micro Jib, Full Jib, 169
hard discs
    See also archiving
    internal/external/RAID, 34–35
Harry Fox Agency, 243–244
headphones, volume controls on, 240
Hi8
    defined, 318
    8mm format, 4, 5
home movies, filming
    See also home movies, editing
    introduction to, 39–40

camera shake, limiting, 53–54
editing handles vs. abrupt endings, 48–49
good sound, importance of, 56
lavalier microphones, use of, 56
less is more (selective shooting), 52–53
lighting, useful tips for, 54–56
multiple angles, use of, 49
narration dos and dont's, 44–45
necessary equipment, 40
overexposure and zebra setting, 55
panning, 54
post production, defined, 45, 321
practice, importance of, 57
pre-production, defined, 322
pre-production planning, checklists for, 40–42
retakes, 48
shot types (wide, close-up, etc.), 50–52
"stepping over" the interviewee, 47–48
storyboards and shot lists, 42–43
tight and wide shots, toggling between, 45
two shots, 52
wide shot, defined, 324
zoom, proper use of, 45–46
home movies, editing
    See also home movies, filming
    catalog (scene) list, creating, 58–59
    the ending, visual/audio techniques for, 60–61
    the "Ferris effect," 61
    finding the beginning (of the narrative), 57–58
    the foreshadowed event, 61
    graphics (credits, titles, etc.), 64
    intercutting, defined, 60
    montages, 61
    music, use of, 62
    narration (voice-over), 62–64
    post production, 61–64, 321
    sound effects, 62
    telling the story (the middle), 59–60
    video effects (fades, dissolves, transitions), 62, 63

I

iDVD
    creating digital movies with, 299–301
    importing chapter markers into, 303
IEEE 1394 (FireWire)
    introduction to, 21–22
    adding to PC (via PCI card), 22
    DirectX compatibility of, 23

Firewire, defined, 317
IEEE 1394, defined, 318
Macintosh compatibility with, 26
and output to analog tape, 293
and output to DV tape, 290
I.Link, defined, 318
iMovie
    introduction to, 27–28
    batch capture using, 210
    color effects using, 256–257
    cropping clips with, 216
    digital movies, export techniques for, 295–296
    editing interviews with, 108–109
    immediate effects, slow rendering of, 257
    and Internet movies, 225
    manual capture using, 207
    tape export commands (DV tape), 291
    time-phased effects in, 261–238
in the can, defined, 318
in the field, defined, 318
intercut, defined, 318
intercuts
    B-roll intercuts, inserting (via NLE), 222–225
    defined, 60, 222
    in home movies, 59
Internet movies
    See also streaming video
    introduction to, 289
    Adobe Premiere in, 307–308
    file size/compression considerations for, 305–306
    Final Cut in, 306–307
    iMovie in, 306
    NLE applications for, 306
    and Quick Time, 306, 309
interviews, filming
    See also interviews, editing
    introduction to, 89–90
    changing (reframing) shots, 99–100
    eyeline and seating, 95–96, 97
    interviewee, choosing, 90–93
    lighting, types of, 100–102
    location, selecting, 94–95
    microphones for, 105–106
    names, importance of, 96
    one-person interview shot, 92–93
    open-ended questions, asking, 97–99
    organizational interviews, 156

pre-interview research and planning, 92
sound/sound recording, 104–105
studios, advantages of, 106–107
three-camcorder shooting, 94
two-camcorder shooting, 93
the two-shot, 93, 324
interviews, editing
    See also interviews, filming
    introduction to, 107–108
    audio tracks, synchronizing/combining, 109–110
    with iMovie (one-camcorder interview), 108–109
    sound editing, 111
    straight cuts and transitions, 110–111
    two-camcorder interview, 109–110

J

jibs
    Micro Jib, full jib, Super jib arm, 169
jump cut, defined, 318

K

key lights
    defined, 318
    use of, 12, 101, 102–103
keyframing
    defined, 318–319
    as special effect, 262, 264, 11;15

L

lavalier microphones
    applications of, 56, 68, 106, 126, 235–236
    defined, 319
Leitech Technology Corp., 24
lighting
    for feature films, 169–170, 195–196
    fill lights, 102–103
    flash capability, 12
    home movies, lighting, 54–56
    interview lighting, types of, 100–102
    in key lights, 12, 101, 102–103
    in night shooting, lighting for, 83
    on-camera, 11
    in small studios, 143, 144, 145, 146
    two-, three-, four-point, 102–103
    for vérité videos, 118

for weddings and events, 73, 78, 82, 83
zebra effect, 55, 83
linear-editing systems, defined, 319
LocationSound (microphones), 236
long shot, defined, 319

M

Macintosh computers
See also Macintosh computers, configuring
Cardbus compatibility of, 26
FireWire compatibility of, 26
iBook, limitations of, 26
iMac G4 and iMac DV models, 26
Power Macintosh G4, 25–26
PowerBook, 26
PowerBook (G3, G4), 26
SoundTrack music software (Apple), 245, 246
Macintosh computers, configuring
hard disc capacity, 26
OS X 10.2, 26
processors, 26
RAM, minimum requirements for, 26
SuperDrives, NLE/DVD integration in, 26, 27
manual overrides, 10–11
manufacturers, camcorder
choosing, 6
digital formats of, 8
websites for, 8
marketing. See exhibiting/marketing
mask, defined, 319
McElwee, Ross, 120
Media 100, Inc., 23, 24
medium shot, defined, 319
megapixel, defined, 319
memory cards, 13
MicroMV format
See also formats, camcorder
advantages of, 5
defined, 319
resolution of, 4
microphones
See also audio/sound
attenuation (sensitivity) controls on, 239–240
balanced XLR connectors for, 11, 233–234
boom, 106, 234_235
breakout boxes for (Beachtek), 234, 240
for documentaries, 116–117, 126
for feature films, 169
handheld, 105

lavalier, 56, 68, 106, 126, 235–236, 319
mic/line inputs, camcorder, 237–238
on-camcorder vs. eternal, 232
pickup patterns of (omnidirectional, cardioid), 232, 236
Minidisc recorders, 241
MiniDV
defined, 320
format, 4, 5
Moore, Michael, 113
MOS, defined, 116, 320
motion effects. See special effects
motivation, defined, 320
movies, digital (DVD/VCD)
See also Internet movies; movies, digital (tape); optical discs
introduction to, 297–298
Adobe Encore DVD, 298
chapter markers, creating, 301–302
creating (in Apple iDVD), 299–301
creating (in Final Cut), 301–304
digital movie, defined, 316
file compression vs. quality, 300
Roxio Creator software, 305
VCDs, creating, 304–305
VCDs, drawbacks of, 304
movies, digital (tape)
See also movies, digital (DVD/VCD)
introduction to, 294
Adobe Premiere export techniques for, 296–297, 298
file size vs. resolution, 295
file types, 294–295
Final Cut export techniques for, 296
iMovie export techniques for, 295–296
MP3 discs, players, 241
MPEG (Motion Picture Experts Group)
See also compression, file
introduction to, 12–13
defined, 320
MPEG-1, 31–32
MPEG-2, 31
MPEG-4, 31, 309–310
MPEG Audio Layer 3 (MP3), 31
music
See also audio/sound
choosing, 241–243
clearances, 243–244
Harry Fox Agency, 243–244

in home movies, 62
mechanical licenses, 243–244
music libraries, 244
music rights, obtaining, 243–244
original music, acquiring/using, 244–245
SoundTrack music software (Apple), 245, 246
synchronization licenses, 243
unlicensed commercial music, using, 244

N

narration
  adding, 248–249
  voice over, discussion of, 249
  voice over, tips for, 249–250
NLE (nonlinear editing) software. See editing
  software, nonlinear (NLE)
NTSC television image
  defined, 320
  interlace in, 198
  resolution (vs. PAL), 198

O

"180-degree rule," 187
optical discs
  See also movies, digital
  introduction to, 297–298
  DVD formats, camcorder, 4, 8
  DVD movies, introduction to, 297–298
  DVD-R, burning to (archiving), 35
  DVD-R, convenience of, 5
  DVD-R, defined, 316
  DVD Studio Pro (Apple), 302
  optical disc, defined, 320
  Pinnacle Expression, Impression, 302–303
  VCDs, creating, 304–305
  VCDs, drawbacks of, 305
optical zoom. See zoom
optics, defined, 321
organizational videos, filming
  See also organizational videos, editing
  introduction to, 141–142
  ambient sound, importance of, 159
  artistic/content control, maintaining,
    147–148
  B-roll, shooting, 158–159
  chromakey (blue screen), use of, 144–145
  color temperature, importance of, 149
  documentary footage, use of, 156

documentary-style interviews in, 148
  emotion/humor, use of, 154–155
  event video, use of, 156–157
  good sound, importance of, 158
  interviews and studio setups, 156
  locations for, selecting, 148–150
  necessary equipment, 142–143
  news producers, learning from, 148
  outlines, importance of, 150–152
  sets and studios for, 143–145
  shooting location, selecting, 157–158
  shooting meetings, tips for, 157–158
  shot angles, varying, 159
  shot lists, 153
  small studio, checklist for, 145–146
  stock footage, use of, 159
  storyboarding, 152
  strong talent, use of, 148
  teaching/motivating function of, 146–147
  training videos, 155
  user interest, maintaining, 153–154
  using multiple techniques for, 156–157
  white balancing, 149
organizational videos, editing
  See also organizational videos, filming
  introduction to, 160
  edit decision list, use of, 161
  fades (between slides), 161, 162
  simple transitions, importance of, 160
  slides, formatting, 162–163
  still images and graphics, use of, 161
  titles, documentary-style, 160–161, 162
output
  See also Internet movies; movies, digital;
    optical discs; tape, analog; tape, digital
  introduction to, 287–288
  to a computer file, 288–289
  to DV camcorders, 222
  to optical discs, 288
  tape output, 288
  timecode, not breaking, 290

P

PAL (Phase Alternating Line) standard
  defined, 321
  resolution (vs. NTSC), 198
  shutter speed, 198
pan, defined, 79, 321

Panasonic Corporation
    digital format of (DVPro), 4
    PV-DC352 camcorder, 12
parties and banquets, shooting, 84–85
PCs, configuring (hardware)
    hard disc capacity, 22
    IEEE 1394 (FireWire) port, 22–23
    P4 processor, 22
    RAM, minimum requirements for, 22
    real-time effects processors, 23
Pinnacle Systems, Inc.
    Commotion, 24
    Pinnacle Edition, 24, 25
    Pinnacle Expression, Impression, 302–303
    Pinnacle Studio, 24
pixel, defined, 321
practicals, defined, 321
pre-production, defined, 322
producer, responsibilities of
    in feature films, 180
    in wedding/event videos, 66
progressive scan frame mode, 198
prosumer, defined, 322
public domain, fair use, 136

Q

Quick Time (Apple)
    defined, 309–310
    digital movie format (Macintosh), 31, 32,
      294, 306
    and Internet streaming video, 322

R

rack focus, defined, 79, 322
real-time effects processors
    Canopus DVRaptor, 23
    DPS/Leitech, 24
    Matrox, 23
    Media 100, 23, 24
RealNetworks, Inc. (Real Media), 32, 311
removable media, introduction to, 13
render, defined, 322
renting vs. buying (camcorders), 14–15
resolution
    analog camcorders, CCD resolutions of, 7
    of camcorder formats, 4
    defined, 322
    of MicroMV format, 4
    NTSC vs. PAL, 198

    still photography and CCD resolution, 7
    vs. file size (digital movies), 295
rough cut
    archiving, 33–34
    defined, 216, 322
    in digital editing, 217
    in feature films, 201–202
Roxio Creator software, 305
rule of thirds
    defined, 322
    in documentaries, 130–131

S

safety tabs, MiniDV tapes, 130
Samson microphones, 236
scripts
    basic elements of, 173–175
    example of (typical), 174
    rehearsals, script readings, 193–194
    script breakdown/master list, developing,
      177–179
    writing/outlining, 121–123
Sennheiser microphones, 236
shoot, defined, 323
Shure microphones, 236
shutter speed
    See also frame rate
    choosing (in feature films), 198
    in PAL standard, 198
    setting (wedding/event videos), 77
16:9 aspect ratio
    camcorder support of, 11
    defined, 313
SkyCrane, 169
SonicFoundry
    Vegas Video, 24
Sony Corporation
    BetacamSP, DigiBeta formats, 3
    Digital8, DVCAM formats, 4–5
    minidisc recorders, 241
    PD150, XLR connector on, 233
    professional microphones from, 236
sound. See audio/sound
sound effects
    effects libraries, 247
    Foley work, 245–247
special effects
    introduction to, 255–256
    color effects (iMovie 3), 256–257

compositing video, introduction to, 281–282
compositing video (Adobe Premiere), 286
compositing video (Final Cut), 282–285
fades (Adobe Premiere), 264, 266
fades (Final Cut), 264, 265–266
graphic overlays, introduction to, 271–272
graphic overlays (Adobe Premiere), 274–275
graphic overlays (Final Cut), 272–274
immediate (Adobe Premiere), 260–261
immediate (Final Cut), 257–260
iMovie effects, slow rendering of, 257
motion effects, introduction to, 267
motion effects (Adobe Premiere), 270–271
motion effects (Final Cut), 267–270
overlays, defined, 227, 321
time-phased, in iMovie, 261–262
time-phased (Adobe Premiere), 262–264
titles (Adobe Premiere), 279–281
titles (Final Cut), 276–279
video effects, rendering, 290
steadying devices, camcorder
saddlebags, 134
steadying device, counterweighted, 134
tripods/monopods, 133–134
Steadytracker (CobraCrane), 169
still photography
and CCD resolution, 7
digital still photography, defined, 316
storyboards and shot lists
for feature films, 180–181
for home movies, 42–43
for organizational videos, 152, 153
for weddings, 87–88
streaming video
defined, 323
and QuickTime, 306, 309
and Real Media, 311
vs. movie files, 306
Windows Media (Microsoft), 311
Studio1 Productions, 169
studios
advantages of (in interviews), 106–107
for organizational videos, 143–145
small studio, checklist for, 145, 146
small studios, lighting in, 143, 144, 145, 146
use of chromakey in, 144, 145
Super Jib Arm, 169

T

take, defined, 323
tape, analog
See also output; tape, digital
output techniques for, 293
Print to Video command (Final Cut, Adobe Premiere), 293
S-video output (camcorder), 293
tape, digital
See also output; tape, analog
exporting to (Adobe Premiere), 291–292
exporting to (Final Cut), 291
exporting to (iMovie), 291
Print to Video dialog box (Final Cut), 292
safety tabs, MiniDV tape, 130
tapestock, defined, 323
Telex microphones, 236
30-degree rule, defined, 313
tight shot, defined, 323
tilt, defined, 79, 323
Timecode/timelines
defined, 324
in image capture, 213
not breaking (in DV tape output), 290
titles
adding, 228–229
in Adobe Premiere, 279–281
centered, 227
in Final Cut, 276–279
lower-third, 227–228, 319
over black, 227, 321
scrolling, 228, 323
training videos, 155
Trew Audio microphones, 236
trimming, defined, 324
tripods/monopods, 133–134
two-shot
in home movies, 52
in interviews, 93

U

USB (Universal Serial Bus)
defined, 324
on camcorders, 13
and MPS players, 241

V

VCDs. See movies, digital; optical discs
Vegas Video, 24
VHS
    defined, A:!2
    Super-VHS, defined, 323
    VHS-C, defined, 323
    VHS formats, 4
video, digital. See digital video, working with
video generator, defined, 324

W

wedding and event videos
    introduction to, 65–66
    assistants, using, 69
    behavior, professional, 80–81
    camcorder placement, 74–75
    camcorder settings, checklist of, 77–78
    camcorder-to-subject distance, 67
    camcorders, multiple (synchronizing/using),
        67–68, 75–77
    camcorders, variation between, 76
    client expectations, clarifying, 66–67
    coordination with principals and pre-shoot
        details, 69, 73–74
    costs and fees, 67
    digital zoom, disabling, 77
    editing the event, 85–86
    good wishes, recording, 81
    lighting, 73, 78, 82, 83
    location scouting, importance of, 72–73, 78
    manual exposure, using, 78
    microphones for, 68
    necessary equipment, planning, 71–72, 74
    night shooting, lighting for, 83
    outdoor shooting, 82–83
    parties and banquets, shooting, 84–85
    pre-shoot problems, typical, 70
    producer, responsibilities of, 66
    shot list, wedding, 87–88
    shutter speed, setting, 77
    sound quality/levels, checking, 68–69, 73
    white balance, setting, 77
    zebra effect (camcorder feature), 83
    zoom, long shot, 78
white balance
    defined, 324
    in feature films, 196
    in organizational videos, 149
    in wedding/event videos, 77
Windows Media (Microsoft), 31, 32, 311
wipes, adding, 225–226

X

XLR connectors, breakout boxes
    applications of, 11, 233–234, 240
    XLR/XLR cable, defined, 324

Z

zebra effect
    overexposure and zebra setting, 55
    in weddings and event videos, 83
zoom
    digital, defined, 316
    digital, disabling (wedding/event videos), 77
    in home movies, 45–46
    lens adapters for, 17
    in long shots (wedding/event videos), 78
    optical, defined, 320–321
    optical, typical ranges of, 10
    optical vs. digital, 10

INTERNATIONAL CONTACT INFORMATION

AUSTRALIA
McGraw-Hill Book Company Australia Pty. Ltd.
TEL +61-2-9900-1800
FAX +61-2-9878-8881
http://www.mcgraw-hill.com.au
books-it_sydney@mcgraw-hill.com

CANADA
McGraw-Hill Ryerson Ltd.
TEL +905-430-5000
FAX +905-430-5020
http://www.mcgraw-hill.ca

GREECE, MIDDLE EAST, & AFRICA
(Excluding South Africa)
McGraw-Hill Hellas
TEL +30-210-6560-990
TEL +30-210-6560-993
TEL +30-210-6560-994
FAX +30-210-6545-525

MEXICO (Also serving Latin America)
McGraw-Hill Interamericana Editores S.A. de C.V.
TEL +525-117-1583
FAX +525-117-1589
http://www.mcgraw-hill.com.mx
fernando_castellanos@mcgraw-hill.com

SINGAPORE (Serving Asia)
McGraw-Hill Book Company
TEL +65-6863-1580
FAX +65-6862-3354
http://www.mcgraw-hill.com.sg
mghasia@mcgraw-hill.com

SOUTH AFRICA
McGraw-Hill South Africa
TEL +27-11-622-7512
FAX +27-11-622-9045
robyn_swanepoel@mcgraw-hill.com

SPAIN
McGraw-Hill/Interamericana de España, S.A.U.
TEL +34-91-180-3000
FAX +34-91-372-8513
http://www.mcgraw-hill.es
professional@mcgraw-hill.es

UNITED KINGDOM, NORTHERN,
EASTERN, & CENTRAL EUROPE
McGraw-Hill Education Europe
TEL +44-1-628-502500
FAX +44-1-628-770224
http://www.mcgraw-hill.co.uk
computing_europe@mcgraw-hill.com

ALL OTHER INQUIRIES Contact:
McGraw-Hill/Osborne
TEL +1-510-420-7700
FAX +1-510-420-7703
http://www.osborne.com
omg_international@mcgraw-hill.com

LICENSE AGREEMENT

THIS PRODUCT (THE "PRODUCT") CONTAINS PROPRIETARY SOFTWARE, DATA AND INFORMATION (INCLUDING DOCUMENTATION) OWNED BY THE McGRAW-HILL COMPANIES, INC. ("McGRAW-HILL") AND ITS LICENSORS. YOUR RIGHT TO USE THE PRODUCT IS GOVERNED BY THE TERMS AND CONDITIONS OF THIS AGREEMENT.

LICENSE: Throughout this License Agreement, "you" shall mean either the individual or the entity whose agent opens this package. You are granted a non-exclusive and non-transferable license to use the Product subject to the following terms:

(i) If you have licensed a single user version of the Product, the Product may only be used on a single computer (i.e., a single CPU). If you licensed and paid the fee applicable to a local area network or wide area network version of the Product, you are subject to the terms of the following subparagraph (ii).

(ii) If you have licensed a local area network version, you may use the Product on unlimited workstations located in one single building selected by you that is served by such local area network. If you have licensed a wide area network version, you may use the Product on unlimited workstations located in multiple buildings on the same site selected by you that is served by such wide area network; provided, however, that any building will not be considered located in the same site if it is more than five (5) miles away from any building included in such site. In addition, you may only use a local area or wide area network version of the Product on one single server. If you wish to use the Product on more than one server, you must obtain written authorization from McGraw-Hill and pay additional fees.

(iii) You may make one copy of the Product for back-up purposes only and you must maintain an accurate record as to the location of the back-up at all times.

COPYRIGHT; RESTRICTIONS ON USE AND TRANSFER: All rights (including copyright) in and to the Product are owned by McGraw-Hill and its licensors. You are the owner of the enclosed disc on which the Product is recorded. You may not use, copy, decompile, disassemble, reverse engineer, modify, reproduce, create derivative works, transmit, distribute, sublicense, store in a database or retrieval system of any kind, rent or transfer the Product, or any portion thereof, in any form or by any means (including electronically or otherwise) except as expressly provided for in this License Agreement. You must reproduce the copyright notices, trademark notices, legends and logos of McGraw-Hill and its licensors that appear on the Product on the back-up copy of the Product which you are permitted to make hereunder. All rights in the Product not expressly granted herein are reserved by McGraw-Hill and its licensors.

TERM: This License Agreement is effective until terminated. It will terminate if you fail to comply with any term or condition of this License Agreement. Upon termination, you are obligated to return to McGraw-Hill the Product together with all copies thereof and to purge all copies of the Product included in any and all servers and computer facilities.

DISCLAIMER OF WARRANTY: THE PRODUCT AND THE BACK-UP COPY ARE LICENSED "AS IS." McGRAW-HILL, ITS LICENSORS AND THE AUTHORS MAKE NO WARRANTIES, EXPRESS OR IMPLIED, AS TO THE RESULTS TO BE OBTAINED BY ANY PERSON OR ENTITY FROM USE OF THE PRODUCT, ANY INFORMATION OR DATA INCLUDED THEREIN AND/OR ANY TECHNICAL SUPPORT SERVICES PROVIDED HEREUNDER, IF ANY ("TECHNICAL SUPPORT SERVICES"). McGRAW-HILL, ITS LICENSORS AND THE AUTHORS MAKE NO EXPRESS OR IMPLIED WARRANTIES OF MERCHANTABILITY OR FITNESS FOR A PARTICULAR PURPOSE OR USE WITH RESPECT TO THE PRODUCT. McGRAW-HILL, ITS LICENSORS, AND THE AUTHORS MAKE NO GUARANTEE THAT YOU WILL PASS ANY CERTIFICATION EXAM WHATSOEVER BY USING THIS PRODUCT. NEITHER McGRAW-HILL, ANY OF ITS LICENSORS NOR THE AUTHORS WARRANT THAT THE FUNCTIONS CONTAINED IN THE PRODUCT WILL MEET YOUR REQUIREMENTS OR THAT THE OPERATION OF THE PRODUCT WILL BE UNINTERRUPTED OR ERROR FREE. YOU ASSUME THE ENTIRE RISK WITH RESPECT TO THE QUALITY AND PERFORMANCE OF THE PRODUCT.

LIMITED WARRANTY FOR DISC: To the original licensee only, McGraw-Hill warrants that the enclosed disc on which the Product is recorded is free from defects in materials and workmanship under normal use and service for a period of ninety (90) days from the date of purchase. In the event of a defect in the disc covered by the foregoing warranty, McGraw-Hill will replace the disc.

LIMITATION OF LIABILITY: NEITHER McGRAW-HILL, ITS LICENSORS NOR THE AUTHORS SHALL BE LIABLE FOR ANY INDIRECT, SPECIAL OR CONSEQUENTIAL DAMAGES, SUCH AS BUT NOT LIMITED TO, LOSS OF ANTICIPATED PROFITS OR BENEFITS, RESULTING FROM THE USE OR INABILITY TO USE THE PRODUCT EVEN IF ANY OF THEM HAS BEEN ADVISED OF THE POSSIBILITY OF SUCH DAMAGES. THIS LIMITATION OF LIABILITY SHALL APPLY TO ANY CLAIM OR CAUSE WHATSOEVER WHETHER SUCH CLAIM OR CAUSE ARISES IN CONTRACT, TORT, OR OTHERWISE. Some states do not allow the exclusion or limitation of indirect, special or consequential damages, so the above limitation may not apply to you.

U.S. GOVERNMENT RESTRICTED RIGHTS: Any software included in the Product is provided with restricted rights subject to subparagraphs (c), (1) and (2) of the Commercial Computer Software-Restricted Rights clause at 48 C.F.R. 52.227-19. The terms of this Agreement applicable to the use of the data in the Product are those under which the data are generally made available to the general public by McGraw-Hill. Except as provided herein, no reproduction, use, or disclosure rights are granted with respect to the data included in the Product and no right to modify or create derivative works from any such data is hereby granted.

GENERAL: This License Agreement constitutes the entire agreement between the parties relating to the Product. The terms of any Purchase Order shall have no effect on the terms of this License Agreement. Failure of McGraw-Hill to insist at any time on strict compliance with this License Agreement shall not constitute a waiver of any rights under this License Agreement. This License Agreement shall be construed and governed in accordance with the laws of the State of New York. If any provision of this License Agreement is held to be contrary to law, that provision will be enforced to the maximum extent permissible and the remaining provisions will remain in full force and effect.